# THE
# COMMERCE AND NAVIGATION
# OF
# THE ERYTHRAEAN SEA

AND

ANCIENT INDIA AS DESCRIBED
BY
KTESIAS THE KNIDIAN

JOHN WATSON McCRINDLE

# THE COMMERCE AND NAVIGATION OF THE ERYTHRAEAN SEA

BEING TRANSLATIONS OF THE
"PERIPLUS MARIS ERYTHRAEI" BY AN ANONYMOUS WRITER
AND PARTLY FROM
ARRIAN'S ACCOUNT OF THE VOYAGE OF NEARKHOS

FOLLOWED BY

## ANCIENT INDIA AS DESCRIBED
BY
## KTESIAS THE KNIDIAN

BEING A TRANSLATION OF THE ABRIDGEMENT OF HIS "INDIKA"
BY PHOTIOS AND OF THE FRAGMENTS
OF THAT WORK PRESERVED IN OTHER WRITERS

Edited, with
historical introductions, commentary, critical notes, and indexes

**PHILO PRESS**
AMSTERDAM

ISBN 9o 6o22 1o8 7

REPRINT 1973 OF THE EDITIONS CALCUTTA-LONDON 1879, 1882

THE

# COMMERCE AND NAVIGATION

OF THE

# ERYTHRÆAN SEA;

BEING A TRANSLATION

OF THE

## PERIPLUS MARIS ERYTHRÆI,

BY AN ANONYMOUS WRITER,

AND OF

## ARRIAN'S ACCOUNT OF THE VOYAGE OF NEARKHOS,

FROM THE MOUTH OF THE INDUS TO THE HEAD OF THE
PERSIAN GULF.

WITH INTRODUCTIONS, COMMENTARY, NOTES,
AND INDEX.

BY

## J. W. McCRINDLE, M.A., Edin.,

PRINCIPAL OF THE GOVERNMENT COLLEGE, PATNA ;
MEMBER OF THE COUNCIL OF THE UNIVERSITY OF EDINBURGH ;
FELLOW OF THE CALCUTTA UNIVERSITY.

*(Reprinted, with additions, from the Indian Antiquary.)*

# PREFACE.

In the Preface to my former work, "Ancient India as described by Megasthenes and Arrian," I informed the reader that it was my intention to publish from time to time translations of the Greek and Latin works which relate to ancient India, until the series should be exhausted, and the present volume is the second instalment towards the fulfilment of that undertaking. It contains a translation of the *Periplûs* (*i. e. Circumnavigation*) *of the Erythræan Sea,* together with a translation of the second part of the *Indika* of Arrian describing the celebrated voyage made by Nearkhos from the mouth of the Indus to the head of the Persian Gulf. Arrian's narrative, copied from the Journal of the voyage written by Nearkhos himself, forms an admirable supplement to the Periplûs, as it contains a minute description of a part of the Erythræan Coast which is merely glanced at by the author of that work. The translations have been prepared from the most approved texts. The notes, in a few instances only, bear upon points of textual criticism, their main object being to present in a concise form for popular reading the most recent results of learned enquiry directed to verify, correct, or otherwise illustrate the contents of the narratives.

The warm and unanimous approbation bestowed upon the first volume of this series, both by the Press in this country and at home, has given me great encouragement to proceed with the undertaking, and a third volume is now in preparation, to contain the *Indika* of Ktêsias and the account of India given by Strabo in the 15th Book of his Geography.

*Patna College, June* 1879.

# ANONYMI [ARRIANI UT FERTUR]

# PERIPLUS MARIS ERYTHRÆI.

## TRANSLATED FROM THE TEXT

As given in the *Geographi Græci Minores*, edited by
C. Muller : Paris, 1855.

### WITH INTRODUCTION AND COMMENTARY.

# PERIPLUS OF THE ERYTHRÆAN SEA.

## INTRODUCTION.[1]

The *Periplûs of the Erythræan Sea* is the title prefixed to a work which contains the best account of the commerce carried on from the Red Sea and the coast of Africa to the East Indies during the time that Egypt was a province of the Roman empire. The E r y t h r æ a n  S e a was an appellation given in those days to the whole expanse of ocean reaching from the coast of Africa to the utmost boundary of ancient knowledge on the East—an appellation in all appearance deduced from the entrance into it by the Straits of the Red Sea, styled E r y t h r a by the Greeks, and not excluding the Gulf of Persia.

The author was a Greek merchant, who in the first century of the Christian era had, it would appear, settled at B e r e n î k ê, a great seaport situated in the southern extremity of Egypt, whence he made commercial voyages which carried him to the seaports of Eastern Africa as far as A z a n i a, and to those of Arabia as far as K a n ê, whence, by taking advantage of the south-west monsoon, he crossed over to the ports lying on the western shores of India. Having made careful

---

[1] The Introduction and Commentary embody the main substance of Müller's Prolegomena and Notes to the *Periplûs*, and of Vincent's *Commerce and Navigation of the Ancients* so far as it relates specially to that work. The most recent authorities accessible have, however, been also consulted, and the result of their inquiries noted. I may mention particularly Bishop Caldwell's Dravidian Grammar, to which I am indebted for the identification of places on the Malabar and Coromandel coasts.

*a*

observations and inquiries regarding the navigation and commerce of these countries, he committed to writing, for the benefit of other merchants,
the knowledge which he had thus acquired. Much
cannot be said in praise of the style in which he
writes. It is marked by a rude simplicity, which
shows that he was not a man of literary culture,
but in fact a mere man of business, who in composing restricts himself to a narrow round of set
phrases, and is indifferent alike to grace, freedom,
or variety of expression. It shows further that
he was a Greek settled in Egypt, and that he must
have belonged to an isolated community of his
countrymen, whose speech had become corrupt by
much intercourse with foreigners. It presents a
very striking contrast to the rhetorical diction
which A g a t h a r k h i d ê s, a great master of all
the tricks of speech, employs in his description of
the Erythræan. For all shortcomings, however,
in the style of the work, there is ample compensa-
tion in the fulness, variety, accuracy, and utility
of the information which it conveys. Such indeed
is its superiority on these points that it must be
reckoned as a most precious treasure : for to it
we are indebted far more than to any other work
for most of our knowledge of the remote shores of
Eastern Africa, and the marts of India, and the
condition of ancient commerce in these parts of
the world.

The name of the author is unknown. In the Heidelberg MS., which alone has preserved the little
work, and contains it after the *Periplûs* of Arrian,
the title given is Ἀρριανοῦ περίπλους τῆς' Ἐρυθρᾶς
θαλάσσης. Trusting to the correctness of this

title, Stuckius attributed the work to A r r i a n of Nikomedia, and Fabricius to another Arrian who belonged to Alexandria. No one, however, who knows how ancient books are usually treated can fail to see what the real fact here is, viz. that since not only the *Periplûs Maris Erythrœi*, but also the *Anonymi Periplûs Ponti Euxini* (whereof the latter part occurs in the Heidelberg MS. before Arrian's *Ponti Periplûs*) are attributed to Arrian, and the different Arrians are not distinguished by any indications afforded by the titles, there can be no doubt that the well-known name of the Nikomedian writer was transferred to the books placed in juxtaposition to his proper works, by the arbitrary judgment of the librarians. In fact it very often happens that short works written by different authors are all referred to one and the same author, especially if they treat of the same subject and are published conjointly in the same volume. But in the case of the work before us, any one would have all the more readily ascribed it to Arrian who had heard by report anything of the *Paraplûs* of the Erythræan Sea described in that author's *Indika*. On this point there is the utmost unanimity of opinion among writers.

That the author, whatever may have been his name, lived in Egypt, is manifest. Thus he says in § 29 : " Several of the trees *with us* in Egypt weep gum," and he joins the names of the Egyptian months with the Roman, as may be seen by referring to §§ 6, 39, 49, and 56. The place in which he was settled was probably Berenîkê, since it was from that port he embarked on his

voyages to Africa and Arabia, and since he speaks
of the one coast as on the right from Berenîkê,
and the other on the left. The whole tenor of the
work proclaims that he must have been a merchant.
That the entire work is not a mere compilation
from the narratives or journals of other merchants
and navigators, but that the author had himself
visited some of the seats of trade which he describes, is in itself probable, and is indicated in § 20,
where, contrary to the custom of the ancient
writers, he speaks in his own person :—" In sailing
south, therefore, *we* stand off from the shore and
keep *our* course down the middle of the gulf."
Compare with this what is said in § 48: τὰ πρὸς
τὴν ἐμπορίαν τὴν ἡμετέραν.

As regards the age to which the writer belonged : it is first of all evident that he wrote after the
times of Augustus, since in § 23 mention is made
of the Roman Emperors. That he was older,
however, than P t o l e m y the Geographer, is
proved by his geography, which knows nothing of
India beyond the Ganges except the traditional
account current from the days of Eratosthenês to
those of Pliny, while it is evident that Ptolemy
possessed much more accurate information regarding these parts. It confirms this view that
while our author calls the island of Ceylon P a l a i-
s i m o u n d o u, Ptolemy calls it by the name
subsequently given to it—S a l i k ê. Again, from
§ 19, it is evident that he wrote before the
kingdom of the Nabathæans was abolished by
the Romans. Moreover Pliny (VI. xxvi. 104), in
proceeding to describe the navigation to the
marts of India by the direct route across the

ocean with the wind called Hippalos, writes to this effect :—" And for a long time this was the mode of navigation, until a merchant discovered a compendious route whereby India was brought so near that to trade thither became very lucrative. For, every year a fleet is despatched, carrying on board companies of archers, since the Indian seas are much infested by pirates. Nor will a description of the whole voyage from Egypt tire the reader, since now for the first time correct information regarding it has been made public." Compare with this the statement of the *Periplûs* in § 57, and it will be apparent that while this route to India had only just come into use in the time of Pliny, it had been for some time in use in the days of our author. Now, as Pliny died in 79 A.D., and had completed his work two years previously, it may be inferred that he had written the 6th book of his *Natural History* before our author wrote his work. A still more definite indication of his date is furnished in § 5, where Zoskalês is mentioned as reigning in his times over the Auxumitæ. Now in a list of the early kings of Abyssinia the name of Za-Hakale occurs, who must have reigned from 77 to 89 A.D. This Za-Hakale is doubtless the Zoskalês of the *Periplûs,* and was the contemporary of the emperors Vespasian, Titus, and Domitian. We conclude, therefore, that the *Periplûs* was written a little after the death of Pliny, between the years A.D. 80-89.

Opinions on this point, however, have varied considerably. Salmasius thought that Pliny and our author wrote at the same time, though their accounts of the same things are often contradictory. In support of this view he adduces the statement of the *Periplûs* (§ 54), "M u z i r i s, a place in India, is in the kingdom of Kêprobotres," when compared with the statement of Pliny (VI. xxvi. 104), " C œ l o b o t h r a s was reigning there when I committed this to writing ;" and argues that since K ê p r o b o t r a s and C œ l o b o t h r a s are but different forms of the same name, the two authors must have been contemporary. The inference is, however, unwarrantable, since the name in question, like that of P a n d î ô n, was a common appellation of the kings who ruled over that part of India.

Dodwell, again, was of opinion that the *Periplûs* was written after the year A. D. 161, when Marcus Aurelius and Lucius Verus were joint emperors. He bases, in the first place, his defence of this view on the statement in § 26 : " Not long before our own times the Emperor (Καῖσαρ) destroyed the place," viz. E u d a i m ô n-A r a b i a, now Aden. This emperor he supposes must have been Trajan, who, according to Eutropius (VIII. 3), reduced Arabia to the form of a province. Eutropius, however, meant by Arabia only that small part of it which adjoins Syria. This Dodwell not only denies, but also asserts that the conquest of Trajan embraced the whole of the Peninsula—a sweeping inference, which he bases on a single passage in the *Periplûs* (§ 16) where the south part of Arabia is called ἡ πρώτη Αραβία, "the First Arabia." From this expression he gathers that Trajan, after his conquest of the country, had divided it into several provinces, designated according to the order in which they were constituted. The language of the *Periplûs*, however, forbids us to suppose that there is here any reference to a Roman province. What the passage states is that A z a n i a (in Africa) was by ancient right subject to the kingdom τῆς πρώτης γινομένης (λεγομένης according to Dodwell) 'Αραβίας, and was ruled by the despot of M a p h a r i t i s.

Dodwell next defends the date he has fixed on by the passage in § 23, where it is said that K h a-r i b a ë l sought by frequent gifts and embassies to gain the friendship of the emperors (τῶν αὐτοκρατόρων). He thinks that the time is here indicated when M. Aurelius and L. Verus were reigning conjointly, A.D. 161-181. There is no need, however, to put this construction on the words, which may without any impropriety be taken to mean '*the emperors for the time being,*' viz. Vespasian, Titus, and Domitian.

Vincent adopted the opinion of Salmasius regarding the date of the work, but thinks that the Kaîsar mentioned in § 26 was Claudius. "The Romans," he says, "from the time they first entered Arabia under Ælius Gallus, had always maintained a footing on the coast of the Red Sea. They had a garrison at L e u k ô K ô m ê, in Naba-thæa, where they collected the customs ; and it is apparent that they extended their power down the gulf and to the ports of the ocean in the reign of C_.udius, as the freedman of A n n i u s P l o c a m u s was in the act of collecting the tributes there when he was carried out to sea and over to T a p r o b a n ê. If we add to this the discovery of Hippalus in the same reign, we find a better reason for the destruction of Aden at this time than at any other." The assertion in this extract that the garrison and custom-house at L e u k ê K ô m ê belonged to the Romans is not warranted by the language of the *Periplûs*, which in fact shows that they belonged to M a l i k h o s the king of the Nabathæans. Again, it is a mere conjecture that the voyage which the freedman of Plocamus (who, according to Pliny, farmed the revenues of the Red Sea) was making along the coast of Arabia, when he was carried away by the monsoon to Taprobanê, was a voyage undertaken to collect the revenues due to the Roman treasury. With regard to the word Καῖσαρ, which has occasioned so much perplexity, it is most probably a corrupt reading in a text notorious for its corruptness. The proper reading may perhaps be ΕΛΙΣΑΡ. At any rate, had one of the emperors in reality destroyed Aden, it is unlikely that their historians would have failed to mention such an important fact.

Schwanbeck, although he saw the weakness of the arguments with which Salmasius and Vincent endeavoured to establish their position, nevertheless thought that our author lived in the age of Pliny and wrote a little before him, because those particulars regarding the Indian navigation which Pliny says became known in his age agree, on the whole, so well with the statement in the *Periplûs* that they must have been extracted therefrom. No doubt there are, he allows, some discrepancies; but those, he thinks, may be ascribed to the haste or negligence of the copyist. A careful examination, however, of parallel passages in Pliny and the *Periplûs* show this assertion to be untenable. Vincent himself speaks with caution on this point :—" There is," he says, " no absolute proof that either copied from the other. But those who are acquainted with Pliny's methods of abbreviation would much rather conclude, if one must be a copyist, that his title to this office is the clearest."

From these preliminary points we pass on to consider the contents of the work, and these may be conveniently reviewed under the three heads Geography, Navigation, Commerce. In the commentary, which is to accompany the translation, the Geography will be examined in detail. Meanwhile we shall enumerate the voyages which are distinguishable in the *Periplús*,[2] and the articles of commerce which it specifies.

### I. Voyages mentioned in the Periplus.

I. A voyage from *Bereníkê,* in the south of Egypt, down the western coast of the Red Sea through the Straits, along the coast of Africa, round Cape Guardafui, and then southward along the eastern coast of Africa as far as Rhâpta, a place about six degrees south of the equator.

II. We are informed of two distinct courses confined to the Red Sea : one from Myos Hormos, in the south of Egypt, across the northern end of the sea to Leukê Kômê, on the opposite coast of Arabia, near the mouth of the Elanitic Gulf, whence it was continued to Mouza, an Arabian port lying not far westward from the Straits ; the other from Bereníkê directly down the gulf to this same port

---

[2] The enumeration is Vincent's, altered and abridged.

*b*

III. There is described next to this a voyage from the mouth of the Straits along the southern coast of Arabia round the promontory now called Ras-el-Had, whence it was continued along the eastern coast of Arabia as far as Apologos (now Oboleh), an important emporium at the head of the Persian Gulf, near the mouth of the river Euphrates.

IV. Then follows a passage from the Straits to India by three different routes : the first by adhering to the coasts of Arabia, Karmania, Gedrosia, and Indo-Skythia, which terminated at B ar u g a z a (Bharôch), a great emporium on the river N a m m a d i o s (the Narmadâ), at a distance of thirty miles from its mouth; the second from Kanê, a port to the west of S u a g r o s, a great projection on the south coast of Arabia, now Cape Fartaque; and the third from Cape Guardafui, on the African side—both across the ocean by the monsoon to M o u z i r i s and N e l k u n d a, great commercial cities on the coast of Malabar.

V. After this we must allow a similar voyage performed by the Indians to Arabia, or by the Arabians to India, previous to the performance of it by the Greeks, because the Greeks as late as the reign of Philomêtôr met this commerce in Sabæa.

VI. We obtain an incidental knowledge of a voyage conducted from ports on the east coast of Africa over to India by the monsoon long before Hippalos introduced the knowledge of that wind to the Roman world. This voyage was connected, no doubt, with the commerce of Arabia, since the Arabians were the great traffickers of antiquity, and held in subjection part of the sea-board of Eastern

Africa. The Indian commodities imported into
Africa were rice, ghee, oil of sesamum, sugar,
cotton, muslins, and sashes. These commodities,
the *Periplûs* informs us, were brought sometimes
in vessels destined expressly for the coast of Africa,
while at others they were only part of the cargo,
out of vessels which were proceeding to another
port. Thus we have two methods of conducting
this commerce perfectly direct; and another
by touching on this coast with a final destination to Arabia. This is the reason that the
Greeks found cinnamon and the produce of India
on this coast, when they first ventured to pass
the Straits in order to seek a cheaper market than
Sabæa.

## II. Articles of Commerce mentioned in the Periplus.

I.  Animals :—

1. Παρθένοι εὐειδεῖς πρὸς παλλακίαν—Handsome
girls for the haram, imported into Barugaza for
the king (49).[3]

2. Δούλικα κρείσσονα—Tall slaves, procured at
Opônê, imported into Egypt (14).

3. Σώματα θηλυκὰ—Female slaves, procured
from Arabia and India, imported into the island
of Dioskoridês (31).

4. Σώματα.—Slaves imported from Omana and
Apologos into Barugaza (36), and from Moundou
and Malaô (8, 9).

5. Ἵπποι—Horses imported into Kanê for the
king, and into Mouza for the despot (23, 24).

---

[3] The numerals indicate the sections of the *Periplûs* in
which the articles are mentioned.

6. ʿ Ἡμίοναι νωτηγοὶ—Sumpter mules imported into Mouza for the despot (24).

II. Animal Products :—

1. Βούτυρον—Butter, or the Indian preparation therefrom called *ghî*, a product of Ariakê (41); exported from Barugaza to the Barbarine markets beyond the Straits (14). The word, according to Pliny (xxviii. 9), is of Skythian origin, though apparently connected with Βοῦς, τυρὸς. The reading is, however, suspected by Lassen, who would substitute Βόσμορον or Βόσπορον, *a kind of grain*.

2. Δέρματα Σηρικὰ—Chinese hides or furs. Exported from Barbarikon, a mart on the Indus (39). Vincent suspected the reading δέρματα, but groundlessly, for Pliny mentions the Sêres sending their iron along with vestments and hides (*vestibus pellibusque*), and among the presents sent to Yudhishṭhira by the Śaka, Tushâra and Kaṅka skins are enumerated.—*Mahâbh.* ii. 50, quoted by Lassen.

3. Ἐλέφας—Ivory. Exported from Adouli (6), Aualitês (8), Ptolemaïs (3), Mossulon (10), and the ports of Azania (16, 17). Also from Barugaza (49), Mouziris and Nelkunda (56); a species of ivory called Βωσαρὴ is produced in Desarênê (62).

4. Ἔριον Σηρικὸν—Chinese cotton. Imported from the country of the Thînai through Baktria to Barugaza, and by the Ganges to Bengal, and thence to Dimurikê (64). By Ἔριον Vincent seems to understand silk in the raw state.

5. Κέρατα—Horns. Exported from Barugaza to the marts of Omana and Apologos (36). Müller suspects this reading, thinking it strange that

such an article as *horns* should be mentioned
between *wooden beams* and *logs*. He thinks, therefore, that Κέρατα is either used in some technical
sense, or that the reading Κορμῶν or Κορμίων
should be substituted—adding that Κορμοὺς ἐβένου,
*planks of ebony*, are at all events mentioned by
Athênaios (p. 201a) where he is quoting Kal-
lixenos of Rhodes.

6. Κοράλλιον—Coral. (Sans. *pravâla*, Hindi
*mûngâ*.) Imported into Kanê (28), Barbarikon
on the Indus (39), Barugaza (49), and Naoura,
Tundis, Mouziris, and Nelkunda (56).

7. Λάκκος χρωμάτινος—Coloured lac. Exported
to Adouli from Ariakê (6). The Sanskrit word
is *lâkshâ*, which is probably a later form of *râkshâ*,
connected, as Lassen thinks, with *râga*, from the
root *ranj*, to dye. The vulgar form is *lâkkha*.
Gum-lac is a substance produced on the leaves
and branches of certain trees by an insect, both
as a covering for its egg and food for its young.
It yields a fine red dye.[*] Salmasius thinks that
by λάκκος χρωμάτινος must be understood not lac
itself, but vestments dyed therewith.

8. Μαργαρίτης—Pearl. (Sans. *mukta*, Hindi,
*moti*.) Exported in considerable quantity and of
superior quality from Mouziris and Nelkunda (56).
Cf. πινικόν.

9. Νῆμα Σηρικόν—Silk thread. From the coun-

[*] Bhagvânlâl Indraji Pandit points out that the colour is
called *alaktaka*, Prakrit *alito* : it is used by women for
dying the nails and feet,—also as a dye. The *gulalî* or
pill-like balls used by women are made with arrowroot
coloured with *alito*, and cotton dipped in it is sold in the
bazars under the name of *pothi*, and used for the same
purposes. He has also contributed many of the Sanskrit
names, and some notes.

try of the Thinai: imported into Barugaza and
the marts of Dimurikê (64). Exported from
Barugaza (49), and also from Barbarikon on the
Indus (39)." It is called μέταξα by Procopius and all
the later writers, as well as by the *Digest*, and was
known without either name to Pliny "—Vincent.

10. Πινίκιος κόγχος—the Pearl-oyster. (Sans.
*śukti.*) Fished for at the entrance to the Persian
Gulf (35). Pearl (πίνικον) inferior to the Indian
sort exported in great quantity from the marts of
Apologos and Omana (36). A pearl fishery (Πινικοῦ
κολύμβησις) in the neighbourhood of Kolkhoi, in
the kingdom of Pandiôn, near the island of Epio-
dôros; the produce transported to Argalou, in the
interior of the country, where muslin robes with
pearl inwoven (μαργαρίτιδες σινδόνες) were fabricated (59). The reading of the MS. is σινδόνες,
ἐβαργαρείτιδες λεγόμεναι, for which Salmasius proposed to read μαργαρίτιδες. Müller suggests
instead αἱ ᾿Αργαρίτιδες, as if the muslin bore the
name of the place *Argarou* or *Argulou*, where it was
made.

Pearl is also obtained in Taprobanê (61); is
imported into the emporium on the Ganges called
Gangê (63).

11. Πορφύρα—Purple. Of a common as well as
of a superior quality, imported from Egypt into
Mouza (24) and Kanê (28), and from the marts of
Apologos and Omana into Barugaza (36).

12. ῾Ρινόκερως—Rhinoceros (Sans. *khadgad*)—
the horn or the teeth, and probably the skin.
Exported from Adouli (16), and the marts of
Azania (7). Bruce found the hunting of the
rhinoceros still a trade in Abyssinia.

13. Χελώνη—Tortoise (Sans. *kachchhapa*) or tortoise-shell. Exported from Adouli (6) and Aualitês (7); a small quantity of the genuine and land tortoise, and a white sort with a small shell, exported from Ptolemaïs (3) ; small shells (Χελανάρια) exported from Mossulon (10); a superior sort in great quantity from Opônê (13); the mountain tortoise from the island of Menouthias (15); a kind next in quality to the Indian from the marts of Azania (16, 17); the genuine, land, white, and mountain sort with shells of extraordinary size from the island of Dioskoridês (30, 31); a good quantity from the island of Serapis (33) ; the best kind in all the. Erythræan—that of the Golden Khersonêsos (63), sent to Mouziris and Nelkunda, whence it is exported along with that of the islands off the coast of Dimurikê (probably the Laccadive islands) (56); tortoise is also procured in Taprobanê (61).

III.—Plants and their products :—

1. Αλόη—the aloe (Sans. *agaru*). Exported from Kanê (28). The sort referred to is probably the bitter cathartic, not the aromatic sort supposed by some to be the sandalwood. It grows abundantly in Sokotra, and it was no doubt exported thence to Kanê. "It is remarkable," says Vincent, "that when the author of the *Periplûs* arrives at Sokotra he says nothing of the aloe, and mentions only Indian cinnabar as a gum or resin distilling from a tree: but the confounding of cinnabar with dragon's-blood was a mistake of ancient date and a great absurdity" (II. p. 689).

2. 'Αρώματα—aromatics (εὐωδία, θυμιάματα.) Exported from Aualitês (7), Mossulon (10). Among

the spices of Tabai (12) are enumerated ἀσύβη καί ἄρωμα καί μάγλα, and similarly among the commodities of Opônê κασσία καὶ ἄρωμα καὶ μότω; and in these passages perhaps a particular kind of aromatic (cinnamon?) may by preëminence be called ἄρωμα. The occurrence, however, in two instances of such a familiar word as ἄρωμα between two outlandish words is suspicious, and this has led Müller to conjecture that the proper reading may be ἀρηβὼ, which Salmasius, citing Galen, notes to be a kind of cassia.

3.  Ασύβη—Asuphê, a kind of cassia. Exported from Tabai (12). "This term," says Vincent, "if not Oriental, is from the Greek ἀσύφηλος, signifiying *cheap* or *ordinary;* but we do not find ἀσύφη used in this manner by other authors: it may be an Alexandrian corruption of the language, or it may be the abbreviation of a merchant in his invoice." (*Asafœtida*, Sans. *hingu* or *báhlika*, Mar, *hing.*)

4.  Βδέλλα, (common form Βδέλλιον). Bdella, Bdellium, produced on the sea-coast of Gedrosia (37); exported from Barbarikon on the Indus (39); brought from the interior of India to Barugaza (48) for foreign export (49). Bdella is the gum of the *Balsamodendron Mukul,* a tree growing in Sind, Káthiáváḍ, and the Dîsâ district.[5] It is used both as an incense and as a cordial medicine. The bdellium of Scripture is a crystal, and has nothing in common with the bdellium of the *Periplûs* but its transparency. Conf. Dioskorid. i. 80; Plin. xii. 9; Galen, *Therapeut: ad Glauc.* II. p. 106; Lassen,

---

[5] Sans. *Guggula,* Guj. *Gûgal,* used as a tonic and for skin and urinary diseases.—B. I. P.

*Ind. Alt.* vol. I. p. 290; Vincent, vol. II. p. 690; Yule's *Marco Polo,* vol. II. p. 387. The etymology of the word is uncertain. Lassen suspects it to be Indian.

5. Γίζειρ—Gizeir, a kind of cassia exported from Tabai (12). This sort is noticed and described by Dioskoridês.

6. Δόκος—Beams of wood. Exported from Barugaza to the marts of Omana and Apologos (36). (? Blackwood.)

7. Δούακα—Douaka, a kind of cassia. Exported from Malao and Moundou (8, 9). It was probably that inferior species which in Dioskorid. i. 12, is called δάκαρ or δακάρ or δάρκα.

8. Ἐβένιναι φάλαγγες—Logs of ebony (*Diospyros melanoxylon.*) Exported from Barugaza to the marts of Omana and Apologos (36).

9. Ελαιον—Oil (*tila*). Exported from Egypt to Adouli (6); ἔλαιον σησάμινον, oil of sêsamê, a product of Ariakê (41). Exported from Barugaza to the Barbarine markets (14), and to Moskha in Arabia (32).[6]

10. Ἰνδικὸν μέλαν—Indigo. (Sans. *nîlî,* Guj. *gulî.*) Exported from Skythic Barbarikon (39). It appears pretty certain that the culture of the indigo plant and the preparation of the drug have been practised in India from a very remote epoch. It has been questioned, indeed, whether the Indicum mentioned by Pliny (xxxv. 6) was indigo, but, as it would seem, without any good reason. He states that it was brought from India, and that when diluted it produced an admirable mixture

---

[6] Mahuwâ oil (Guj. *doliuñ,* Sans. *madhuka*) is much exported from Bharoch.—B. I. P.

c

of blue and purple colours. *Vide* McCulloch's *Commer. Dict.* s. v. *Indigo.* Cf. Salmas. in *Exerc.* Plin. p. 181. The dye was introduced into Rome only a little before Pliny's time.

11. Κάγκαμον—Kankamon. Exported from Malao and Moundou (8, 10). According to Dioskoridês i. 23, it is the exudation of a wood, like myrrh, and used for fumigation. Cf. Plin. xii. 44. According to Scaliger it was gum-lac used as a dye. It is the "dekamalli" gum of the bazars.

12. Κάρπασος—Karpasus (Sans. *kárpása*; Heb. *karpas*,) *Gossypium arboreum*, fine muslin—a product of Ariakê (41). "How this word found its way into Italy, and became the Latin *carbasus*, fine linen, is surprising, when it is not found in the Greek language. The Καρπάσιον λίνον of Pausanias (*in Atticis*), of which the wick was formed for the lamp of Pallas, is asbestos, so called from Karpasos, a city of Crete—Salmas. Plin. *Exercit.* p. 178. Conf. Q. Curtius viii. 9 :—' Carbaso Indi corpora usque ad pedes velant, eorumque rex lecticâ margaritis circumpendentibus recumbit distinctis auro et purpurâ carbasis quâ indutus est.' " Vincent II. 699.

13. Κασσία or Κασία (Sans. *kuta*, Heb. *kiddah* and *keziah*). Exported from Tabai (12) ; a coarse kind exported from Malao and Moundou (8, 9) ; a vast quantity exported from Mossulon and Opônê (10, 13).

"This spice," says Vincent, " is mentioned frequently in the *Periplûs*, and with various additions, intended to specify the different sorts properties, or appearances of the commodity. It is a species of cinnamon, and manifestly the same as what we call cinnamon at this day; but dif-

ferent from that of the Greeks and Romans,
which was not a bark, nor rolled up into pipes,
like ours. Theirs was the tender shoot of the
same plant, and of much higher value." " If our
cinnamon," he adds, "is the ancient casia, our casia
again is an inferior sort of cinnamon." Pliny
(xii. 19) states that the cassia is of a larger size
than the cinnamon, and has a thin rind rather
than a bark, and that its value consists in being
hollowed out. Dioskoridês mentions cassia as a
product of Arabia, but this is a mistake, Arabian
cassia having been an import from India. Herodotos (iii.) had made the same mistake, saying
that cassia grew in Arabia, but that cinnamon
was brought thither by birds from the country
where Bacchus was born (India). The cassia
shrub is a sort of laurel. There are ten kinds of
cassia specified in the *Periplûs*.[7] Cf. Lassen, *Ind.
Alt.* I. 279, 283; Salmas. Plin. *Exercit.* p. 1304;
Galen, *de Antidotis*, bk. i.

14. Κιννάβαρι Ἰνδικὸν—Dragon's-blood, *damu'l
akhawein* of the Arabs, a gum distilled from
*Pterocárpus Draco*, a legumiuous tree[8] in the
island of Dioskoridês or Sokotra (30). Cinnabar, with which this was confounded, is the red
sulphuret of mercury. Pliny (lib. xxix. c. 8)
distinguishes it as ' Indian cinnabar.' Dragon's-
blood is one of the concrete balsams, the produce
of *Calamus Draco*, a species of rattan palm of
the Eastern Archipelago, [of *Pterocarpus Draco*,
allied to the Indian Kino tree or *Pt. marsupium* of

[7] May not some of these be the fragrant root of the *kusâ*
grass, *Andropogon calamus—aromaticus ?*—J. B.
[8] A similar gum is obtained from the *Pâlâsa* (Guj. *khâ-
khara*), the *Dhâka* of Râjputâna.—B. I. P.

South India, and of *Dracæna Draco*, a liliaceous tree of Madeira and the Canary Islands].

15. Κόστος (Sansk. *kushṭa*, Mar. *choka*, Guj. *katha* and *pushkara mûla*,)—Kostus. Exported from Barbarikon, a mart on the Indus (39), and from Barugaza, which procured it from Kâbul through Proklaïs, &c. This was considered the best of aromatic roots, as nard or spikenard was the best of aromatic plants. Pliny (xii. 25) describes this root as hot to the taste and of consummate fragrance, noting that it was found at the head of Patalênê, where the Indus bifurcates to form the Delta, and that it was of two sorts¦ black and white, black being of an inferior quality. Lassen states that two kinds are found in India—one in Multân, and the other in Kâbul and Kâsmîr. "The Costus of the ancients is still exported from Western India, as well as from Calcutta to China, under the name of *Putchok*, to be burnt as an incense in Chinese temples. Its identity has been ascertained in our own days by Drs. Royle and Falconer as the root of a plant which they called *Aucklandia Costus*. . . . . . . Alexander Hamilton, at the beginning of last century, calls it *ligna dulcis* (sic), and speaks of it as an export from Sind, as did the author of the *Periplûs* 1600 years earlier." Yule's *Marco Polo*, vol. II. p. 388.

16. Κρόκος—Crocus, Saffron. (Sans. *kaśmîraja*, Guj. *kesir*, Pers. *zafrán*.) Exported from Egypt to Mouza (24) and to Kanê (28).

17. Κύπερος—Cyprus. Exported from Egypt to Mouza (24). It is an aromatic rush used in medicine (Pliny xxi. 18). Herodotos (iv. 71) describes

it as an aromatic plant used by the Skythians
for embalming. Κύπερος is probably Ionic for
Κύπειρος—Κύπειρος ἰνδικὸς of Dioskoridês, and
*Cypria herba indica* of Pliny.—Perhaps Turmeric,
*Curcuma longa,* or Galingal possibly.

18. Λέντια, (Lat. *lintea*)—Linen. Exported from
Egypt to Adouli (6).

19. Λίβανος (Heb. *lebonah,* Arab. *luban,* Sans.
*śrivása*)—Frankincense. Peratic or Libyan frankincense exported from the Barbarine markets—
Tabai (12), Mossulon (10), Malaô and Moundou, in
small quantities (8, 9); produced in great abundance and of the best quality at Akannai (11);
Arabian frankincense exported from Kanê (28). A
magazine for frankincense on the Sakhalitic Gulf
near Cape Suagros (30). Moskha, the port whence
it was shipped for Kanê and India (32) and Indo-
Skythia (39).

Regarding this important product Yule thus
writes :—"The coast of Hadhramaut is the true
and ancient Χώρα λιβανοφόρος or λιβανωτοφόρος,
indicated or described under those names by The-
ophrastus, Ptolemy, Pliny, Pseudo-Arrian, and
other classical writers, *i.e.* the country producing
the fragrant gum-resin called by the Hebrews *Lebonah,* by the Arabs *Luban* and *Kundur,* by the Greeks
*Libanos,* by the Romans *Thus,* in mediæval Latin
*Olibanum* (probably the Arabic *al-luban,* but popu-
larly interpreted as *oleum Libani*), and in English
frankincense, *i.e.* I apprehend, ' genuine incense'
or ' incense proper.'[9]  It is still produced in this

---

[9] What the Brâhmans call *kundaru* is the gum of a tree
called the *Dhûpa-salai ;* another sort of it, from Arabia,
they call *Isêsa,* and in Kâthiâvâd it is known as *Sesa-
gundar.*—B. I. P.

region and exported from it, but the larger part of that which enters the markets of the world is exported from the roadsteads of the opposite Sumâlî coast. Frankincense when it first exudes is milky white; whence the name *white incense* by which Polo speaks of it, and the Arabic name *luban* apparently refers to milk. The elder Niebuhr, who travelled in Arabia, depreciated the Libanos of Arabia, representing it as greatly inferior to that brought from India, called Benzoin. He adds that the plant which produces it is not native, but originally from Abyssinia."—*Marco Polo*, vol. II. p. 443, &c.

20. Λύκιον—Lycium. Exported from Barbarikon in Indo-Skythia (39), and from Barugaza (49). Lycium is a thorny plant, so called from being found in Lykia principally. Its juice was used for dying yellow, and a liquor drawn from it was used as a medicine (Celsus v. 26, 30, and vi. 7). It was held in great esteem by the ancients. Pliny (xxiv. 77) says that a superior kind of Lycium produced in India was made from a thorn called also *Pyxacanthus* (box-thorn) *Chironia*. It is known in India as *Ruzot*, an extract of the *Berberis lycium* and *B. aristata*, both grown on the Himâlayas. Conf. the λύκιον ἰνδικὸν of Dioskor. i. 133. (? Gamboge.)

21. Μάγλα—Magla—a kind of cassia mentioned only in the *Periplûs*. Exported from Tabai (12).

22. Μάκειρ—Macer. Exported from Malaô and Moundou (8, 9). According to Pliny, Dioskoridês, and others, it is an Indian bark—perhaps a kind of cassia. The bark is red and the root large. The bark was used as a medicine in dysenteries. Pliny

xii. 8; Salmasius, 1302. ( ? The *Karachâlâ* of the
bâzârs, *Kutajatvak*).

23. Μαλάβαθρον (Sans. *tamâlapattra,* the leaf
of the *Laurus Cassia*), Malabathrum, Betel. Obtained by the Thinai from the Sesatai and exported to
India[10] (65); conveyed down the Ganges to Gangê
near its mouth (63); conveyed from the interior
of India to Mouziris and Nelkunda for export (56).
That Malabathrum was not only a masticatory, but
also an unguent or perfume, may be inferred from
Horace (*Odes,* II. vii. 89):—

. . . " coronatus nitentes
Malabathro Syrio capillos",
and from Pliny (xii. 59): "Dat et Malabathrum
Syria, arborum folio convoluto, arido colore, ex
quo exprimitur oleum ad unguenta: fertiliore
ejusdem Egypto : laudatius tamen ex India venit."
From Ptolemy (VII. ii. 16) we learn that the best
Malabathrum was produced in Kirrhadia—that is,
Rangpur. Dioskoridês speaks of it as a masticatory, and was aware of the confusion caused by
mistaking the nard for the betel.

24. Μέλι τὸ καλάμινον, τὸ λεγόμενον σάκχαρ
(Sans. *śarkarâ,* Prâkṛit *sâkara,* Arab. *sukkar,*
Latin *saccharum*)—Honey from canes, called
Sugar. Exported from Barugaza to the marts
of Barbaria (14). The first Western writer
who mentions this article was Theophrastos, who
continued the labours of Aristotle in natural history. He called it a sort of honey extracted from
reeds. Strabo states, on the authority of Nearkhos,
that reeds in India yield honey without bees.

[10] More likely from Nepâl, where it is called *tejapât.*—
B. I. P.

Ælian (*Hist. Anim.*) speaks of a kind of honey pressed from reeds which grew among the Prasii. Seneca (Epist. 84) speaks of sugar as a kind of honey found in India on the leaves of reeds, which had either been dropped on them from the sky as dew, or had exuded from the reeds themselves. This was a prevalent error in ancient times, *e.g.* Dioskoridês says that sugar is a sort of concreted honey found upon canes in India and Arabia Felix, and Pliny that it is collected from canes like a gum. He describes it as white and brittle between the teeth, of the size of a hazel-nut at most, and used in medicine only. So also Lucan, alluding to the Indians near the Ganges, says that they quaff sweet juices from tender reeds. Sugar, however, as is well known, must be extracted by art from the plant. It has been conjectured that the sugar described by Pliny and Dioskoridês was sugar candy obtained from China.

25. Μελίλωτον—Melilot, Honey-lotus. Exported from Egypt to Barugaza (49). Melilot is the Egyptian or Nymphæa Lotus, or Lily of the Nile, the stalk of which contained a sweet nutritive substance which was made into bread. So Vincent ; but Melilot is a kind of clover, so called from the quantity of honey it contains. The nymphæa lotus, or what was called the Lily of the Nile, is not a true lotus, and contains no edible substance.

26. Μοκρότον. Exported from Moundou (9) and Mossulon (10). It is a sort of incense, mentioned only in the *Periplûs*.

27. Μότω—Motô—a sort of cassia exported from Tabai and Opônê (13).

28. Μύρον—Myrrh. (Sans. *bola*.) Exported from

Egypt to Barugaza as a present for the king (49).
It is a gum or resin issuing from a thorn found
in Arabia Felix, Abyssinia, &c., *vide σμύρνη inf.*

29. Νάρδος (Sans. *nalada,* ' kaskas,' Heb. *nerd*)
Nard, Spikenard.[11] Gangetic spikenard brought
down the Ganges to Gangê, near its mouth (63), and
forwarded thence to Mouziris and Nelkunda (56).
Spikenard produced in the regions of the Upper
Indus and in Indo-Skythia forwarded through
Ozênê to Barugaza (48). Imported by the Egyp-
tians from Barugaza and Barbarikon in Indo-
Skythia (49, 39).

The *Nardos* is a plant called (from its root
being shaped like an ear of corn) νάρδου στάχυς,
also ναρδόσταχυς, Latin *Spica nardi*, whence ' spikenard.' It belongs to the species *Valeriana.* " No
Oriental aromatic," says Vincent, " has caused
greater disputes among the critics or writers on
natural history, and it is only within these few
years that we have arrived at the true knowledge
of this curious odour by means of the inquiries
of Sir W. Jones and Dr. Roxburgh. Pliny describes the nard with its *spica,* mentioning also
that both the leaves and the *spica* are of high
value, and that the odour is the prime in all
unguents ; the price 100 denarii for a pound. But
he afterwards visibly confounds it with the Malabathrum or Betel, as will appear from his usage
of *Hadrosphœrum, Mesosphœrum,* and *Microsphœ-
rum,* terms peculiar to the Betel"—II. 743-4. See
Sir W. Jones on the spikenard of the ancients in
*As. Res.* vol. II. pp. 416 *et seq.,* and Roxburgh's

---

[11] Obtained from the root of *Nardostachys jatamansi,* a
native of the eastern Himâlayas.—J. B.

additional remarks on the spikenard of the ancients, vol. IV. pp. 97 *et seq.*, and botanical observations on the spikenard, pp. 433. See also Lassen,
*Ind. Alt.* vol. I. pp. 288 *et seq.*

30. Ναύπλιος—Nauplius. Exported in small
quantity from the marts of Azania (17). The
signification of the word is obscure, and the reading suspected. For ΝαΥΠλιος Müller suggests
ΝαΡΓΙλιος, the Indian cocoanut, which the Arabians
call *Nargil* (Sansk. *nárikéla* or *nálikéra*, Guj.
*náliyér*, Hindi *náliyar*). It favours this sugges-
tion that cocoanut oil is a product of Zangibar, and
that in four different passages of Kosmas Indiko-
pleustês nuts are called ἀργέλλια, which is either a
corrupt reading for ναργέλλια, or Kosmas may not
have known the name accurately enough.

31. 'Οθόνιον—Muslin. Séric muslin sent from
the Thînai to Barugaza and Dimurikê (64). Coarse
cottons produced in great quantity in Ariakê,
carried down from Ozênê to Barugaza (48); large
supplies sent thither from Tagara also (51);
Indian muslins exported from the markets of
Dimurikê to Egypt (56). Muslins of every description, Seric and dyed of a mallow colour, exported from Barugaza to Egypt (49); Indian muslin
taken to the island of Dioskoridês (31); wide Indian
muslins called μοναχή, *monákhé*, i. e. of the best
and finest sort; and another sort called σαγματογήνη, *sagmatogéné*, i. e. coarse cotton unfit for
spinning, and used for stuffing beds, cushions, &c.,
exported from Barugaza to the Barbarine markets
(14), and to Arabia, whence it was exported to
Adouli (6). The meanings given to *monákhé* and
*sagmatogéné* (for which other readings have

been suggested) are conjectural. Vincent defends the meaning assigned to *sagmatogêné* by a quotation from a passage in Strabo citing Nearkhos :—" Fine muslins are made of cotton, but the Makedonians use cotton for flocks, and stuffing of couches."

32. 'Οἶνος—Wine. Laodikean and Italian wine exported in small quantity to Adouli (6); to Aualitês (7), Malaô (8), Mouza (24), Kanê (28), Barbarikon in Indo-Skythia (39); the same sorts, together with Arabian wine, to Barugaza (49); sent in small quantity to Mouziris and Nelkunda (56); the region inland from Oraia bears the vine (37), which is found also in the district of Mouza (24), whence wine is exported to the marts of Azania, not for sale, but to gain the good will of the natives (17). Wine is exported also from the marts of Apologos and Omana to Barugaza (36). By Arabian wine may perhaps be meant palm or toddy wine, a great article of commerce.

33. "Ομφακος Διοσπολιτικῆς χυλός—the juice of the sour grape of Diospolis. Exported from Egypt to Aualitês (7). This, says Vincent, was the *dipse* of the Orientals, and still used as a relish all over the East. *Dipse* is the rob of grapes in their unripe state, and a pleasant acid.— II. 751. This juice is called by Dioskoridês (iv. 7) in one word Ομφάκιον, and also (v. 12) 'Οἶνος 'Ομφακίτης. Cf. Plin. xii. 27.

34. "Ορυζα (Sansk. *vrîhi*)—Rice. Produced in Oraia and Ariakê (37, 41), exported from Barugaza to the Barbarine markets (14), and to the island of Dioskoridês (31).

35. Πέτερι (Sansk. *pippalî*,) long pepper—Pep-

per. Kottonarik pepper exported in large quantities from Mouziris and Nelkunda (56); long pepper from Barugaza (49). *Kottonara* was the name of the district, and *Kottonarikon* the name of the pepper for which the district was famous. Dr. Buchanan identifies Kottonara with Kadattanâḍu, a district in the Calicut country celebrated for its pepper. Dr. Burnell, however, identifies it with Kolatta-Nâḍu, the district about Tellicherry, which, he says, is the pepper district.

36. Πυρὸs—Wheat. Exported in small quantity from Egypt to Kanê (28), some grown in the district around Mouza (24).

37. Σάκχαρι—Sugar : see under Μέλι.

38. Σανδαράκη—Sandarakê (*chandrasa* of the bazars) ; a resin from the *Thuja articulata* or *Callitris quadrivalvis*, a small coniferous tree of North Africa; it is of a faint aromatic smell and is used as incense. Exported from Egypt to Barugaza (49); conveyed to Mouziris and Nelkunda (56).[12]

Sandarakê also is a red pigment—red sulphuret of arsenic, as orpiment is the yellow sulphuret. Cf. Plin. xxxv. 22, Hard. "Juba informs us that sandarace and ochre are found in an island of the Red Sea, Topazas, whence they are brought to us."

39. Σαντάλινα and σασάμινα ξύλα—Logs of Sandal and Sasame (*santalum album*). Exported from Barugaza to the marts of Omana and Apologos (36). Σαντάλινα is a correction of the MS. reading σαγάλινα proposed by Salmasius. Kosmas Indiko-

---

[12] It is brought now from the Eastern Archipelago.— B. I. P.

pleustes calls sandalwood τζαδάνα. For σασάμινα
of the MS. Stuckius proposed σησάμινα—a futile
emendation, since sesame is known only as a
leguminous plant from which an oil is expressed,
and not as a tree. But possibly Red Saunders
wood (*Pterocarpus Santalinus*) may be meant.

40. Σησάμινον ἔλαιον. See *Ελαιον.

41. Σινδόνες διαφορώταται αἱ Γαγγητικᾶι. The finest
Bengal muslins exported from the Ganges (63);
other muslins in Taprobanê (61); Μαργαρίτιδες (?),
made at Argalou and thence exported (59);
muslins of all sorts and mallow-tinted (μολόχιναι)
sent from Ozênê to Barugaza (48), exported thence
to Arabia for the supply of the market at Adouli
(6).

42. Σῖτος—Corn. Exported from Egypt to
Adouli (7), Malaô (8); a little to Mouza (24), and to
Kanê (28), and to Muziris and Nelkunda for ships'
stores (56); exported from Dimurikê and Ariakê
into the Barbarine markets (14), into Moskha (32)
and the island of Dioskoridês (31); exported also
from Mouza to the ports of Azania for presents (17).

43. Σμύρνη—Myrrh (vide μύρον). Exported from
Malaô,Moundou, Mossulon (8, 9, 10); from Aualitês
a small quantity of the best quality (7); a choice
sort that trickles in drops, called *Abeirminaia*
(ἐκλεκτὴ καὶ στακτὴ ἀβειρμιναία), exported from Mouza
(24). For ᾽Αβειρμιναία of the MS. Müller suggests
to read γαβειρμιναία, inclining to think that two
kinds of myrrh are indicated, the names of which
have been erroneously combined into one, viz. the
Gabiræan and Minæan, which are mentioned by
Dioskoridês, Hippokratês, and Galen. There is a
*Wadi Gabir* in Omân.

44. Στύραξ—Storax (Sans. *turuska, selarasa* of the bazars),—one of the balsams. Exported from Egypt to Kanê (28), Barbarikon on the Indus (39), Barugaza (40). Storax is the produce of the tree *Liquidambar orientale,* which grows in the south of Europe and the Levant.[13] The purest kind is storax in grains. Another kind is called *styrax calamita,* from being brought in masses wrapped up in the leaves of a certain reed. Another kind, that sold in shops, is semi-fluid.

45. Φοῖνιξ—the Palm or Dates. Exported from the marts of Apologos and Omana to Barugaza (36, 37).

IV.—Metals and Metallic Articles :—

1. Ἀργυρᾶ σκεύη, ἀργυρώματα—Vessels of silver. Exported from Egypt to Mossulon (10), to Barbarikon on the Indus (39). Silver plate chased or polished (τορνευτὰ or τετορνευμένα) sent as presents to the despot of Mouza (24), to Kanê for the king (28). Costly (βαρύτιμα) plate to Barugaza for the king (49). Plate made according to the Egyptian fashion to Adouli for the king (6).

2. Ἀρσενικὸν—Arsenic (*somal*). Exported from Egypt to Mouziris and Nelkunda (56).

3. Δηνάριον—Denary. Exported in small quantity from Egypt to Adouli (6). Gold and silver denarii sent in small quantity to the marts of Barbaria (8, 13); exchanges with advantage for native money at Barugaza (49).

The *denary* was a Roman coin equal to about $8\frac{1}{2}d.$, and a little inferior in value to the Greek drachma.

4. Κάλτις—Kaltis. A gold coin (νομισμὰ) cur-

---

[13] In early times it was obtained chiefly from *Styrax officinalis,* a native of the same region.—J. B.

rent in the district of the Lower Ganges (63);
Benfey thinks the word is connected with the
Sanskrit *kalita,* i.e. *numeratum.*

5. Κασσίτερος (Sans. *banga, kathila*)—Tin.
Exported from Egypt to Aualitês (7), Malaô (8)
Kanê (28), Barugaza (49), Mouziris and Nelkunda
(56). India produced this metal, but not in those
parts to which the Egyptian trade carried it.

6. Μόλυβδος—Lead (Sansk. *nága,* Guj. *sísun*).
Exported from Egypt to Barugaza, Muziris, and
Nelkunda (49, 56).

7. 'Ορείχαλκος—Orichalcum (Sans. *tripus,* Prak.
*pítala*)—Brass. Used for ornaments and cut into
small pieces by way of coin. Exported from Egypt
to Adouli (6).

The word means 'mountain copper.' Ramusio
calls it white copper from which the gold and
silver have not been well separated in extracting
it from the ore. Gold, it may be remarked, does
not occur as an export from any of the African
marts, throughout the *Periplûs.*

8. Σίδηρος, σιδηρᾶ σκεύη—Iron, iron utensils.
Exported from Egypt to Malaô, Moundou, Tabai,
Opônê (8, 9, 12, 13). Iron spears, swords and
adzes exported to Adouli (6). Indian iron and
sword-blades (στόμωμα) exported to Adouli from
Arabia (Ariakê?). Spears (λόγχαι) manufactured
at Mouza, hatchets (πελύκια), swords (μάχαιραι),
awls (ὀπέτια) exported from Mouza to Azania
(17).

On the Indian sword see Ktêsias, p. 80, 4.
The Arabian poets celebrate swords made of Indian
steel. Cf. Plin. xxxiv. 41 :—" Ex omnibus autem
generibus palma Serico ferro est." This iron, as

has already been stated, was sent to India along with skins and cloth. Cf. also Edrisi, vol. I. p. 65, ed. Joubert. Indian iron is mentioned in the Pandects as an article of commerce.

9. Στίμμι—Stibium (Sans. *sauvîrânjana*, Prâk. *surmâ*). Exported from Egypt to Barugaza (49), to Mouziris and Nelkunda (56).

Stibium is a sulphuret of antimony, a dark pigment, called *kohol*, much used in the East for dyeing the eyelids.

10. Χαλκὸς—Copper (Sans. *tâmra*) or Brass. Exported from Egypt to Kanê (28), to Barugaza (49), Mouziris and Nelkunda (56). Vessels made thereof (Χαλκουργήματα) sent to Mouza as presents to the despot (24). Drinking-vessels (ποτήρια) exported to the marts of Barbaria (8, 13). Big and round drinking-cups to Adouli (6). A few (μελίεφθα ὀλίγα) to Malaô (8) ; μελίεφθα χαλκᾶ for cooking with, and being cut into bracelets and anklets for women to Adouli (6).

Regarding μελίεφθα Vincent says : " No usage of the word occurs elsewhere ; but metals were prepared with several materials to give them colour, or to make them tractable, or malleable. Thus χολόβαφα in Hesychius was brass prepared with ox's gall to give it the colour of gold, and used, like our tinsel ornaments or foil, for stage dresses and decorations. Thus common brass was neither ductile nor malleable, but the Cyprian brass was both. And thus perhaps brass, μελίεφθα was formed with some preparation of honey." Müller cannot accept this view. " It is evident," he says, " that the reference is to ductile copper from which, as Pliny says, all impurity has been

carefully removed by smelting, so that pots, bracelets, and articles of that sort could be fabricated
from it. One might therefore think that the reading should be περίεφθα or πυρίεφθα, but in such a
case the writer would have said περίεφθον
χαλκόν. In vulgar speech μελίεφθα is used as
a substantive noun, and I am therefore almost
persuaded that, just as molten copper, ὁ χαλκὸς
ὁ χυτὸς, cuprum caldarium, was called τρόχιος, from
the likeness in shape of its round masses to
hoops, so laminæ of ductile copper (plaques de
cuivre) might have been called μελίεφθα, because
shaped like thin honey-cakes, πέμματα μελίεφθα."

11. Χρυσὸς—Gold. Exported from the marts of
Apologos and Omana to Barugaza (36). Gold
plate—χρυσώματα—exported from Egypt to Mouza
for the despot (24), and to Adouli for the king (6).

V.  Stones :—

1. Λιθία διαφανὴς—Gems (carbuncles ?) found in
Taprobanê (63) ; exported in every variety from
Mouziris and Nelkunda (56).

2. Αδάμας—Diamonds. (Sans. vajra, pîraka).
Exported from Mouziris and Nelkunda (56).

3. Καλλεανὸς λίθος—Gold-stone, yellow crystal,
chrysolith ? Exported from Barbarikon in Indo-
Skythia (39).

It is not a settled point what stone is meant.
Lassen says that the Sanskrit word kalyâṇa means
gold, and would therefore identify it with the
chrysolith or gold-stone. If this view be correct,
the reading of the MS. need not be altered into
καλλαϊνὸς, as Salmasius, whom the editors of the
Periplûs generally follow, enjoins. In support of
the alteration Salmasius adduces Pliny, xxxvii.

e

56 :—" Callais sapphirum imitatur, candidior et litoroso mari similis. Callainas vocant e turbido Callaino", and other passages. Schwanbeck, however, maintaining the correctness of the MS. reading, says that the Sanskṛit word *kalyâṇa* generally signifies *money*, but in a more general sense *anything beautiful*, and might therefore have been applied to this gem. *Kalyâṇa*, he adds, would appear in Greek as καλλιανὸς or καλλεανὸς rather than καλλαϊνὸς. In like manner *kalyâṇî* of the Indians appears in our author not as καλλάϊνα, but, as it ought to be, καλλίενα.

4. Λύγδος—Alabaster. Exported from Mouza (24). Salmasius says that an imitation of this alabaster was formed of Parian marble, but that the best and original *lygdus* was brought from Arabia, that is, Mouza, as noted in the *Periplûs*. Cf. Pliny (xxxvi. 8) :— " Lygdinos in Tauro repertos . . . antea ex Arabia tantum advehi solitos candoris eximii."

5. 'Ονυχινὴ λίθια—Onyx (*akika*—agate). Sent in vast quantities (πλείστη) from Ozênê and Paithana to Barugaza (48, 51), and thence exported to Egypt (49). Regarding the onyx mines of Gujarât *vide* Ritter, vol. VI. p. 603.

6. Μουρρίνη, sup. λιθία—Fluor-spath. Sent from Ozênê to Barugaza, and exported to Egypt (49). Porcelain made at Diospolis (μουρρίνη λιθία ἡ γενομένη ἐν Διοσπόλει) exported from Egypt to Adouli (6).

The reading of the MS. is μορρίνης. By this is to be understood *vitrum murrhinum*, a sort of china or porcelain made in imitation of cups or vases of *murrha*, a precious fossil-stone resembling, if not identical with, *fluor-spath,* such as is found in Derbyshire. Vessels of this stone were exported from India, and also, as we learn from Pliny, from Karmania, to the Roman market, where they fetched extravagant prices.[14] The " cups baked in Parthian fires" (*pocula Parthis focis cocta*) mentioned by Propertius (IV. v. 26) must be referred to the former class. The whole subject is one which has much exercised the pens of the learned. " Six hundred writers," says Müller, " emulously apply-ing themselves to explain what had the best claim to be considered the *murrha* of the ancients, have advanced the most conflicting opinions. Now it is pretty well settled that the murrhine vases were made of that stone which is called in German *flusspath (spato-fluore)*". He then refers to the following as the principal authorities on the subject :—Pliny—xxxiii. 7 *et seq. ;* xxxiii. *proœm.* Suetonius—*Oct.* c. 71; Seneca—*Epist.* 123; Martial—iv. 86; xiv. 43; *Digest*—xxxiii. 10, 3; xxxiv. 2. 19 ; Rozière—*Mémoire sur les Vases mur-rhins,* &c. ; in *Description de l'Égypt,* vol. VI. pp. 277 *et seq. ;* Corsi—*Delle Pietre antiche,* p. 106 ; Thiersch—*Ueber die Vasa Murrhina der Alten, in Abhandl. d. Munchn. Akad.* 1835, vol. I. pp. 443-509; A learned Englishman in the *Classical Journal* for 1810, p. 472; Witzsch in Pauly's *Real 'Encycl.* vol. V. p. 253 ; See also Vincent, vol. II. pp. 723-7.

7. 'Οψιανὸς λίθος—the Opsian or Obsidian stone, found in the Bay of Hanfelah (5). Pliny says,— "The opsians or obsidians are also reckoned as a

---

[14] Nero gave for one 300 talents = £58,125. They were first seen at Rome in the triumphal procession of Pompey. [May these not have been of emerald, or even ruby ?—J. B.]

sort of glass bearing the likeness of the stone
which Obsius (or Obsidius) found in Ethiopia, of
a very black colour, sometimes even translucent,
hazier than ordinary glass to look through, and
when used for mirrors on the walls reflecting
but shadows instead of distinct images." (Bk.
xxxvi. 37). The only Obsius mentioned in history
is a M. Obsius who had been Prætor, a friend of
Germanicus, referred to by Tacitus (*Ann*. IV. 68,
71). He had perhaps been for a time prefect of
Egypt, and had coasted the shore of Ethiopia at
the time when Germanicus traversed Egypt till
he came to the confines of Ethiopia. Perhaps,
however, the name of the substance is of Greek
origin—'οψιανὸς, from its reflecting power.

8. Σάπφειρος—the Sapphire. Exported from
Barbarikon in Indo-Skythia (39). "The ancients
distinguished two sorts of dark blue or purple,
one of which was spotted with gold. Pliny says it
is never pellucid, which seems to make it a
different stone from what is now called sapphire."—
Vincent (vol. II. p. 757), who adds in a note, "Dr.
Burgess has specimens of both sorts, the one with
gold spots like lapis lazuli, and not transparent."[15]

9. Ὑάκινθος—Hyacinth or Jacinth. Exported
from Mouziris and Nelkunda (56). According to
Salmasius this is the Ruby. In Solinus xxx.
it would seem to be the Amethyst (Sansk.
*pushkarája*.)

10. Ὕαλος 'αργὴ—Glass of a coarse kind. Exported from Egypt to Barugaza (49), to Mouziris
and Nelkunda (56). Vessels of glass (ὑαλὰ σκεύη) ex-

---

[15] Possibly the Lapis Lazuli is meant.—J. B.

ported from Egypt to Barbarikon in Indo-Skythia
(39). Crystal of many sorts (λιθίας ὑαλῆς πλεῖστα
γένη) exported from Egypt to Adouli, Aualitês,
Mossulon (6, 7, 10); from Mouza to Azania (17).

11. Χρυσόλιθος—Chrysolite. Exported from
Egypt to Barbarikon in Indo-Skythia (39), to
Barugaza (43), to Mouziris and Nelkunda (56).
Some take this to be the topaz (Hind. *pîrojâ*).

VI. Wearing Apparel :—

1. 'Ιμάτια ἄγναφα—Cloths undressed. Manufactured in Egypt and thence exported to Adouli (6).
These were disposed of to the tribes of Barbaria
—the Troglodyte shepherds of Upper Egypt,
Nubia and Ethiopia.

2. 'Ιμάτια βαρβαρικὰ σύμμικτα γεγναμμένα—
Cloths for the Barbarine markets, dressed and
dyed of various colours. Exported to Malaô and
Aualitês (8, 7).

3. 'Ιματισμὸς 'Αραβικὸς—Cloth or coating for the
Arabian markets. Exported from Egypt (24).
Different kinds are enumerated :—Χειριδωτὸς, with
sleeves reaching to the wrist; ᾽Οτε ἁπλοῦς καὶ ὁ
κοινὸς, with single texture and of the common sort;
σκοτουλάτος, wrought with figures, checkered; the
word is a transliteration of the Latin *scutulatus*,
from *scutum*, the checks being lozenge-shaped, like
a shield: see Juvenal, Sat. ii. 79; διάχρυσος, shot
with gold; πολυτελὴς, a kind of great price sent
to the despot of Mouza; Κοινὸς καὶ ἁπλοῦς καὶ
ὁ νόθος, cloth of a common sort, and cloth of simple
texture, and cloth in imitation of a better commodity, sent to Kanê (28); Διάφορος ἁπλοῦς, of
superior quality and single texture, for the king
(28); 'Απλοῦς, *of single texture*, in great quantity, and

νόθος, an inferior sort imitating a better, in small quantity, sent to Barbarikon in Indo-Skythia (39), ἁπλοῦς καὶ νόθος παντοῖος, and for the king ἁπλοῦς πολυτελὴς, sent to Barugaza (49); Ἱματισμὸς οὐ πολύς—cloth in small quantity sent to Muziris and Nelkunda (56); ἐντόπιος, of native manufacture, exported from the marts of Apologos and Omana to Barugaza (36).

4. Ἀβόλλαι—Riding or watch cloaks. Exported from Egypt to Mouza (34), to Kanê (28). This word is a transliteration of the Latin Abolla. It is supposed, however, to be derived from Greek: ἀμβολλη, i. e. ἀμφιβολή. It was a woollen cloak of close texture—often mentioned in the Roman writers: e.g. Juven. Sat. iii. 115 and iv. 76; Sueton. Calig. c. 35. Where the word occurs in sec. 6 the reading of the MS. is ἄβολοι, which Müller has corrected to ἀβόλλαι, though Salmasius had defended the original reading.

5. Δικρόσσια (Lat. Mantilia utrinque fimbriata) —Cloths with a double fringe. Exported from Egypt to Adouli (6). This word occurs only in the Periplús. The simple Κρόσσιον, however, is met with in Herodian, Epim. p. 72. An adjective δίκροσσος is found in Pollux vii. 72. "We cannot err much," says Vincent, "in rendering the δικρόσσια of the Periplús either cloth fringed, with Salmasius, or striped, with Apollonius. Meursius says λεντία ἄκροσσα are plain linens not striped.

6. Ζῶναι πολύμιτοι πηχυαῖοι—Flowered or embroidered girdles, a cubit broad. Exported from Egypt to Barugaza (49). Σκιωταὶ—girdles (kácha) shaded of different colours, exported to Mouza (24). This word occurs only in the Periplús.

7. Καννάκαι—Garments of frieze. Exported from Arabia to Adouli (6); a pure sort—ἁπλοῖ— exported to the same mart from Egypt (6). In the latter of these two passages the MS. reading is γαυνάκαι. Both forms are in use: conf. Latin *gaunace*—Varro, *de L. L.* 4, 35. It means also *a fur garment* or *blanket—vestis stragula*.

8. Λώδικες—Quilts or coverlids. Exported in small quantity from Egypt to Mouza (24) and Kanê (28).

9. Περιζώματα—Sashes, girdles, or aprons. Exported from Barugaza to Adouli (6), and into Barbaria (14).

10. Πολύμιτα—Stuffs in which several threads were taken for the woof in order to weave flowers or other objects : Latin *polymita* and *plumatica*. Exported from Egypt to Barbarikon in Indo-Sky-thia (39), to Mouziris and Nelkunda (56).

11. Σάγοι 'Αρσινοητικοὶ γεγναμμένοι καὶ βεβαμμένοι —Coarse cloaks made at Arsinoê, dressed and dyed. Exported from Egypt to Barbaria (8, 13).

12. Στολαὶ 'Αρσινοητικὰι—Women's robes made at Arsinoê. Exported from Egypt to Adouli (6).

13. Χιτῶνες—Tunics. Exported from Egypt to Malaô, Moundou, Mossulon (8, 9, 10).

VII. In addition to the above, works of art are mentioned.

'Ανδριάντες—Images, sent as presents to Khari-baël (48). Cf. Strabo (p. 714), who among the articles sent to Arabia enumerates τόρευμα, γραφὴν, πλάσμα, pieces of sculpture, painting, statues.

Μουσικὰ—Instruments of music, for presents to the. king of Ariakê (49).

## ANONYMI [ARRIANI UT FERTUR] PERIPLUS MARIS ERYTHRÆI.

1. The first of the important roadsteads established on the Red Sea, and the first also of the great trading marts upon its coast, is the port of M y o s-h o r m o s in Egypt. Beyond it

*Commentary.*

(1) M y o s H o r m o s.—Its situation is determined by the cluster of islands now called J i f â t î n [lat. 27° 12′ N., long. 33° 55′ E.] of which the three largest lie opposite an indenture of the coast of Egypt on the curve of which its harbour was situated [near Ras Abu Somer, a little north of Safâjah Island]. It was founded by Ptolemy Philadelphos B. C. 274, who selected it as the principal port of the Egyptian trade with India in preference to Arsinoe,[16] N. N. E. of Suez, on account of the difficulty and tediousness of the navigation down the Heroöpolite Gulf. The vessels bound for Africa and the south of Arabia left its harbour about the time of the autumnal equinox, when the North West wind which then prevailed carried them quickly down the Gulf. Those bound for the Malabar Coast or Ceylon left in July, and if they cleared the Red Sea before the 1st of

---

[16] There was another Arsinoe between Ras Dh'ib and Ras Shukhair, lat. 28° 3′ N. The few geographical indications added by Mr. Burgess to these comments as they passed through the press are enclosed in brackets. [ ]

at a distance of 1800 stadia is B e r e n î k ê, which is to your right if you approach it by sea.

---

September, they had the monsoon to assist their passage across the ocean. M y o s H o r m o s was distant from K o p t o s [lat. 26° N.], the station on the Nile through which it communicated with Alexandria, a journey of seven or eight days along a road opened through the desert by Philadelphos. The name M y o s H o r m o s is of Greek origin, and may signify either the Harbour of the Mouse, or, more probably, of the Mussel, since the pearl mussel abounded in its neighbourhood. A g a t h a r k h i d ê s calls it A p h r o d i t ē s H o r m o s, and Pliny V e n e r i s P o r t u s. [Veneris Portus however was probably at Sherm Sheikh, lat. 24° 36′ N. Off the coast is Wade Jemâl Island, lat. 24° 39′ N., long. 35° 8′ E., called Iambe by Pliny, and perhaps the Aphroditês Island of Ptolemy IV. v. 77.] Referring to this name Vincent says: "Here if the reader will advert to Aphroditê, the Greek title of Venus, as springing from the foam of the ocean, it will immediately appear that the Greeks were translating here, for the native term to this day is *Suffange-el-Bahri*, 'sponge of the sea'; and the vulgar error of the sponge being the foam of the sea, will immediately account for Aphroditê."

The rival of Myos-Hormos was B e r e n i k ê, a city built by Ptolemy Philadelphos, who so named it in honour of his mother, who was the daughter of Ptolemy Lagos and Antigonê. It was in the same parallel with Syênê and therefore not far from the Tropic [lat. 23° 55′ N.]. It stood nearly

*f*

These roadsteads are both situate at the furthest
end of Egypt, and are bays of the Red Sea.

2. The country which adjoins them on the
right below Berenîkê is B a r b a r i a. Here the
sea-board is peopled by the I k h t h y o p h a g o i,
who live in scattered huts built in the narrow
gorges of the hills, and further inland are the

---

at the bottom of *Foul Bay* (ἐν βάθει τοῦ ʼΑκαθάρτου
Κόλπου), so called from the coast being foul with
shoals and breakers, and not from the impurity of
its water, as its Latin name, *Sinus Immundus*, would
lead us to suppose. Its ruins are still per-
ceptible even to the arrangement of the streets,
and in the centre is a small Egyptian temple
adorned with hieroglyphics and bas-reliefs of
Greek workmanship. Opposite to the town is
a very fine natural harbour, the entrance of which
has been deep enough for small vessels, though
the bar is now impassable at low water. Its prosperity under the Ptolemies and afterwards under
the Romans was owing to its safe anchorage and
its being, like Myos-Hormos, the terminus of a
great road from Koptos along which the traffic
of Alexandria with Ethiopia, Arabia, and India
passed to and fro. Its distance from K o p t o s
was 258 Roman miles or 11 days' journey. The
distance between Myos-Hormos and Berenikê is
given in the *Periplûs* at 225 miles, but this is
considerably above the mark. The difficulty of
the navigation may probably have made the
distance seem greater than it was in reality.

(2) Adjoining B e r e n i k ê was B a r b a r i a

Berbers, and beyond them the Agriophagoi and Moskhophagoi, tribes under regular government by kings. Beyond these again, and still further inland towards the west [is situated the metropolis called Meroê].

3. Below the Moskhophagoi, near the sea, lies a little trading town distant from Bere-

---

(ἡ Βαρβαρικὴ χώρα)—the land about Ras Abû Fatima [lat. 22° 26′ N.—Ptol. IV. vii. 28]. The reading of the MS. is ἡ Τισηβαρικὴ which Müller rejects because the name nowhere occurs in any work, and because if Barbaria is not mentioned here, our author could not afterwards (Section 5) say ἡ ἄλλη Βαρβαρία. The Agriophagoi who lived in the interior are mentioned by Pliny (vi. 35), who says that they lived principally on the flesh of panthers and lions. Vincent writes as if instead of Αγριοφάγων the reading should be Ακριδοφάγων locust-eaters, who are mentioned by Agatharkhidês in his *De Mari Erythraeo,* Section 58. Another inland tribe is mentioned in connection with them—the Moskhophagoi, who may be identified with the Rizophagoi or Spermatophagoi of the same writer, who were so named because they lived on roots or the tender suckers and buds of trees, called in Greek μόσχοι. This being a term applied also to the young of animals, Vincent was led to think that this tribe fed on the brinde or flesh cut out of the living animal as described by Bruce.

(3) To the south of the Moskhophagoi lies Ptolemaïs Thêrôn, or, as it is called by

nîkê about 4000 stadia, called Ptolemaïs Thêrôn, from which, in the days of the Ptolemies, the hunters employed by them used to go up into the interior to catch elephants. In this mart is procured the true (or marine) tortoise-shell, and the land kind also, which, however, is scarce, of a white colour, and smaller size. A little ivory is also sometimes obtainable, resembling that of Adouli. This place has no port, and is approachable only by boats.

---

Pliny, Ptolemaïs Epitheras. [On Er-rih island, lat. 18° 9′ N., long 38° 27′ E., are the ruins of an ancient town—probably Ptolemaïs Therôn,—Müller however places Suche here.—Ptol. I. viii. 1.; IV. vii. 7 ; VIII. xvi. 10]. It was originally an Ethiopian village, but was extended and fortified by Ptolemy Philadelphos, who made it the depôt of the elephant trade, for which its situation on the skirts of the great Nubian forest, where these animals abounded, rendered it peculiarly suitable. The Egyptians before this had imported their elephants from Asia, but as the supply was precarious, and the cost of importation very great, Philadelphos made the most tempting offers to the Ethiopian elephant-hunters (Elephantophagoi) to induce them to abstain from eating the animal, or to reserve at least a portion of them for the royal stables. They rejected however all his solicitations, declaring that even for all Egypt they would not forego the luxury of their repast. The king resolved thereupon to procure his supplies by employing hunters of his own.

4. Leaving Ptolemaïs Thêrôn we are conducted, at the distance of about 3000 stadia, to
A d o u l i, a regular and established port of trade
situated on a deep bay the direction of which is

---

(4) Beyond P t o l e m a ï s   T h ê r ô n occur
A d o u l ê, at a distance, according to the *Periplûs*,
of 3000 stadia—a somewhat excessive estimate.
The place is called also A d o u l e i and more
commonly Adoulis by ancient writers (Ptol. IV.
vii. 8; VIII. xvi. 11). It is represented by the
modern Thulla or Zula [pronounced Azule,—lat.
15° 12'—15° 15' N., long. 39° 36' E.].—To the West
of this, according to Lord Valentia and Mr. Salt,
there are to be found the remains of an ancient
city. It was situated on the A d o u l i k o s
K o l p o s (Ptol. I. xv. 11.; IV. vii. 8), now called
Annesley Bay, the best entrance into Abyssinia.
It was erroneously placed by D'Anville at Dokhnau
or Harkiko, close to Musawwâ [lat. 15° 35' N.]
There is much probability in the supposition that
it was founded by a party of those Egyptians who,
as we learn from Herodotos (II. 30), to the number
of 240,000 fled from their country in the days of
Psammêtikhos (B. c. 671—617) and went to as great
a distance beyond Meroë, the capital of Ethiopia, as
Meroë is beyond Elephantinê. This is the account
which Pliny (VI. 3-4) gives of its foundation,
adding that it was the greatest emporium of the
T r o g l ó d y t e s, and distant from P t o l e m a ï s
a five days' voyage, which by the ordinary reckon-
ing is 2,500 stadia. It was an emporium for
rhinoceros' hides, ivory and tortoise-shell. It had
not only a large sea-borne traffic, but was also **a**

due south. Facing this, at a distance seaward
of about 200 stadia from the inmost recess of
the bay, lies an island called O r e i n ê (or ' the
mountainous'), which runs on either side parallel

caravan station for the traffic of the interior of
Africa. Under the Romans it was the haven
of A u x u m ê (Ptol. IV. vii. 25,—written also
Auxumis, Axumis), now Axum, the capital of the
kingdom of Tigre in Abyssinia. A u x u m ê was
the chief centre of the trade with the interior of
Africa in gold-dust, ivory, leather, hides and
aromatics. It was rising to great prosperity
and power about the time the *Periplûs* was
written, which is the earliest work extant in which
it is mentioned. It was probably founded by the
Egyptian exiles already referred to. Its remaining monuments are perfectly Egyptian and not
pastoral, Troglodytik, Greek, or Arabian in their
character. Its name at the same time retains
traces of the term A s m a k, by which, as we
learn from Herodotos, those exiles were designated, and Heeren considers it to have been one
of the numerous priest-colonies which were sent
out from Meroë.

At Adouli was a celebrated monument, a
throne of white marble with a slab of basanite
stone behind it, both covered with Greek characters, which in the sixth century of our era were
copied by K o s m a s I n d i k o p l e u s t ê s. The
passage in Kosmos relating to this begins
thus: "A d u l ê is a city of Ethiopia and the
port of communication with A x i ô m i s, and the
whole nation of which that city is the capital.

with the mainland. Ships, that come to trade
with Adouli, now-a-days anchor here, to avoid
being attacked from the shore ; for in former
times when they used to anchor at the very
head of the bay, beside an island called
D i o d ô r o s, which was so close to land that the
sea was fordable, the neighbouring barbarians,
taking advantage of this, would run across to
attack the ships at their moorings. At the
distance of 20 stadia from the sea, opposite
O r e i n ê, is the village of Adouli, which is not
of any great size, and inland from this a three

---

In this port we carry on our trade from
Alexandria and the Elanitik Gulf. The town
itself is about a mile from the shore, and as you
enter it on the Western side which leads from
A x i ô m i s, there is still remaining a chair or
thrône which appertained to one of the Ptolemys
who had subjected this country to his authority."
The first portion of the inscription records that
Ptolemy Euergetês (247-222 B.C.) received from
the Troglodyte Arabs and Ethiopians certain
elephants which his father, the second king of the
Makedonian dynasty, and himself had taken in
hunting in the region of A d u l ê and trained to
war in their own kingdom. The second portion of
the inscription commemorates the conquests of an
anonymous Ethiopian king in Arabia and Ethiopia
as far as the frontier of Egypt. A d o u l i, it is
known for certain, received its name from a tribe
so designated which formed a part of the D a n a-
k i l shepherds who are still found in the neigh-

days' journey is a city, K o l ö ê, the first market where ivory can be procured. From Kolöê it takes a journey of five days to reach the metropolis of the people called the A u x u m i-t a i, whereto is brought, through the province called K y ê n e i o n, all the ivory obtained on the other side of the Nile, before it is sent on to Adouli. The whole mass, I may say, of the ele-phants and rhinoceroses which are killed *to supply the trade* frequent the uplands *of the interior*, though at rare times they are seen near the coast, even in the neighbourhood of Adouli. Besides the islands already mentioned, a cluster consist-

---

bourhood of Annesley Bay, in the island of Diset [lat. 15° 28', long. 39° 45', the Diodôros perhaps of the *Periplûs*] opposite which is the town or station of Masawâ (anc. Saba) [lat. 15° 37' N., long. 39° 28' E.], and also in the archipelago of D h a l a k, called in the *Periplûs*, the islands of A l a l a i o u. The merchants of Egypt, we learn from the work, first traded at Masawwâ but after-wards removed to Oreine for security. This is an islet in the south of the Bay of Masawwâ, lying 20 miles from the coast; it is a rock as its name imports, and is of considerable elevation.

A d u l i being the best entrance into Abyssinia, came prominently into notice during the late Abyssinian war. Beke thus speaks of it, " In our recent visit to Abyssinia I saw quite enough to confirm the opinion I have so long entertained, that when the ancient Greeks founded Adule or Adulis at the mouth of the river Hadâs, now only

ing of many small ones lies out in the sea to the right of this port. They bear the name of Alalaiou, and yield the tortoises with which the Ikhthyophagoi supply the market.

5. Below Adouli, about 800 stadia, occurs another very deep bay, at the entrance of which on the right are vast accumulations of sand, wherein is found deeply embedded the Opsian stone, which is not obtainable anywhere else. The king of all this country, from the Moskhophagoi to the other end of Barbaria, is Zôskalês, a man at once of penurious

---

a river bed except during the rains, though a short way above there is rain all the year round, they knew that they possessed one of the keys of Abyssinia."

(5) At a distance of about 100 miles beyond Adouli the coast is indented by another bay now known as Hanfelah bay [near Râs Hanfelah in lat. 14° 44′, long. 40° 49′ E.] about 100 miles from Annesley Bay and opposite an island called Daramsas or Hanfelah. It has wells of good water and a small lake of fresh water after the rains ; the coast is inhabited by the Dummoeta, a tribe of the Danakil]. This is the locality where, and where only, the Opsian or Obsidian stone was to be found. Pliny calls it an unknown bay, because traders making for the ports of Arabia passed it by without deviating from their course to enter it. He was aware, as well as our author, that it contained the Opsian stone, of which he gives an account, already produced in the introduction.

g

habits and of a grasping disposition, but otherwise honourable in his dealings and instructed in the Greek language.

6. The articles which these places import are the following :—

Ἱμάτια βαρβαρικὰ, ἄγναφα τὰ ἐν Ἀιγύπτῳ γινόμενα —Cloth undressed, of Egyptian manufacture, for the Barbarian market.

Στολὰι Ἀρσινοητικὰι—Robes manufactured at Arsinoê.

Ἀβόλλαι νόθοι χρωμάτιναι—Cloaks, made of a poor cloth imitating a better quality, and dyed.

Λέντια—Linens.

Δικρόσσια—Striped cloths and fringed. Mantles with a double fringe.

Λιθίας ὑαλῆς πλείονα γένη καὶ ἄλλης μορρίνης, τῆς γινομένης ἐν Διοσπόλει—Many sorts of glass or crystal, and of that other transparent stone called Myrrhina, made at Diospolis.

Ὀρείχαλκος—Yellow copper, for ornaments and cut into pieces to pass for money.

Μελίεφθα χαλκᾶ—Copper fused with honey : for

---

(6, 7) From this bay the coast of the gulf, according to our author, has a more easterly direction to the Straits, the distance to which from Adouli is stated at 4,000 stadia, an estimate much too liberal. In all this extent of coast the *Periplûs* mentions only the bay of the Opsianstones and conducts us at once from thence to Aualites at the straits. Strabo however, and Juba, and Pliny, and Ptolemy mention several places in this tract, such as A r s i n o ë, B e r e-

culinary vessels and cutting into bracelets and
anklets worn by certain classes of women.

Σίδηρος—Iron. Consumed in making spear-
heads for hunting the elephant and other animals
and in making weapons of war.

Πελύκια—Hatchets.

Σκέπαρνα—Adzes.

Μάχαιραι—Swords.

Ποτήρια χαλκᾶ στρογγύλα μεγάλα—Drinking
vessels of brass, large and round.

Δηνάριον ὀλίγον—A small quantity of denarii :
for the use of merchants resident in the country.

Οἶνος Λαοδικηνὸς καὶ Ἰταλικὸς οὐ πολὺς—Wine,
Laodikean, i.e. Syrian, from Laodike, (now Latakia)
and Italian, but not much.

Ἔλαιον οὐ πολύ—Oil, but not much.

Ἀργυρώματα καὶ χρυσώματα τοπικῷ ῥυθμῷ
κατεσκευασμέναι—Gold and silver plate made according to the fashion of the country for the king.

Ἀβόλλαι—Cloaks for riding or for the camp.

Καυνάκαι ἁπλοῖ—Dresses simply made of skins
with the hair or fur on. These two articles of dress
are not of much value.

---

nîkê, Epideirês, the Grove of Eumenês,
the Chase of Puthangelos, the Territory of the
Elephantophagoi, &c. The straits are called by
Ptolemy Deirê or Dêrê (i. e. the neck), a word
which from its resemblance in sound to the Latin
Dirae has sometimes been explained to mean
"the terrible." (I. xv. 11 ; IV. vii. 9 ; VIII.
xvi. 12). "The Periplûs," Vincent remarks,
"makes no mention of Deirê, but observes that
the point of contraction is close to Abalitês

These articles are imported from the interior parts of Ariakê :—

Σίδηρος Ἰνδικὸς—Indian iron.

Στόμωμα—Sharp blades.

Ὀθόνιον Ἰνδικὸν τὸ πλατύτερον, ἡ λεγομένη μοναχή.
—Monakhê,[17] Indian cotton cloth of great width.

Σαγματογῆναι—Cotton for stuffing.

Περιζώματα— Sashes or girdles.

Καυνάκαι—Dresses of skin with the hair or fur on.

Μολόχινα—Webs of cloth mallow-tinted.

Σινδόνες ʼολίγαι—Fine muslins in small quantity.

Λάκκος χρωμάτινος—Gum-lac : yielding Lake.

The articles locally produced for export are ivory, tortoise-shell, and rhinoceros. Most of the goods which supply the market arrive any time from January to September—that is, from Tybi to Thôth. The best season, however, for ships from Egypt to put in here is about the month of September.

---

or the Abalitik mart; it is from this mart that the coast of Africa falling down first to the South and curving afterwards towards the East is styled the Bay of A u a l i t ê s by Ptolemy, (IV. vii. 10, 20, 27, 30, 39,) but in the *Periplûs* this name is confined to a bay immediately beyond the straits which D'Anville has likewise inserted in his map, but which I did not fully understand till I obtained Captain Cook's chart and found it perfectly consistent with the *Periplûs.*" It is the gulf of Tejureh or Zeyla.

---

[17] Bruce, *Travels,* vol. III., p. 62.—J. B.

7. From this bay the Arabian Gulf trends
eastward, and at A u a l i t ê s is contracted to
its narrowest. At a distance of about 4000
stadia (*from Adouli*), if you still sail along the
same coast, you reach other marts of B a r b a r i a,
called the marts beyond (*the Straits*), which occur
in successive order, and which, though harbourless, afford at certain seasons of the year good
and safe anchorage. The first district you come
to is that called A u a l i t ê s, where the passage
across the strait to the opposite point of Arabia
is shortest. Here is a small port of trade,
called, like the district, A u a l i t ê s, which
can be approached only by little boats and rafts.
The imports of this place are—

Ὑαλὴ λίθια σύμμικτος—Flint glass of various
sorts.

[Χυλός] Διοσπολιτικῆς ὄμφακος—Juice of the sour
grape of Diospolis.

---

The tract of country extending from the Straits
to Cape Arômata (now Guardafui) is called
at the present day A d e l. It is described by
Strabo (XVI. iv. 14), who copies his account of it
from Artemidoros. He mentions no emporium,
nor any of the names which occur in the *Periplûs*
except the haven of Daphnous. [Bandar Mariyah,
lat. 11° 46′ N., long. 50° 38′ E.] He supplies
however many particulars regarding the region
which are left unnoticed by our author as having
no reference to commerce—particulars, however,
which prove that these parts which were resorted
to in the times of the Ptolemies for elephant-hunt-

Ἱμάτια βαρβαρικὰ σύμμικτα γεγναμμένα—Cloths of different kinds worn in Barbaria dressed by the fuller.

Σῖτος—Corn.

Οἶνος—Wine.

Κασσίτερος ὀλίγος—A little tin.

The exports, which are sometimes conveyed on rafts across the straits by the B e r b e r s themselves to O k ê l i s and M o u z a on the opposite coast, are—

Ἀρώματα—Odoriferous gums.

Ἐλέφας ʼολίγος—Ivory in small quantity.

Χελώνη—Tortoise-shell.

Σμύρνα ἐλαχίστη διαφέρουσα δὲ τῆς ἄλλης—Myrrh in very small quantity, but of the finest sort.

Μάκειρ—Macer.

The barbarians forming the population of the place are *rude and* lawless men.

---

ing were much better known to the ancients than they were till quite recently known to ourselves. Ptolemy gives nearly the same series of names (IV. vii. 9, 10) as the *Periplûs*, but with some discrepancies in the matter of their distances which he does not so accurately state. His list is: D ê r e, a city; A b a l i t ê s or Aualitês, a mart; M a l a ô, a mart; M o u n d o u or M o n d o u, a mart; Mondou, an island; Mosulon, a cape and a mart; K o b ê, a mart; E l e p h a s, a mountain; A k-k a n a i or Akannai, a mart; A r o m a t a, a cape and a mart.

The mart of A b a l i t ê s is represented by the modern Z e y l a [lat. 11° 22ʹ N., long. 43° 29ʹ E.,

8. Beyond Aualitês there is another mart,
superior to it, called M a l a ô, at a distance
by sea of 800 stadia. The anchorage is an
open road, sheltered, however, by a cape protrud-
ing eastward. The people are of a more peace-
able disposition than their neighbours. The
imports are such as have been already specified,
with the addition of—

Πλείονες χιτῶνες—Tunics in great quantity.

Σάγοι Ἀρσινοητικοὶ γεγναμμένοι καὶ βεβαμμένοι—
Coarse cloaks (or blankets) manufactured at Arsinoê, prepared by the fuller and dyed.

Μελίεφθα ὀλίγα.—A few utensils made of copper
fused with honey.

Σίδηρος—Iron.

Δηνάριον οὐ πολὺ χρυσοῦντε καὶ ἀργυροῦν—Specie,
—gold and silver, but not much.

The exports from this locality are—

Σμύρνα—Myrrh.

Λίβανος ὁ περατικὸς ὀλίγος—Frankincense *which
we call peratic, i.e.* from beyond the straits, a little
only.

---

79 miles from the straits.] On the N. shore of the
gulf are Abalit and Tejureh. Abalit is 43 miles
from the straits, and Tejureh 27 miles from
Abalit. This is the Z o u i l e h of Ebn Haukal
and the Z a l e g h of Idrisi. According to the
*Periplûs* it was near the straits, but Ptolemy
has fixed it more correctly at the distance from
them of 50 or 60 miles.

(8) M a l a ô as a mart was much superior to
Abalitês, from which our author estimates its
distance to be 800 stadia, though it is in reality

Κασσία σκληροτέρα—Cinnamon of a hard grain.

Δούακα—Douaka (*an inferior kind of cinnamon*).

Κάγκαμον—The gum (*for fumigation*) *kangka-mon.* ' Dekamalli,' gum.

Μάκειρ—The spice *macer*, which is carried to Arabia.

Σώματα σπανίως—Slaves, a few.

9. Distant from M a l a ô a two days' sail is the trading port of M o u n d o u, where ships find a safer anchorage by mooring at an island which lies very close to shore. The exports and imports are similar to those of the preceding marts, with the addition of the fragrant gum called *Mokrotou*, a peculiar product of the place. The native traders here are uncivilized in their manners.

10. After M o u n d o u, if you sail eastward as before for two or three days, there comes

---

greater. From the description he gives of its situation it must be identified with Berbereh [lat. 10° 25′ N., long. 45° 1′ E.] now the most considerable mart on this part of the coast. Vincent erroneously places it between Zeyla and the straits.

(9) The next mart after Malaô is M o u n d o u, which, as we learn from Ptolemy, was also the name of an adjacent island—that which is now called Meyet or Burnt-island [lat. 11° 12′ N., long. 47° 17′ E., 10 miles east of Bandar Jedid].

(10) At a distance beyond it of two or three days' sail occurs M o s u l o n, which is the name both of a mart and of a promontory. It is mentioned

next M o s ʊ l l o n, where it is difficult to anchor.
It imports the same sorts of commodities as
have been already mentioned, and also utensils
of silver and others of iron but not so many,
and glass-ware. It exports a vast amount
of cinnamon (whence it is a port requiring
ships of heavy burden) and other fragrant
and aromatic products, besides tortoise shell,
but in no great quantity, and the incense
called *mokrotou* inferior to that of Moundou, and
frankincense brought from parts further dis-

---

by Pliny (VI. 34), who says : "Further on is the
bay of A b a l i t ê s, the island of D i o d ô r u s
and other islands which are desert. On the mainland, which has also deserts, occur a town G a z a
[Bandar Gazim, long. 49° 13′ E.], the promontory
and port of M o s y l o n, whence cinnamon is
exported. Sesostris led his army to this point
and no further. Some writers place one town of
Ethiopia beyond it, Baricaza, which lies on the
coast. According to Juba the Atlantic Sea
begins at the promontory of Mossylon." Juba
evidently confounded this promontory with Cape
Arômata, and Ptolemy, perhaps in consequence,
makes its projection more considerable than it is.
D'Anville and Gosselin thought M o s s u l o n
was situated near the promontory Mete, where
is a river, called the Soal, which they supposed
preserved traces of the name of Mossulon. This
position however cannot be reconciled with the
distances given in the *Periplûs*, which would lead
us to look for it where Guesele is placed in the

*h*

tant, and ivory and myrrh though in small
quantity.

11. After leaving M o s u l l o n, and sailing
past a place called N e i l o p t o l e m a i o s, and
past T a p a t ê g ê and the Little Laurel-grove,
you are conducted in two days to Cape E l e-

---

latest description given of this coast. Vincent on
very inadequate grounds would identify it with
Barbara or Berbera. [Müller places it at Bandar
Barthe and Ras Antarah, long. 49° 35′ E.]

(11) After Mosulon occurs Cape Elephant,
at some distance beyond N e i l o p t o l e m a i o s,
T a p a t e g ê, and the Little Laurel-grove. At the
Cape is a river and the Great Laurel-grove called
A k a n n a i. Strabo in his account of this coast
mentions a Neilospotamia which however can
hardly be referred to this particular locality
which pertains to the region through which the
Khori or San Pedro flows, of which Idrisi (I. 45)
thus writes: "At two journeys' distance from
Markah in the desert is a river which is subject
to risings like the Nile and on the banks of which
they sow dhorra." Regarding Cape Elephant
Vincent says, "it is formed by a mountain conspicuous in the Portuguese charts under the name
of Mount Felix or Felles from the native term
Jibel Fîl, literally, Mount Elephant. The cape
[Ras Filik, 800 ft. high, lat. 11° 57′ N., long. 50°
37′ E.] is formed by the land jutting up to the
North from the direction of the coast which is
nearly East and West, and from its northern-
most point the land falls off again South-East to
Râs 'Asir—Cape Guardafun, the Arômata of the

p h a n t. Here is a stream called E l e p h a n t
River, and the Great Laurel-grove called A k a n-
n a i, where, and where only, is produced the
*peratic* frankincense. The supply is most abundant, and it is of the very finest quality.

12. After this, the coast now inclining to the
south, succeeds the mart of A r ô m a t a, and a

---

ancients. We learn from Captain Saris, an English navigator, that there is a river at Jibel Fîl.
In the year 1611 he stood into a bay or harbour
there which he represents as having a safe
entrance for three ships abreast : he adds also that
several sorts of gums very sweet in burning were
still purchased by the Indian ships from Cambay
which touched here for that purpose in their
passage to Mocha." The passage in the *Periplûs*
where these places are mentioned is very corrupt.
Vincent, who regards the greater D a p h n ô n
(Laurel-grove) as a river called A k a n n a i, says,
"Neither place or distance is assigned to any
of these names, but we may well allot the rivers
Daphnôn and Elephant to the synonymous town
and cape; and these may be represented by the
modern Mete and Santa Pedro." [Müller places
Elephas at Ras el Fîl, long. 50° 37′ E., and Akannai at Ulûlah Bandar, long. 50° 56′ E., but they
may be represented by Ras Ahileh, where a river
enters through a lagoon in 11° 46′, and Bonah
a town with wells of good water in lat. 11° 58′ N.,
long. 50° 51′ E.]

(12) We come now to the great projection
Cape Arômata, which is a continuation of Mount
Elephant. It is called in Arabic J e r d  H a f û n

bluff headland running out eastward which
forms the termination of the Barbarine coast.
The roadstead is an open one, and at certain
seasons dangerous, as the place lies exposed to

---

or Ras Asir; in Idrisi, C a r f o u n a,. whence the
name by which it is generally known. [The South
point 11° 40′ is Râs Shenarif or Jerd Hafûn :
the N. point 11° 51′ is Râs 'Asir.] It formed
the limit of the knowledge of this coast in the
time of Strabo, by whom it is called N o t o u
K e r a s or South Horn. It is described as a
very high bluff point and as perpendicular as if
it were scarped. [Jerd Hafûn is 2500 feet high.]
The current comes round it out of the gulf with
such violence that it is not to be stemmed without a brisk wind, and during the South-West
Monsoon, the moment you are past the Cape to
the North there is a stark calm with insufferable
heat. The current below Jerd Hafûn is noticed by
the *Periplûs* as setting to the South, and is there
perhaps equally subject to the change of the
monsoon. With this account of the coast from
the straits to the great Cape may be compared
that which has been given by Strabo, XVI. iv. 14 :

" From D e i r ê the next country is that which
bears aromatic plants. The first produces myrrh
and belongs to the I c h t h y o p h a g i and
C r e o p h a g i. It bears also the persea, peach or
Egyptian almond, and the Egyptian fig. Beyond is
L i c h a, a hunting ground for elephants. There
are also in many places standing pools of rain-
water. When these are dried up, the elephants
with their trunks and tusks dig holes and find

the north wind. A coming storm gives warning
of its approach by a peculiar prognostic, for the
sea turns turbid at the bottom and changes its
colour. When this occurs, all hasten for refuge

---

water. On this coast there are two very large
lakes extending as far as the promontory Pytho-
laus. One of them contains salt water and is
called a sea; the other fresh water and is the
haunt of hippopotami and crocodiles. On the
margin grows the papyrus. The ibis is seen in
the neighbourhood of this place. Next is the
country which produces frankincense; it has a
promontory and a temple with a grove of poplars.
In the inland parts is a tract along the banks of a
river bearing the name of I s i s, and another that
of N i l u s, both of which produce myrrh and frankincense. Also a lagoon filled with water from the
mountains. Next the watch-post of the Lion and
the port of P y t h a n g e l u s. The next tract
bears the false cassia. There are many tracts
in succession on the sides of rivers on which
frankincense grows, and rivers extending to the
cinnamon country. The river which bounds this
tract produces rushes (φλους) in great abundance.
Then follows another river and the port of
D a p h n u s, and a valley called A p o l l o's which
bears besides frankincense, myrrh and cinnamon.
The latter is more abundant in places far in the
interior. Next is the mountain E l e p h a s, a
mountain projecting into the sea and a creek; then
follows the large harbour of P s y g m u s, a water-
ing place called that of C y n o c e p h a l i and the
last promontory of this coast N o t u-c e r a s (or the

to the great promontory called T a b a i, which
affords a secure shelter. The imports into this
mart are such as have been already mentioned;
while its products are cinnamon, gizeir (*a finer
sort of cinnamon*), asuphê (*an ordinary sort*),

---

Southern Horn). After doubling this cape towards
the south we have no more descriptions of harbours
or places because nothing is known of the sea-coast
beyond this point." [Bohn's *Transl.*] According
to Gosselin, the Southern Horn corresponds with
the Southern Cape of Bandel-caus, where com-
mences the desert coast of Ajan, the ancient
A z a n i a.

According to the *Periplûs* Cape A r ô m a t a
marked the termination of B a r b a r i a and the
beginning of A z a n i a. Ptolemy however distinguishes them differently, defining the former as
the interior and the latter as the sea-board of the
region to which these names were applied.

The description of the Eastern Coast of Africa
which now follows is carried, as has been already
noticed, as far as R h a p t a, a place about 6 degrees
South of the Equator, but which Vincent places
much farther South, identifying it with Kilwa.

The places named on this line of coast are:
a promontory called T a b a i, a Khersonesos;
O p ô n e, a mart; the Little and the Great A p o-
k o p a; the Little and the Great Coast; the
D r o m o i or courses of A z a n i a (first that of
S e r a p i ô n, then that of N i k ô n); a number of
rivers; a succession of anchorages, seven in number; the P a r a l a o i islands; a strait or canal;
the island of M e n o u t h i a s; and then R h a p t a,

fragrant gums, magla, motô (*an inferior cinnamon*), and frankincense.

13.  If, on sailing from T a b a i, you follow the coast of the peninsula *formed by the promontory*, you are carried by the force of a strong current to another mart 400 stadia distant, called O p ô n ê, which imports the commodities already mentioned, but produces most abundantly cin-

---

beyond which, as the author conceived, the ocean curved round Africa until it met and amalgamated with the Hesperian or Western Ocean.

(13)  Tabai, to which the inhabitants of the Great Cape fled for refuge on the approach of a storm, cannot, as Vincent and others have supposed, be Cape Orfui, for it lay at too great a distance for the purpose. The projection is meant which the Arabs call Banna. [Or, Tabai may be identified with Râs Shenarif, lat. 11° 40′ N.] Tabai, Müller suggests, may be a corruption for Tabannai.

"From the foreign term Banna," he says, "certain Greeks in the manner of their countrymen invented P a n o s or P a n ô n or Panô or Panôna Kômê. Thus in Ptolemy (I. 17 and IV. 7) after Arômata follows P a n ô n K ô m ê, which Mannert has identified with Benna. [Khor Banneh is a salt lake, with a village, inside Râs Ali Beshgêl, lat. 11° 9′ N., long. 51° 9′ E.] Stephen of Byzantium may be compared, who speaks of P a n o s as a village on the Red Sea which is also called P a n ô n." The conjecture, therefore, of Letronnius that P a n ô n K ô m ê derived its name from the large apes found there, called P â n e s, falls to the ground.

namon, spice, *motô*, slaves of a very superior
sort, chiefly for the Egyptian market, and tortoise-shell of small size but in large quantity
and of the finest quality known.

14. Ships set sail from Egypt for all these
ports beyond the straits about the month of
July—that is, Epiphi. The same markets are
also regularly supplied with the products of
places far beyond them—A r i a k ê and B a r u-
g a z a. These products are—

Σῖτος—Corn.

*Ὄρυζα[18]—Rice.

Βούτυρον—Butter, i. e. *ghî.*

῎Ελαιον σησάμινον—Oil of sesamum.

᾿Οθόνιον ἥ τε μοναχὴ καὶ ἡ σαγματογήνη—Fine

O p ô n ê was situated on the Southern shores
of what the *Periplûs* calls a Khersonese, which
can only be the projection now called R a s
H a f û n or Cape D'Orfui (lat. 10° 25′ N.).
Ptolemy (I. 17) gives the distance of O p ô n ê
from P a n ô n K ô m ê at a 6 days' journey, from
which according to the *Periplûs* it was only
400 stadia distant. That the text of Ptolemy is
here corrupt cannot be doubted, for in his tables
the distance between the two places is not far from
that which is given in the *Periplûs.* Probably,
as Müller conjectures, he wrote ὁδόν ἡμέρας (a day's
journey) which was converted into ὁδόν ἡμερ. ς́ (a
six-days' journey).

(14) At this harbour is introduced the mention
of the voyage which was annually made between

---

[18] From the Tamil *ariśi*, rice deprived of the husk.—
*Caldwell.*

cotton called *Monakhê*, and a coarse kind for stuffing called *Sagmatogene*.

Περιζώματα—Sashes or girdles.

Μέλι τὸ καλάμινον τὸ λεγόμενον σάκχαρι.—The honey of a reed, called *sugar*.

Some traders undertake voyages for this commerce expressly, while others, as they sail along the coast *we are describing*, exchange their cargoes for such others as they can procure. There is no king who reigns paramount over all this region, but each separate seat of trade is ruled by an independent despot of its own.

15.  After O p ô n ê, the coast now trending more to the south, you come first to what are called the little and the great A p o k o p a (or Bluffs) of A z a n i a, where there are no har-

---

the coast of India and Africa in days previous to the appearance of the Greeks on the Indian Ocean, which has already been referred to.

(15)  After leaving O p ô n ê the coast first runs due south, then bends to the south-west, and here begins the coast which is called the Little and the Great A p o k o p a or Bluffs of A z a n i a, the voyage along which occupies six days.  This rocky coast, as we learn from recent explorations, begins at Râs Mab b e r [about lat. 9° 25′ N.], which is between 70 and 80 miles distant from Ras Hafûn and extends only to R â s-u l-K h e i l [about lat. 7° 45′ N.], which is distant from Râs Mabber about 140 miles or a voyage of three or four days only.  The length of this rocky coast (called H a z i n e by the Arabs) is therefore much exaggerated in the *Peri-*

ε

bours, but only roads in which ships can conveniently anchor.  The navigation of this coast,
the direction of which is now to the south-
west, occupies six days.  Then follow the Little
Coast and the Great Coast, occupying other six
days, when in due order succeed the D r o m o i

---

*plûs*.  From this error we may infer that our author,
who was a very careful observer, had not personally
visited this coast.  Ptolemy, in opposition to Marî-
nos as well as the *Periplûs*, recognizes but one
A p o k o p a, which he speaks of as a bay.  Müller
concludes an elaborate note regarding the A p o-
k o p a by the following quotation from the work of
Owen, who made the exploration already referred to,
" It is strange that the descriptive term H a z i n e
should have produced the names  A j a n,  A z a n
and  A z a n i a  in many maps and charts, as the
country never had any other appellation  than
B a r r a  S o m â l i  or the land of the  S o m â l i,
a people who have never yet  been collected under
one government, and whose limits of subjection
are only within bow-shot of individual chiefs.
The coast of Africa from the Red Sea to the river
Juba is inhabited by the tribe called  S o m â l i.
They are a mild people of pastoral habits and
confined entirely to the coast ; the whole of the
interior being occupied by an untameable tribe of
savages called  G a l l a."
The coast which follows the A p o k o p a, called
the Little and the Great  A i g i a l o s  or Coast,
is so desolate that, as Vincent remarks, not a
name occurs on it, neither is there an anchorage
noticed, nor the least trace of commerce to be

(or Courses) of A z a n i a, the one going
by the name of S a r a p i ô n, and the other
by that of N i k ô n. Proceeding thence, you
pass the mouths of numerous rivers, and a succession of other roadsteads lying apart one
from another a day's distance either by sea or by

---

found. Yet it is of great extent—a six days'
voyage according to the *Periplûs*, but, according
to Ptolemy, who is here more correct, a voyage of
eight days, for, as we have seen, the *Periplûs* has
unduly extended the A p o k o p a to the South.

Next follow the D r o m o i or Courses of
A z a n i a, the first called that of S e r a p i ô n
and the other that of N i k ô n. Ptolemy interposes a bay between the Great Coast and the port
of S e r a p i ô n, on which he states there was
an emporium called E s s i n a—a day's sail distant from that port. Essina, it would therefore
appear, must have been somewhere near where
M a k d a s h û [Magadoxo, lat. 2° 3′ N.] was built
by the Arabs somewhere in the eighth century A.D.
The station called that of N i k ô n in the *Periplûs*
appears in Ptolemy as the mart of T o n i k ê.
These names are not, as some have supposed, of
Greek origin, but distortions of the native appel-
lations of the places into names familiar to Greek
ears. That the Greeks had founded any settle-
ments here is altogether improbable. At the
time when the *Periplûs* was written all the trade
of these parts was in the hands of the Arabs of
M o u z a. The port of S e r a p i ô n may be
placed at a promontory which occurs in 1° 40′
of N. lat. From this, T o n i k ê, according to

land. There are seven of them altogether, and
they reach on to the P u r a l a o i islands and the
*narrow strait* called the Canal, beyond which,
where the coast changes its direction from south-
west slightly more to south, you are conducted
by a voyage of two days and two nights to M e-

---

the tables of Ptolemy, was distant 45′, and its
position must therefore have agreed with that of
T o r r e or Torra of our modern maps.

Next occurs a succession of rivers and roadsteads, seven in number, which being passed we
are conducted to the P u r a l a ä n Islands, and
what is called a canal or channel (δεώρυξ). These
islands are not mentioned elsewhere. They can
readily be identified with the two called M a n d a
and L a m o u, which are situate at the mouths of
large rivers, and are separated from the mainland
and from each other by a narrow channel. Vincent would assign a Greek origin to the name of
these islands. "With a very slight alteration,"
he says, "of the reading, the Puralian Islands
(Πῦρ ἅλιον, *marine fire,*) are the islands of the
Fiery Ocean, and nothing seems more consonant
to reason than for a Greek to apply the name of
the Fiery Ocean to a spot which was the centre
of the Torrid Zone and subject to the perpendicular rays of an equinoctial sun." [The Juba
islands run along the coast from Juba to about
Lat. 1° 50′ S., and Manda bay and island is in Lat.
2° 12′ S.]

Beyond these islands occurs, after a voyage
of two days and two nights, the island of M e-
n o u t h i a s or M e n o u t h e s i a s, which it has

n o u t h i a s, an island stretching towards sunset,
and distant from the mainland about 300 stadia.
It is low-lying and woody, has rivers, and a
vast variety of birds, and yields the mountain
tortoise, but it has no wild beasts at all, except
only crocodiles, which, however, are quite

---

been found difficult to identify with any certainty.
" It is," says Vincent, " the *Eitenediommenouthesias*
of the *Periplús*, a term egregiously strange and
corrupted, but out of which the commentators
unanimously collect Menoothias, whatever may be
the fate of the remaining syllables. That this Menoothias," he continues, " must have been one of
the Zangibar islands is indubitable; for the distance from the coast of all three, Pemba, Zangibar,
and Momfia, affords a character which is indelible;
a character applicable to no other island from
Guardafui to Madagascar." He then identifies
it with the island of Zangibar, lat. 6° 5′ S., in preference to Pemba, 5° 6′ S., which lay too far out
of the course, and in preference to Momfia, 7° 50′
S. (though more doubtfully), because of its being
by no means conspicuous, whereas Zangibar was
so prominent and obvious above the other two,
that it might well attract the particular attention
of navigators, and its distance from the mainland
is at the same time so nearly in accordance with
that given in the *Periplús* as to counterbalance all
other objections. A writer in Smith's *Classical
Geography*, who seems to have overlooked the indications of the distances both of Ptolemy and the
*Periplús*, assigns it a position much further to the
north than is reconcilable with these distances.

harmless.    The boats are here made of planks
sewn together attached to a keel formed of a
single log of wood, and these are used for fishing
and for catching turtle.    This is also caught in
another mode, peculiar to the island, by lower-
ing wicker-baskets instead of nets, and fixing

---

He places it about a degree south from the mouth
of the River Juba or Govind, just where an opening in the coral-reefs is now found.    "The coasting voyage," he says, "steering S. W., reached the
island on the east side—a proof that it was close
to the main.  .  .  .    It is true the navigator
says it was 300 stadia from the mainland ; but as
there is no reason to suppose that he surveyed
the island, this distance must be taken to signify
the estimated width of the northern inlet separat-
ing the island from the main, and this estimate
is probably much exaggerated.    The mode of
fishing with baskets is still practised in the Juba
islands and along this coast.    The formation of
the coast of E. Africa in these latitudes—where
the hills or downs upon the coast are all formed
of a coral conglomerate comprising fragments
of madrepore, shell and sand, renders it likely
that the island which was close to the main 16 or
17 centuries ago, should now be united to it.
Granting this theory of gradual transformation of
the coast-line, the M e n o u t h i a s of the *Periplûs*
may be supposed to have stood in what is now
the rich garden-land of S h a m b a, where the
rivers carrying down mud to mingle with the
marine deposit of coral drift covered the choked-
up estuary with a rich soil."

them against the mouths of the cavernous
rocks which lie out in the sea confronting the
beach.

16. At the distance of a two days' sail from
this island lies the last of the marts of A z a n i a,
called R h a p t a, a name which it derives
from the sewn boats just mentioned. Ivory is
procured here in the greatest abundance, and
also turtle. The indigenous inhabitants are

---

The island is said in the *Periplûs* to extend
towards the West, but this does not hold good
either in the case of Zangibar or any other island
in this part of the coast. Indeed there is no one
of them in which at the present day all the
characteristics of M e n o u t h i a s are found combined. M o m f i a, for instance, which resembles
it somewhat in name, and which, as modern
travellers tell us, is almost entirely occupied with
birds and covered with their dung, does not
possess any streams of water. These are found
in Zangibar. The author may perhaps have con-
fusedly blended together the accounts he had
received from his Arab informants.

(16) We arrive next and finally at R h a p t a, the
last emporium on the coast known to the author.
Ptolemy mentions not only a city of this name,
but also a river and a promontory. The name
is Greek (from ῥάπτειν, *to sew*), and was applied
to the place because the vessels there in use
were raised from bottoms consisting of single
trunks of trees by the addition of planks which
were sewn together with the fibres of the cocoa.

men of huge stature, who live *apart from each other*, every man ruling like a lord his own domain.  The whole térritory is governed by the despot of M o p h a r i t i s, because the sovereignty over it, by some right of old standing, is vested in the kingdom of what is called the First Arabia.  The merchants of M o u z a farm its revenues from the king, and employ in trading with it a great many ships of heavy burden, on board of which they have Arabian command-ers and factors who are intimately acquainted with the natives and have contracted marriage

---

"It is a singular fact," as Vincent remarks, "that this peculiarity should be one of the first objects which attracted the attention of the Portuguese upon their reaching this coast.  They saw them first at Mozambique, where they were called *Almeidas*, but the principal notice of them in most of their writers is generally stated at Kilwa, the very spot which we have supposed to receive its name from vessels of the same con-struction."  Vincent has been led from this coinci-dence to identify Rhapta with Kilwa [lat. 8° 50′ S.].  Müller however would place it not so far south, but somewhere in the Bay of Zangibar.  The promontory of R h a p t u m, he judges from the indications of the *Periplûs* to be the projection which closes the bay in which lies the island of Zangibar, and which is now known as M o i n a n o-k a l û or Point Pouna, lat. 7° S.  The parts beyond this were unknown, and the southern coast of Africa, it was accordingly thought by the ancient

with them, and know their language and the
navigation of the coast.

17. The articles imported into these marts
are principally javelins manufactured at Mouza,
hatchets, knives, awls, and crown glass of various
sorts, to which must be added corn and wine
in no small quantity landed at particular ports,
not for sale, but to entertain and thereby con-
ciliate the barbarians. The articles which these
places export are ivory, in great abundance
but of inferior quality to that obtained at
Adouli, rhinoceros, and tortoise-shell of fine
quality, second only to the Indian, and a little
*nauplius*.

---

geographers, began here. Another cape however
is mentioned by Ptolemy remoter than Rhaptum
and called P r a s u m (that is the Green Cape)
which may perhaps be Cape Delgado, which is
noted for its luxuriant vegetation. The same author
calls the people of R h a p t a, the R h a p s i o i
A i t h i o p e s. They are described in the *Periplús*
as men of lofty stature, and this is still a characteristic of the Africans of this coast. The
R h a p s i i were, in the days of our author, subject
to the people of M o u z a in Arabia just as their
descendants are at the present day subject to the
Sultan of Maskat. Their commerce moreover still
maintains its ancient characteristics. It is the
African who still builds and mans the ships while
the Arab is the navigator and supercargo. The
ivory is still of inferior quality, and the turtle is
still captured at certain parts of the coast.

*j*

18. These marts, we may say, are about the last on the coast of A z a n i a—the coast, that is, which is on your right as you sail *south* from B e r e n î k ê. For beyond these parts an ocean, hitherto unexplored, curves round towards sunset, and, stretching along the southern extremities of Ethiopia, Libya, and Africa, amalgamates with the Western Sea.

19. To the left, again, of B e r e n i k ê, if you

---

(18, 19) Our author having thus described the African coast as far southward as it was known on its Eastern side, reverts to B e r e n i k ê and enters at once on a narrative of the second voyage—that which was made thence across the Northern head of the gulf and along the coast of Arabia to the emporium of M o u z a near the Straits. The course is first northward, and the parts about B e r e n i k ê as you bear away lie therefore now on your left hand. Having touched at M y o s H o r m o s the course on leaving it is shaped eastward across the gulf by the promontory P h a r a n, and L e u k ê K ô m ê[19] is reached after three or four days' sailing. This was a port in the kingdom of the Nabathæans (the Nebaioth of Scripture), situated perhaps near the mouth of the Elanitic Gulf or eastern arm of the Red Sea, now called the Gulf of Akabah. Much difference of opinion has prevailed as to its exact position, since the encroachment of the land upon the sea has much altered the line of coast here. Mannert identified it with the modern Y e n b o [lat. 24° 5′ N., long. 38° 3′ E., the port

---

[19] Meaning *white village.*

sail eastward from M y o s-H o r m o s across the
adjacent gulf for two days, or perhaps three, you
arrive at a place having a port and a fortress
which is called L e u k ê  K ô m ê, and forming the
point of communication with Petra, the residence
of M a l i k h a s, the king of the Nabatæans.  It
ranks as an emporium of trade, since small
vessels come to it laden with merchandize from
Arabia; and hence an officer is deputed to

---

of Medina], Gosselin with M o w i l a h  [lat. 27°
38′ N., long. 35° 28′ E.,] Vincent with E y n o u n a h
[lat. 28° 3′ N., long. 35° 13′ E.—the O n n e  of
Ptolemy], Reichhard with I s t a b e l  A n t a i, and
Rüppel with W e j h  [lat. 26° 13′ N., long. 36°
27′ E]. Müller prefers the opinion held by Bochart,
D'Anville, Quatremêre, Noel des Vergers, and
Ritter, who agree in placing it at the port called
H a u a r a  [lat. 24° 59′ N., long. 37° 16′ E.) mentioned by Idrisi (I. p. 332), who describes it as a
village inhabited by merchants carrying on a considerable trade in earthen vases manufactured at
a clay-pit in their neighbourhood.  Near it lies
the island of H a s s a n i  [lat. 24° 59′ N., long.
37° 3′ E.], which, as Wellsted reports, is conspicuous from its *white* appearance.  L e u k ê
K ô m ê  is mentioned by various ancient authors,
as for instance Strabo, who, in a passage wherein he recounts the misfortunes which befel the
expedition which Aelius led into Nabathaea,
speaks of the place as a large mart to which and
from which the camel traders travel with ease
and in safety from P e t r a  and back to P e t r a

collect the duties which are levied on imports
at the rate of twenty-five per cent. of their
value, and also a centurion who commands the
garrison by which the place is protected.

20. Beyond this mart, and quite contiguous
to it, is the realm of Arabia, which stretches to a
great distance along the coast of the Red Sea.
It is inhabited by various tribes, some speaking
the same language with a certain degree of

---

with so large a body of men and camels as to
differ in no respect from an army.

The merchandize thus conveyed from L e u k ê
K ô m ê to P e t r a was passed on to R h i-
n o k o l o u r a in Palestine near Egypt, and
thence to other nations, but in his own time the
greater part was transported by the Nile to
A l e x a n d r i a. It was brought down from India
and Arabia to M y o s H o r m o s, whence it was
first conveyed on camels to K o p t o s and thence
by the Nile to A l e x a n d r i a. The Nabathaean
king, at the time when our author visited L e u k ê
K ô m ê, was, as he tells us, M a l i k h a s, a name
which means ' king.' Two Petraean sovereigns so
called are mentioned by Josêphos, of whom the latter
was contemporary with Herod. The Malikhas of
the *Periplûs* is however not mentioned in any other
work. The Nabathaean kingdom was subverted
in the time of Trajan, A.D. 105, as we learn from Dio
Cassius (cap. lxviii. 14), and from Eutropius
(viii. 2, 9), and from Ammianus Marcellinus (xiv. 8).

(20) At no great distance from L e u k ê K ô m ê
the Nabathaean realm terminates and Arabia

uniformity, and others a language totally different. Here also, *as on the opposite continent*, the
sea-board is occupied by I k h t h y o p h a g o i,
who live in dispersed huts ; while the men of the
interior live either in villages, or where pasture
can be found, and are an evil race of men,
speaking two different languages. If a vessel
is driven from her course upon this shore she
is plundered, and if wrecked the crew on
escaping to land are reduced to slavery. For
this reason they are treated as enemies and captured by the chiefs and kings of Arabia. They
are called K a n r a i t a i. Altogether, therefore,
the navigation of this part of the Arabian coast
is very dangerous : for, *apart from the barbarity
of its people*, it has neither harbours nor good
roadsteads, and it is foul with breakers, and
girdled with rocks which render it inaccessible.
For this reason when sailing south we stand off

---

begins. The coast is here described as most dismal, and as in every way dangerous to navigation.
The inhabitants at the same time are barbarians,
destitute of all humanity, who scruple not to
attack and plunder wrecked ships and to make
slaves of their crews if they escaped to land. The
mariner therefore, shunned these inhospitable
shores, and standing well out to sea, sailed down
the middle of the gulf. The tribe here spoken of
was that perhaps which is represented by the
H u t e m i of the present day, and the coast belonged to the part of Arabia now called H e j i d.

from a shore in every way so dreadful, and
keep our course down the middle of the gulf,
straining our utmost to reach *the more civilized
part* of Arabia, which begins at Burnt Island.
From this onward the people are under a regular government, and, as their country is pastoral,
they keep herds of cattle and camels.

21. Beyond this tract, and on the shore of a
bay which occurs at the termination of the left
(or east) side of the gulf, is M o u z a, an established and notable mart of trade, at a distance

---

A more civilized region begins at an island
called Burnt island, which answers to the modern
Zebâyir [about lat. 15° 5′ N., long. 42° 12′ E.],
an island which was till recently volcanic.

(21) Beyond this is the great emporium called
M o u z a, [lat. 13° 43′ N., long. 43° 5′ 14″ E.] situated
in a bay near the termination of the Gulf, and at a
distance from B e r e n i k ê of 12,000 stadia. Here
the population consists almost entirely of merchants
and mariners, and the place is in the highest degree
commercial. The commodities of the country are
rich and numerous (though this is denied by
Pliny), and there is a great traffic in Indian
articles brought from B a r u g a z a (Bharoch).
This port, once the most celebrated and most frequented in Yemen, is now the village Musa about
twenty-five miles north from Mokhâ, which has
replaced it as a port, the foundation of which dates
back no more than 400 years ago. "Twenty miles
inland from Mokhâ," says Vincent, "Niebuhr discovered a Musa still existing, which he with great

south from Berenikê of not more than 12,000
stadia. The whole place is full of Arabian ship-
masters and common sailors, and is absorbed
in the pursuits of commerce, for with ships of its
own fitting out, it trades with the marts beyond
the Straits on the opposite coast, and also with
B a r u g a z a.

22. Above this a three days' journey off lies the
city of S a u ê, in the district called M o p h a-
r i t i s. It is the residence of K h o l a i b o s, the
despot of that country.

---

probability supposes to be the ancient mart now
carried inland to this distance by the recession of
the coast." [He must have confounded it with
J e b e l M u s a, due east of Mokhâ, at the commencement of the mountain country.] It is a
mere village badly built. Its water is good, and
is said to be drunk by the wealthier inhabitants
of Mokhâ. Bochart identified M o u z a with the
M e s h a mentioned by Moses.

(22) The *Periplûs* notices two cities that lay
inland from M o u z a—the 1st S a u ê, the S a v ê
of Pliny (VI. xxvi., 104), and also of Ptolemy
(VI. vii., p. 411), who places it at a distance of
500 stadia S. E. of M o u z a. The position and
distance direct us to the city of T a a e s, which lies
near a mountain called S a b e r. Sauê belonged to a
district called M a p h a r i t i s or M o p h a r e i t ê s,
a name which appears to survive in the modern
M h a r r a s, which designates a mountain lying
N. E. from T a a e s. It was ruled by K h o l a i b o s
(Arabicé—Khaleb), whom our author calls a tyrant,

23. A journey of nine days more conducts us to S a p h a r, the metropolis of K h a r i b a ê l, the rightful sovereign of two contiguous tribes, the H o m ê r i t e s and the S a b a ï t a i, and, by means of frequent embassies and presents, the friend of the Emperors.

---

and who was therefore probably a Sheikh who had revolted from his lawful chief, and established himself as an independent ruler.

(23) The other city was S a p h a r, the metropolis of the H o m e r î t a i, *i.e.* the H i m a r y i— the Arabs of Yemen, whose power was widely extended, not only in Yemen but in distant countries both to the East and West. Saphar is called S a p p h a r by Ptolemy (VI. vii.), who places it in 14° N. lat. Philostorgios calls it T a p h a r o n, and Stephen of Byzantium T a r p h a r a. It is now D h a f a r or Dsoffar or Zaphar. In Edrisi (I. p. 148) it appears as D h o f a r, and he thus writes of it :—" It is the capital of the district Jahsseb. It was formerly one of the greatest and most famous of cities. The kings of Yemen made it their residence, and there was to be seen the palace of Zeidan. These structures are now in ruins, and the population has been much decreased, nevertheless the inhabitants have preserved some remnants of their ancient riches." The ruins of the city and palace still exist in the neighbourhood of J e r i m, which Niebuhr places in 14° 30′ N. lat. The distance from S a u ê to S a p h a r in the *Periplûs* is a nine days' journey. Niebuhr accomplished it however in six. Perhaps, as Müller suggests, the nine days' journey is from

24. The mart of M o u z a has no harbour, but its sea is smooth, and the anchorage good, owing to the sandy nature of the bottom. The commodities which it imports are—

Πορφύρα, διάφορος καὶ χυδαία—Purple cloth, fine and ordinary.

Ἱματισμὸς Ἀραβικὸς χειριδωτὸς, ὅτε ἁπλοῦς καὶ ὁ κοινὸς καὶ σκοτουλάτος καὶ διάχρυσος—Garments made up in the Arabian fashion, some plain and common, and others wrought in needlework and inwoven with gold.

Κρόκος—Saffron.

Κύπερος—The aromatic rush Kyperos. (Turmeric?)

Ὀθόνιον—Muslins.

Ἀβόλλαι—Cloaks.

Λώδικες οὐ πολλαὶ, ἁπλοῖ τε καὶ ἐντόπιοι—Quilts, in small quantity, some plain, others adapted to the fashion of the country.

Ζῶναι σκιωταὶ—Sashes of various shades of colour.

Μύρον μέτριον—Perfumes, a moderate quantity.

Χρῆμα ἱκανὸν—Specie as much as is required.

Οἶνος—Wine.

Σῖτος οὐ πολύς—Corn, but not much.

---

M o u z a to S a p h a r. The sovereign of Saphar is called by our author K h a r i b a ê l, a name which is not found among the Himyaritic kings known from other sources. In Ptolemy the region is called E l i s a r ô n, from a king bearing that name.

(24) Adjacent to the Homeritai, and subject to them when the *Periplûs* was written, were the Sabaeans, so famous in antiquity for their wealth,

k

The country produces a little wheat and a
great abundance of wine. Both the king and
the despot above mentioned receive presents
consisting of horses, pack-saddle mules, gold
plate, silver plate embossed, robes of great value,
and utensils of brass. M o u z a exports its
own local products—myrrh of the finest quality
that has oozed in drops from the trees, both the
Gabiræan and Minœan kinds; white marble (or
alabaster), in addition to commodities brought
from the other side of the Gulf, all such as were
enumerated at A d o u l i. The most favourable
season for making a voyage to Mouza is the month
of September,—that is Thoth,—but there is
nothing to prevent it being made earlier.

25. If on proceeding from M o u z a you sail
by the coast for about a distance of 300 stadia,

luxury and magnificence. Their country, the
S h e b a of Scripture, was noted as the land of
frankincense. Their power at one time extended
far and wide, but in the days of our author they
were subject to the Homerites ruled over by
Kharibaêl, who was assiduous in courting the
friendship of Rome.

(25) At a distance of 300 stadia beyond M o u z a
we reach the straits where the shores of Arabia
and Africa advance so near to each other that the
passage between them has only, according to the
*Periplûs,* a width of 60 stadia, or 7½ miles. In the
midst of the passage lies the island of D i o-
d ô r o s (now Perim), which is about 4⅓ miles long
by 2 broad, and rises 230 feet above the level of the

there occurs, where the Arabian mainland and the opposite coast of B a r b a r i a at A u a- l i t ê s now approach each other, a channel of no great length which contracts the sea and encloses it within narrow bounds. This is 60 stadia wide, and in crossing it you come midway upon the island of D i o d ô r o s, to which it is owing that the passage of the straits is in its neighbourhood exposed to violent winds which blow down from the adjacent mountains. There is situate upon the shore of the straits an Arabian village subject to the same ruler (as Mouza), O k ê l i s by name, which is not so much a mart of com- merce as a place for anchorage and supplying water, and where those who are bound for the interior first land and halt to refresh themselves.

---

sea. The straits, according to Moresby, are 14½ geographical miles wide at the entrance between Bab-el-Mandab Cape (near which is Perim) and the opposite point or volcanic peak called J i b e l S i j a n. The larger of the two entrances is 11 miles wide, and the other only 1½. Strabo, Agathêmeros, and Pliny all agree with the *Periplús* in giving 60 stadia as the breadth of the straits. The first passage of those dreaded straits was regarded as a great achievement, and was naturally ascribed to Sesostris as the voyage though the straits of Kalpê was ascribed to Heraklês.

Situated on the shores of the straits was a place called O k ê l i s. This was not a mart of commerce, but merely a bay with

26.  Beyond O k ê l i s, the sea again widening
out towards the east, and gradually expanding
into the open main, there lies, at about the distance of 1,200 stadia, E u d a i m ô n A r a b i a,
a maritime village subject to that kingdom of
which Kharibaêl is sovereign—a place with good
anchorage, and supplied with sweeter and better
water than that of Okêlis, and standing at
the entrance of a bay where the land begins to

---

good anchorage and well supplied with water.
It is identical with the modern Ghalla or
Cella, which has a bay immediately within the
straits.  Strabo following Artemidoros notes here
a promontory called A k i l a. Pliny (VI. xxxii. 157)
mentions an emporium of the same name "ex
quo in Indiam navigatur."  In xxvi., 104 of the
same Book he says : "Indos petentibus utilis-
simum est ab O c e l i egredi."  Ptolemy mentions
a P s e u d o k ê l i s, which he places at the distance of half a degree from the emporium of
O k ê l i s.

(26)  At a distance beyond O k ê l i s of 1,200
stadia is the port of E u d a i m ô n A r a b i a, which
beyond doubt corresponds to 'A d e n, [lat. 12°
45′ N., long. 45° 21′ E.] now so well-known as
the great packet station between Suez and India.
The opinion held by some that Aden is the Eden
mentioned by the Prophet Ezekiel (xxvii. 23) is
opposed by Ritter and Winer.  It is not mentioned by Pliny, though it has been erroneously
held that the A t t a n a e, which he mentions
in the following passage, was Aden. "Homnae

retire inwards. It was called Eudaimôn ('rich and prosperous'), because in bygone days, when the merchants from India did not proceed to Egypt, and those from Egypt did not venture to cross over to the marts further east, but both came only as far as this city, it formed the common centre of their commerce, as Alexandria receives the wares which pass to and fro between Egypt and the ports of the Mediter-

---

et Attanae (v. l. Athanae) quæ nunc oppida maxime celebrari a˙ Persico mari negotiatores dicunt." (vi. 32.) Ptolemy, who calls it simply Arabia, speaks of it as an emporium, and places after it at the distance of a degree and a half Melan Horos, or Black Hill, 17 miles from the coast, which is in long. 46° 59′ E. The place, as the *Periplûs* informs us, received the name of Eudaimôn from the great prosperity and wealth which it derived from being the great entrepôt of the trade between India and Egypt. It was in decay when that work was written, but even in the time of Ptolemy had begun to show symptoms of returning prosperity, and in the time of Constantine it was known as the 'Roman Emporium,' and had almost regained its former consequence, as is gathered from a passage in the works of the ecclesiastical historian Philostorgios. It is thus spoken of by Edrisi (I. p. 51) : "'Âden is a small town, but renowned for its seaport whence ships depart that are destined for Sind, India, and China." In the middle ages it became again the centre of the trade between India and

ranean. Now, however, it lies in ruins, the
Emperor having destroyed it not long before
our own times.

27. To E u d ạ i m ô n  A r a b i a at once succeeds a great length of coast and a bay extending 2,000 stadia or more, inhabited by nomadic
tribes and Ikhthyophagoi settled in villages.
On doubling a cape which projects from it you
come to another trading seaport, K a n ê, which

---

the Red Sea, and thus regained that wonderful
prosperity which in the outset had given it its
name. In this flourishing condition it was found
by Marco Polo, whose account of its wealth,
power and influence is, as Vincent remarks,
almost as magnificent as that which Agatharkhidês
attributed to the Sabæans in the time of the
Ptolemies, when the trade was carried on in the
same manner. Agatharkhidês does not however
mention the place by name, but it was probably
the city which he describes without naming it as
lying on the White Sea without the straits, whence,
he says, the Sabæans sent out colonies or factories
into India, and where the fleets from Persis,
Karmania and the Indus arrived. The name of
A d e n is supposed to be a corruption from
E u d ạ i m ô n.

(27) The coast beyond Aden is possessed partly
by wandering tribes, and partly by tribes settled
in villages which subsist on fish. Here occurs a
bay—that now called Ghubhet-al-Kamar, which
extends upwards of 2,000 stadia, and ends in a
promontory—that now called Râs-al-Asîdah or

is subject to Eleazos, king of the incense
country. Two barren islands lie opposite to it,
120 stadia off—one called Orneôn, and the
other Troullas. At some distance inland
from Kanê is Sabbatha, the principal city
of the district, where the king resides. At
Kanê is collected all the incense that is produced in the country, this being conveyed to it
partly on camels, and partly *by sea* on floats

---

Bâ-l-hâf [lat. 13° 58′ N., long 48° 9′ S.—a cape
with a hill near the fishing village of Gillah].
Beyond this lies another great mart called Kanê.
It is mentioned by Pliny, and also by Ptolemy,
who assigns it a position in agreement with the
indications given in the *Periplûs*. It has been
identified with the port now called Hisn Ghorâb
[lat. 14° 0′ N. long. 48° 19′ E.]. Not far from this
is an island called Halanî, which answers to the
Troullas of our author. Further south is another island, which is called by the natives of the
adjacent coast Sikkah, but by sailors Jibûs.
This is covered with the dung of birds which in
countless multitudes have always frequented it,
and may be therefore identified with the Orneôn
of the *Periplûs*. Kanê was subject to Eleazos, the
king of the Frankincense Country, who resided at
Sabbatha, or as it is called by Pliny (VI. xxxii.
155) Sabota, the capital of the Atramîtae or
Adramitae, a tribe of Sabæans from whom the
division of Arabia now known as Hadhramaut
takes its name. The position of this city cannot
be determined with certainty. Wellsted, who pro-

supported on inflated skins, a local invention,
and also in boats. Kanê carries on trade
with ports across the ocean—B a r u g a z a,
S k y t h i a, and O m a n a, and the adjacent
coast of P e r s i s.

28. From Egypt it imports, like Mouza,
corn and a little wheat, cloths for the Arabian

---

ceeded into the interior from the coast near Hisn
Ghorab through Wadi Meifah, came after a day's
journey and a half to a place called Nakb-el-
Hajar, situated in a highly cultivated district,
where he found ruins of an ancient city of the
Himyarites crowning an eminence that rose gently
with a double summit from the fertile plain.  The
city appeared to have been built in the most solid
style of architecture, and to have been protected by
a very lofty wall formed of square blocks of black
marble, while the inscriptions plainly betokened
that it was an old seat of the Himyarites.  A
close similarity could be traced between its ruins
and those of K a n ê, to which there was an easy
communication by the valley of M e i f a h.  This
place, however, can hardly be regarded as S a b-
b a t h a  without setting aside the distances given
by Ptolemy, and Wellsted moreover learned from
the natives that other ruins of a city of not less
size were to be met with near a village called
Esan, which could be reached by a three days'
journey.—(See Haines, *Mem. of the S. Coast of
Arab.*)

(28)  With regard to the staple product of this
region—frankincense, the *Periplûs* informs us that

market, both of the common sort and the plain,
and large quantities of a sort that is adulterated;
also copper, tin, coral, styrax, and all the other
articles enumerated at Mouza. Besides these
there are brought also, principally for the king,
wrought silver plate, and specie as well as
horses and carved images, and plain cloth of
a superior quality. Its exports are its indigenous products, frankincense and aloes, and such
commodities as it shares in common with other
marts on the same coast. Ships sail for this
port at the same season of the year as those
bound for Mouza, but earlier.

29. As you proceed from K a n ê the land

---

it was brought for exportation to K a n ê. It was
however in the first place, if we may credit Pliny,
conveyed to the Metropolis. He says (xv. 32)
that when gathered it was carried into S a b o t a
on camels which could enter the city only by
one particular gate, and that to take it by any
other route was a crime punished by death. The
priests, he adds, take a tithe for a deity named
S a b i s, and that until this impost is paid, the
article cannot be sold.

Some writers would identify S a b b a t h a
with M a r i a b o (Marab), but on insufficient
grounds. It has also been conjectured that the
name may be a lengthened form of S a b a (Sheba),
a common appellation for cities in Arabia Felix.
[Müller places Sabbatha at Sawa, lat. 16° 13´ N.,
long. 48° 9´ E.]

(29) The next place mentioned by our author

l

retires more and more, and there succeeds
another very deep and far-stretching gulf,
S a k h a l i t ê s by name, and also the frankincense country, which is mountainous and
difficult of access, having a dense air loaded
with vapours [and] the frankincense exhaled
from the trees. These trees, which are not of any
great size or height, yield their incense in the
form of a concretion on the bark, just as several
of our trees in Egypt exude gum. The incense
is collected by the hand of the king's slaves, and
malefactors condemned to this service as a
punishment. The country is unhealthy in the
extreme :—pestilential even to those who sail
along the coast, and mortal to the poor wretches
who gather the incense, who also suffer from
lack of food, which readily cuts them off.

30. Now at this gulf is a promontory, the
greatest in the world, looking towards the east,

---

after K a n ê is a Bay called S a k h a l î t e s, which
terminates at S u a g r o s, a promontory which
looks eastward, and is the greatest cape in the
whole world. There was much difference of
opinion among the ancient geographers regarding
the position of this Bay, and consequently regarding that of Cape S u a g r o s.

(30) Some would identify the latter with Râs-
el-Ḥad, and others on account of the similarity
of the name with Cape S a u g r a or S a u k i r a h
[lat. 18° 8′ N., long. 56° 35′ E.], where Ptolemy
places a city S u a g r o s at a distance of 6 degrees

and called S u a g r o s, at which is a fortress
which protects the country, and a harbour, and
a magazine to which the frankincense which is
collected is brought. Out in the open sea,
facing this promontory, and lying between it
and the promontory of A r ô m a t a, which projects from the opposite coast, though nearer to
S u a g r o s, is the island going by the name of
D i o s k o r i d ê s, which is of great extent, but

---

from K a n ê. But S u a g r o s is undoubtedly Ras
Fartak [lat. 15° 39 N., long. 52° 15′ E.], which is
at a distance of 4 degrees from H i s n G h o r a b,
or K a n ê, and which, rising to the height of
2,500 feet on a coast which is all low-lying, is a
very conspicuous object, said to be discernible
from a distance of 60 miles out at sea. Eighteen
miles west from this promontory is a village
called Saghar, a name which might probably
have suggested to the Greeks that of S u a g r o s.
Consistent with this identification is the passage
of Pliny (VI. 32) where he speaks of the island
D i o s c o r i d i s (Sokotra) as distant from
S u a g r o s, which he calls the utmost projection
of the coast, 2,240 stadia or 280 miles, which is
only about 30 miles in excess of the real distance,
2,000 stadia.

With regard to the position of the Bay of
Sakhalitês, Ptolemy, followed by Marcianus,
places it to the East of Suagros. Marinos on the
other hand, like the *Periplûs,* places it to the west
of it. Müller agrees with Fresnel in regarding
S a k h l ê, mentioned by Ptolemy (VI. vii. 41) as

desert and very moist, having rivers and crocodiles and a great many vipers, and lizards of
enormous size, of which the flesh serves for food,
while the grease is melted down and used as a
substitute for oil. This island does not, however, produce either the grape or corn. The
population, which is but scanty, inhabits the
north side of the island—that part of it which
looks towards the mainland (of Arabia). It

---

$1\frac{1}{2}$ degree East of Makalleh [lat. 14° 31' N., long.
49° 7' W.] as the same with Shehr—which is now
the name of all that mountainous region extending
from the seaport of Makalleh to the bay in which
lie the islands of Kurya Murya. He therefore
takes this to be in the Regio Sakhalîtês, and
rejects the opinion of Ptolemy as inconsistent
with this determination. With regard to Shehr
or Shehar [lat. ·14° 38' N., long. 49° 22' E.] Yule
(M. Polo, II. vol. p. 440, note) says : "Shihr or Shehr
still exists on the Arabian Coast as a town and
district about 330 miles east of Aden." The name
Shehr in some of the oriental geographies in-
cludes the whole Coast up to Oman. The hills of
the Shehr and Dhafâr districts were the great
source of produce of the Arabian frankincense.

The island of Dioskoridês (now Sokotra)
is placed by the Periplús nearer to Cape Suagros than to Cape Arômata—although its distance from the former is nearly double the distance
from the latter. The name, though in appearance
a Greek one, is in reality of Sanskrit origin ; from
Dvîpa Sukhâddra, i.e. insula fortunata, ' Island abode

consists of an intermixture of foreigners, Arabs, Indians, and even Greeks, who resort hither for the purposes of commerce. The island produces the tortoise,—the genuine, the land, and the white sort: the latter very abundant, and distinguished for the largeness of its shell; also the mountain sort which is of extraordinary size and has a very thick shell, whereof the under-part cannot be used, being too hard to .cut,

---

of Bliss.' The accuracy of the statements made regarding it in the *Periplûs* is fully confirmed by the accounts given of it by subsequent writers. Kosmas, who wrote in the 6th century, says that the inhabitants spoke Greek, and that he met with people from it who were on their way to Ethiopia, and that they spoke Greek. " The ecclesiastical historian Nikephoros Kallistos," says Yule, " seems to allude to the people of Sokotra when he says that among the nations visited by the Missionary Theophilus in the time of Constantius, were 'the Assyrians on the verge of the outer Ocean, towards the East . . . whom Alexander the Great, after driving them from Syria, sent thither to settle, and to this day they keep their mother tongue, though all of the blackest, through the power of the sun's rays.' The Arab voyagers of the 9th century say that the island was colonized with Greeks by Alexander the Great, in order to promote the culture of the Sokotrine aloes ; when the other Greeks adopted Christianity these did likewise, and they had continued to retain their profession of it. The colonizing by

while the serviceable part is made into money-boxes, tablets, escritoires, and ornamental articles of that description. It yields also the vegetable dye (κιννάβαρι) called Indicum (or Dragon's-blood), which is gathered as it distils from trees.

31. The island is subject to the king of the frankincense country, in the same way as Azania is subject to Kharibaël and the despot of Mopharitis. It used to be visited by some (*merchants*) from Mouza, and others on the homeward voyage from Limurikê and Barugaza would occasionally touch at it, importing rice, corn, Indian cotton and female-slaves, who, being rare, always commanded a ready market. In exchange for these commodities they would receive as fresh cargo great quantities of tortoise-shell. The revenues of the island are at the present day farmed out by its sovereigns, who, however, maintain a garrison in it for the protection of their interests.

---

Alexander is probably a fable, but invented to account for facts." (*Marco Polo* II. 401.) The aloe, it may be noted, is not mentioned in the *Periplûs* as one of the products of the island. The islanders, though at one time Christians, are now Muhammadans, and subject as of yore to Arabia. The people of the interior are still of distinct race with curly hair, Indian complexion, and regular features. The coast people are mongrels of Arab and mixed descent. Probably in old times

32. Immediately after S u a g r o s follows a gulf deeply indenting the mainland of O m a n a, and having a width of 600 stadia. Beyond it are high mountains, rocky and precipitous, and inhabited by men who live in caves. The range extends onward for 500 stadia, and beyond where it terminates lies an important harbour called M o s k h a, the appointed port to

---

civilization and Greek may have been confined to the littoral foreigners. Marco Polo notes that so far back as the 10th century it was one of the stations frequented by the Indian corsairs called B a w â r i j, belonging to Kachh and Gujarat.

(32) Returning to the mainland the narrative conducts us next to M o s k h a, a seaport trading with K a n ê, and a wintering place for vessels arriving late in the season from Malabar and the Gulf of Khambât. The distance of this place from Suagros is set down at upwards of 1,100 stadia, 600 of which represent the breadth of a bay which begins at the Cape, and is called O m a n a A l-K a m a r. The occurrence of the two names Omana and Moskha in such close connexion led D'Anville to suppose that M o s k h a is identical with M a s k a t, the capital of O m a n, the country lying at the south-east extremity of Arabia, and hence that Ras-el-Ḥad, beyond which Maskat lies, must be Cape Suagros. This supposition is, however, untenable, since the identification of Moskha with the modern A u s e r a is complete. For, in the first place, the Bay of Seger, which begins at Cape Fartak, is of exactly the same measure-

which the *Sakhalitik* frankincense is forwarded. It is regularly frequented by a number
of ships from Kanê; and such ships as come
from Limurikê and Barugaza too late in the
season put into harbour here for the winter,
where they dispose of their muslins, corn, and
oil to the king's officers, receiving in exchange
frankincense, which lies in piles throughout the

---

ment across to Cape Thurbot Ali as the Bay of
O m a n a, and again the distance from Cape Thurbot Ali [lat. 16° 38′ N., long. 53° 3′ E.] to Ras-al-
Sair, the A u s a r a of Ptolemy, corresponds almost
as exactly to the distance assigned by our author
from the same Cape to M o s k h a. Moreover
Pliny (XII. 35) notices that one particular kind
of incense bore the name of *Ausaritis*, and, as the
*Periplûs* states that M o s k h a was the great
emporium of the incense trade, the identification
is satisfactory.

There was another Moskha on this coast which
was also a port. It lay to the west of Suagros,
and has been identified with K e s h î n [lat. 15° 21′
N. long. 51° 39′ E.]. Our author, though correct in
his description of the coast, may perhaps have erred
in his nomenclature; and this is the more likely
to have happened as it scarcely admits of doubt
that he had no personal knowledge of South
Arabia beyond K a n ê and Cape S u a g r o s.
Besides no other author speaks of an Omana
so far to westward as the position assigned to
the Bay of that name. The tract immediately
beyond M o s k h a or Ausera is low and fertile,

whole of S a k h a l i t i s without a guard to
protect it, as if the locality were indebted to
some divine power for its security. Indeed, it
is impossible to procure a cargo, either publicly or
by connivance, without the king's permission.
Should one take furtively on board were it but
a single grain, his vessel can by no possibility
escape from harbour.

---

and is called D o f a r or Z h a f â r, after a famous
city now destroyed, but whose ruins are still to be
traced between Al-hâfâh and Addahariz. "This
Dhafâr," says Yule (*Marco Polo* II. p. 442 note)
"or the bold mountain above it, is supposed to
be the S e p h a r of *Genesis* X. 30." It is certain
that the Himyarites had spread their dominion as
far eastward as this place. Marco Polo thus describes Dhafâr :—" It stands upon the sea, and has
a very good haven, so that there is a great traffic
of shipping between this and India; and the merchants take hence great numbers of Arab horses
to that market, making great profits thereby. . . .
Much white incense is produced here, and I will
tell you how it grows. The trees are like small
fir-trees ; these are notched with a knife in several
places, and from these notches the incense is
exuded. Sometimes, also, it flows from the tree
without any notch, this is by reason of the great
heat of the sun there." Müller would identify
M o s k h a with Zhafâr, and accounts for the discre-
pancy of designation by supposing that our author
had confounded the name M a s k a t, which was
the great seat of the traffic in frankincense with

*m*

33. From the port of **M o s k h a** onward to **A s i k h**, a distance of about 1,500 stadia, runs a range of hills pretty close to the shore, and at its termination there are seven islands bearing the name of **Z ê n o b i o s**, beyond which again we come to another barbarous district not subject to any power in Arabia, but to Persis. If when sailing by this coast you stand well out

---

the name of the greatest city in the district which actually produced it. A similar confusion he thinks transferred the name of Oman to the same part of the country. The climate of the incense country is described as being extremely unhealthy, but its unhealthiness seems to have been designedly exaggerated.

(33) Beyond **M o s k h a** the coast is mountainous as far as **A s i k h** and the islands of Zenobios—a distance excessively estimated at 1,500 stadia. The mountains referred to are 5,000 feet in height, and are those now called Subaha. **A s i k h** is readily to be identified with the **H â s e k** of Arabian geographers. Edrisi (I. p. 54) says: " Thence (from Marbat) to the town of Hâsek is a four days' journey and a two days' sail. Before **H a s e k** are the two islands of **K h a r t a n** and **M a r t a n**. Above **H â s e k** is a high mountain named **S o u s**, which commands the sea. It is an inconsiderable town but populous." This place is now in ruins, but has left its name to the promontory on which it stood [Râs Hâsek, lat. 17° 23 N. long. 55° 20 E. opposite the island of Hasiki]. The islands of **Z ê n o b i o s** are mentioned by Ptolemy as seven in

to sea so as to keep a direct course, then at about a distance from the island of Z ê n o b i o s of 2,000 stadia you arrive at another island, called that of S a r a p i s, lying off shore, say, 120 stadia. It is about 200 stadia broad and 600 long, possessing three villages inhabited by a *savage* tribe of I k h t h y o p h a g o i, who speak the Arabic language, and whose clothing con-

---

number, and are those called by Edrisi K h a r t a n and M a r t a n, now known as the K u r i y â n M u r i y â n islands. The inhabitants belonged to an Arab tribe which was spread from Hasek to Râs-el-Ḥad, and was called B e i t or Beni J e n a b i, whence the Greek name. M. Polo in the 31st chapter of his travels "discourseth of the two islands called Male and Female," the position of which he vaguely indicates by saying that "when you leave the kingdom of K e s m a c o r a n (Mekran) which is on the mainland, you go by sea some 500 miles towards the south, and then you find the 2 islands Male and Female lying about 30 miles distant from one another" (See also *Marco Polo*, vol. II. p. 396 note.)

Beyond A s i k h is a district inhabited by barbarians, and subject not to Arabia but to Persis. Then succeeds at a distance of 200 stadia beyond the islands of Z e n o b i o s the island of S a r a p i s, (the Ogyris of Pliny) now called Masira [lat. 20° 10′ to 20° 42′ N., long. 58° 37 to 58° 59′ E.] opposite that part of the coast where Oman now begins. The *Periplus* exaggerates both its breadth and its distance from the continent. It was still insists of a girdle made from the leaves of the cocoa-palm. The island produces in great plenty tortoise of excellent quality, and the merchants of K a n ê accordingly fit out little boats and cargo-ships to trade with it.

34. If sailing onward you wind round with the adjacent coast to the north, then as you approach the entrance of the Persian Gulf you

---

habited by a tribe of fish-eaters in the time of Ebn Batuta, by whom it was visited.

On proceeding from S a r a p i s the adjacent coast bends round, and the direction of the voyage changes to north. The great cape which forms the south-eastern extremity of Arabia called R â s-el-H a d [lat. 22° 33′ N. long. 59° 48′ E.] is here indicated, but without being named; Ptolemy calls it K o r o d a m o n (VI. vii. 11.)

(34) Beyond it, and near the entrance to the Persian Gulf, occurs, according to the *Periplûs*, a group of many islands, which lie in a range along the coast over a space of 2,000 stadia, and are called the islands of K a l a i o u. Here our author is obviously in error, for there are but three groups of islands on this coast, which are not by any means near the entrance of the Gulf. They lie beyond Maskat [lat. 23° 38′ N. long. 58° 36′ E.] and extend for a considerable distance along the Batinah coast. The central group is that of the Deymâniyeh islands (probably the Damnia of Pliny) which are seven in number, and lie nearly opposite Birkeh [lat. 23° 42′ N. long. 57° 55′ E.]. The error, as Müller suggests, may be accounted

fall in with a group of islands which lie in a
range along the coast for 2,000 stadia, and are
called the islands of K a l a i o u. The inhabitants of the adjacent coast are cruel and
treacherous, and see imperfectly in the daytime.

35. Near the last headland of the islands of
K a l a i o u is the mountain called K a l o n

---

for by supposing that the tract of country called
El Baṭinah was mistaken for islands. This tract,
which is very low and extremely fertile, stretches
from Birkeh [lat. 23° 42′ N. long. 57° 55′ E.]
onward to Jibba, where high mountains approach
the very shore, and run on in an unbroken chain
to the mouth of the Persian Gulf. The islands
are not mentioned by any other author, for the
C a l a e o u i n s u l a e of Pliny (VI. xxxii. 150)
must, to avoid utter confusion, be referred to the
coast of the Arabian Gulf. There is a place called
E l K i l ḥ a t, the Akilla of Pliny [lat. 22° 40′ N.
long. 59° 24′ E.]—but whether this is connected with
the K a l a i o u islands of the *Periplûs* is uncertain
[Conf. *Ind. Ant.* vol. IV. p. 48. El Kilhât, south
of Maskat and close to Ṣûr, was once a great
port.]

(35) Before the mouth of the Persian Gulf is
reached occurs a height called K a l o n (Fair Mount)
at the last head of the islands of Papias—τῶν
Παπίου νήσων. This reading has been altered by
Fabricius and Schwanbeck to τῶν Καλάιου
νήσων. The Fair Mount, according to Vincent,
would answer sufficiently to Cape Fillam, if

(Pulcher),[20] to which succeeds, at no great
distance, the mouth of the Persian Gulf,
where there are very many pearl fisheries.
On the left of the entrance, towering to a
vast height, are the mountains which bear
the name of A s a b o i, and directly opposite

---

that be high land, and not far from Fillam are
the straits. The great cape which Arabia
protrudes at these straits towards Karmania is
now called Ras Mussendom. It was seen from the
opposite coast by the expedition under Nearkhos,
to whom it appeared to be a day's sail distant.
The height on that coast is called Semiramis, and
also Strongylê from its round shape. Mussendom, the ' Asabôn akron' of Ptolemy, Vincent says,
" is a sort of Lizard Point to the Gulf; for all the
Arabian ships take their departure from it with
some ceremonies of superstition, imploring a bless-
ing on their voyage, and setting afloat a toy
like a vessel rigged and decorated, which if it is
dashed to pieces by the rocks is to be accepted by
the ocean as an offering for the escape of the vessel."
[The straits between the island of Mussendom
and the mainland are called El Bab, and this is
the origin of the name of the Papiæ islands.—
Miles' *Jour. R. A. Soc.* N. S. vol. x. p. 168.]

The actual width of the straits is 40 miles.
Pliny gives it at 50, and the *Periplûs* at 75. Cape
Mussendom is represented in the *Periplûs* as in

---

[20] " This" (Mons Pulcher) says Major-General Miles, " is
Jebel Lahrim or Shaum, the loftiest and most conspicuous
peak on the whole cape (Mussendom), being nearly 7,000
feet high."—*Jour. R. As. Soc.* (N.S.) vol. X. p. 168.—ED.

on the right you see another mountain high and round, called the hill of S e m i r a m i s.   The strait which separates them has a width of 600 stadia, and through this opening the Persian Gulf pours its vast expanse of waters far up into the interior.   At the very head of this gulf

---

Ptolemy by the Mountains of the Asabi which are described as tremendous heights, black, grim, and abrupt.   They are named from the tribe of B e n i   A s a b.

We enter now the Gulf itself, and here the *Periplûs* mentions only two particulars: the famous Pearl Fisheries which begin at the straits and extend to Bahrein, and the situation of a regular trading mart called A p o l o g o s, which lies at the very head of the Gulf on the Euphrates, and in the vicinity of S p a s i n o u   K h a r a x.   This place does not appear to be referred to in any other classical work, but it is frequently mentioned by Arabian writers under the name of Oboleh or Obolegh.   As an emporium it took the place of T e r ê d ô n or D i r i d ô t i s, just as B a s r a (below which it was situated) under the second Khaliphate took the place of O b o l e h itself.   According to Vincent, Oboleh, or a village that represents it, still exists between Basra and the Euphrates.   The canal also is called the canal of Oboleh.   K h a r a x   P a s i n o u was situated where the K a r u n (the E u l a e u s of the ancients) flows into the P a s i t i g r i s, and is represented by the modern trading town M u h a m m a r a h. It was founded by Alexander the Great, and after its

there is a regular mart of commerce, called the
city of A p o l o g o s, situate near P a s i n o u-
K h a r a x and the river Euphrates.

36. If you coast along the mouth of the
gulf you are conducted by a six days' voyage to
another seat of trade belonging to Persis, called
O m a n a.[21]  Barugaza maintains a regular
commercial intercourse with both these Persian

---

destruction, was rebuilt by Antiokhos Epiphanes,
who changed its name from Alexandreia to Antio-
kheia. It was afterwards occupied by an Arab
Chief called Pasines, or rather S p a s i n e s, who
gave it the name by which it is best known.   Pliny
states that the original town was only 10 miles
from the sea, but that in his time the existing
place was so much as 120 miles from it.   It was
the birth-place of two eminent geographers—
Dionysius Periegetes and Isidôros.

(36) After this cursory glance at the great
gulf, our author returns to the straits, and at once

---

[21] " The city of Omana is Soḥar, the ancient capital of
Omana, which name, as is well known, it then bore, and
Pliny is quite right in correcting *former writers* who had
placed it in Caramania, on which coast there is no good
evidence that there was a place of this name.  Nearchus
does not mention it, and though the author of the *Periplûs
of the Erythræan Sea* does locate it in Persis, it is pretty
evident he never visited the place himself, and he must
have mistaken the information he obtained from others.
It was this city of Soḥar most probably that bore the appellation of Emporium Persarum, in which, as Philostorgius
relates, permission was given to Theophilus, the ambassador
of Constantine, to erect a Christian church."   The Homna
of Pliny may be a repetition of Omana or Soḥar, which
he had already mentioned.—Miles in *Jour. R. As. Soc.*
(N. S.) vol. X. pp. 164-5.—ED.

ports, despatching thither large vessels freighted with copper, sandalwood, beams for rafters, horn, and logs of sasamina and ebony. Omana imports also frankincense from Kanê, while it exports to Arabia a particular species of vessels called *madara*, which have their planks sewn together. But both from A p o l o g o s and O m a n a there are exported to Barugaza and to Arabia great quantities of pearl, of mean quality however compared with the Indian sort, together with purple, cloth for the natives, wine, dates in great quantity, and gold and slaves.

37. After leaving the district of O m a n a

---

conducts us to the Eastern shores of the Ery-thraean, where occurs another emporium belonging to Persis, at a distance from the straits of 6 courses or 3,000 stadia. This is Omana. It is mentioned by Pliny (VI. xxxii. 149) who makes it belong to Arabia, and accuses preceding writers for placing it in Karmania.

The name of O m a n a has been corrupted in the MSS. of Ptolemy into Nommana, Nombana, K o m m a n a, Kombana, but Marcian has pre-served the correct spelling. From Omana as from Apologos great quantities of pearl of an inferior sort were exported to Arabia and Barugaza. No part however of the produce of India is mentioned as among its exports, although it was the centre of commerce between that country and Arabia.

(37) The district which succeeds Omana belongs to the P a r s i d a i, a tribe in Gedrosia next neigh-

n

the country of the **Parsidai** succeeds, which belongs to another government, and the bay which bears the name of **Terabdoi**, from the midst of which a cape projects. Here also is a river large enough to permit the entrance of ships, with a small mart at its mouth called **Oraia**. Behind it in the interior, at the distance of a seven days' journey from the coast, is the city where the king resides, called Rhambakia. This district, in addition to corn, produces wine, rice, and dates, though in the tract near the sea, only the fragrant gum called bdellium.

---

bours to the **Arbitae** on the East. They are mentioned by Ptolemy (VI. xx., p. 439) and by Arrian (*Indika* xxvi.) who calls them **Pasirees**, and notes that they had a small town called **Pasira**, distant about 60 stadia from the sea, and a harbour with good anchorage called **Bagisara**. The Promontory of the *Periplûs* is also noted and described as projecting far into the sea, and being high and precipitous. It is the Cape now called **Arabah** or **Urmarah**. The Bay into which it projects is called **Terabdôn**, a name which is found only in our author. Vincent erroneously identifies this with the **Paragôn** of Ptolemy. It is no doubt the Bay which extends from Cape Guadel to Cape Monze. The river which enters this Bay, at the mouth of which stood the small mart called **Oraia**, was probably that which is now called the Akbor. The royal city

38.  After this region, where the coast is
already deeply indented by gulfs caused by the
land advancing with a vast curve from the east,
succeeds the seaboard of Skythia, a region
which extends to northward.  It is very
low and flat, and contains the mouths of the
S i n t h o s (Indus), the largest of all the rivers
which fall into the Erythræan Sea, and which,
indeed, pours into it such a vast body of water
that while you are yet far off from the land at
its mouth you find the sea turned of a white
colour by its waters.

The  sign by which voyagers before sighting

---

which lay inland from the sea a seven days' journey
was  perhaps,  as  Mannert  has  conjectured,
R a m b a k i a, mentioned by Arrian (*Anab.* vi. 21)
as the capital of the O r e i t a i or H o r i t a i.

(38)  We now approach the  mouths  of  the
Indus which our author calls the S i n t h o s, transliterating  the  native  name of it—S i n d h u.   In
his time the wide tract which was watered by this
river in the lower  part  of  its  course  was  called
I n d o s k y t h i a.   It derived its name from the
Skythian tribes (the Ś â k a of Sansk.) who after
the  overthrow  of  the  Graeco-Baktrian  empire
gradually  passed  southward to the coast, where
they established themselves about the year 120
B. C., occupying all the region between the Indus
and the Narmadâ.   They are called  by Dionysios
Periegetes  N o t i o i  S k y t h a i,  the  Southern
Skythians.  Our author mentions two cities which

land know that it is near is their meeting with
serpents floating on the water; but higher up
and on the coasts of Persia the first sign of land
is seeing them of a different kind, called *graai*.
[Sansk. *graha*—an alligator.] The river has seven
mouths, all shallow, marshy and unfit for navigation except only the middle stream, on which
is B a r b a r i k o n, a trading seaport. Before
this town lies a small islet, and behind it in the
interior is M i n n a g a r, the metropolis of
Skythia, which is governed, however, by Parthian
princes, who are perpetually at strife among
themselves, expelling each the other.

39. Ships accordingly anchor near B a r b a-
r i k ê, but all their cargoes are conveyed by the
river up to the king, who resides in the metropolis.

The articles imported into this emporium are—
Ἱματισμὸς ἁπλοῦς ἱκανὸς—Clothing, plain and
in considerable quantity.

---

belonged to them—B a r b a r i k o n and M i n n a-
g a r; the former of which was an emporium
situated near the sea on the middle and only navigable branch of the Indus. Ptolemy has a B a r -
b a r e i in the Delta, but the position he assigns
to it, does not correspond with that of B a r b a r i -
k o n. M i n n a g a r was the Skythian metropolis.
It lay inland, on or near the banks of the Indus.

(39) Ships did not go up to it but remained at
B a r b a r i k o n, their cargoes being conveyed up
the river in small boats. In Ptolemy (VII. i. 61)

Ἱματισμὸς νόθος οὐ πολὺς—Clothing, mixed, not much.

Πολύμιτα—Flowered cottons.

Χρυσόλιθον—Yellow-stone, topazes.

Κοράλλιον—Coral.

Στύραξ—Storax.

Λίβανος—Frankincense (*Lóbán*).

Ὑαλά σκεύη—Glass vessels.

Ἀργυρώματα—Silver plate.

Χρῆμα—Specie.

Οἶνος οὐ πολύς—Wine, but not much.

The exports are :—

Κόστος—Costus, a spice.

Βδέλλα—Bdellium, a gum.

Λύκιον—A yellow dye (*Ruzót*).

Νάρδος—Spikenard.

Λίθος καλλάϊνος.—Emeralds or green-stones.

Σάπφειρος—Sapphires.

Σηρικὰ δέρματα—Furs from China.

Ὀθόνιον—·Cottons.

Νῆμα Σηρικὸν—Silk thread.

Ἰνδικὸν μέλαν—Indigo.

---

the form of the name is B i n a g a r a, which is less correct since the word is composed of *Min*, the Indian name for the Skythians, and *nagar*, a city. Ritter considers that T h a ṭ h a is its modern representative, since it is called S a m i n a g a r by the Jâḍejâ Rajputs who, though settled in Kachh. derive their origin from that city. To this view it is objected that Ṭhaṭha is not near the position which Ptolemy assigns to his B i n a g a r a. Mannert places it at B a k k a r, D'Anville at M a n - s u r a, and Vincent at M e n h a b e r y mentioned

Ships destined for this port put out to sea when the Indian monsoon prevails—that is, about the month of July or Epiphi. The voyage at this season is attended with danger, but being shorter is more expeditious.

by Edrisi (I. p. 164) as distant two stations or 60 miles from D a b i l, which again was three stations or 90 miles from the mouth of the Indus, that is it lay at the head of the Delta. Our author informs us that in his time M i n a g a r was ruled by Parthian princes. The Parthians (the Parada of Sanskrit writers) must therefore have subverted a Skythian dynasty which must have been that which (as Benfey has shown) was founded by Y e u k a o t s c h i n between the years 30 and 20 B.C., or about 30 years only after the famous Indian Æra called *Sâkâbda* (the year of the Sâka) being that in which Vikramâditya expelled the Skythians from Indian soil. The statement of the *Periplús* that Parthian rulers succeeded the Skythian is confirmed by Parthian coins found everywhere in this part of the country. These sovereigns must have been of consequence, or the trade of their country very lucrative to the merchant as appears by the presents necessary to ensure his protection—plate, musical instruments, handsome girls for the Harem, the best wine, plain cloth of high price, and the finest perfumes. The profits of the trade must therefore have been great, but if Pliny's account be true, that every pound laid out in India produced a hundred at Rome, greater exactions than these might easily have been supported.

40. After the river S i n t h o s is passed we reach another gulf, which cannot be easily seen. It has two divisions,—the Great and the Little by name,—both shoal with violent and continuous eddies extending far out from the shore, so that before ever land is in sight ships are often grounded on the shoals, or being caught within the eddies are lost. Over this gulf hangs a promontory which, curving from E i r i n o n first to the east, then to the south, and finally to the west, encompasses the gulf called B a r a k ê, in the bosom of which lie seven islands. Should a vessel approach the entrance of this gulf, the only chance of escape for those on board is at once to alter their course and stand out to sea, for it is all over with them if they are once fairly within the womb of B a r a k ê,

---

(40) The first place mentioned after the Indus is the Gulf of E i r i n o n, a name of which traces remain in the modern appellation the R a n of Kachh. This is no longer covered with water except during the monsoon, when it is flooded by sea water or by rains and inundated rivers. At other seasons it is not even a marsh, for its bed is hard, dry and sandy; a mere saline waste almost entirely devoid of herbage, and frequented but by one quadruped—the wild ass. Burnes conjectured that its desiccation resulted from an upheaval of the earth caused by one of those earthquakes which are so common in that part of India. The R a n is connected with the Gulf of Kachh,

which surges with vast and mighty billows,
and where the sea, tossing in violent commotion,
forms eddies and impetuous whirlpools in every
direction. The bottom varies, presenting in
places sudden shoals, in others being scabrous
with jagged rocks, so that when an anchor
grounds its cable is either at once cut through,
or soon broken by friction at the bottom. The
sign by which voyagers know they are approaching this bay is their seeing serpents floating
about on the water, of extraordinary size and of
a black colour, for those met with lower down
and in the neighbourhood of Barugaza are of
less size, and in colour green and golden.

41. To the gulf of B a r a k ê succeeds that

---

which our author calls the Gulf of B a r a k ê.
His account of it is far from clear. Perhaps, as
Müller suggests, he comprehended under E i r i-
n o n the interior portion of the Gulf of Kachh,
limiting the Gulf of B a r a k ê to the exterior portion or entrance to it. This gulf is called that of
Kanthi by Ptolemy, who mentions B a r a k ê only
as an island, [and the south coast of Kachh is
still known by the name of Kantha]. The islands
of the *Periplûs* extend westward from the neighbourhood of N a v a n a g a r to the very entrance
of the Gulf.

(41) To B a r a k ê succeeds the Gulf of B a r u-
g a z a (Gulf of K h a m b h â t) and the sea-board
of the region called A r i a k ê. The reading of the
MS. here ἡ πρὸς Ἀραβικῆς χώρας is considered corrupt. Müller substitutes ἡ ἤπειρος τῆς Ἀριακῆς

of B a r u g a z a and the mainland of A r i a k ê,
a district which forms the frontier of the kingdom of M o m b a r o s and of all India. The
interior part of it which borders on S k y t h i a
is called A b ê r i a, and its sea-board S u r a s-
t r ê n ê. It is a region which produces abundantly corn and rice and the oil of sesamum,
butter, muslins and the coarser fabrics which are

---

χώρας, though Mannert and others prefer Λαρικῆς
χώρας, relying on Ptolemy, who places A r i a k ê to
the south of L a r i k ê, and says that L a r i k ê
comprehends the peninsula (of Gujarât) Barugaza
and the parts adjacent. As A r i a k ê was however previously mentioned in the *Periplûs* (sec.
14) in connexion with Barugaza, and is afterwards
mentioned (sec. 54) as trading with Muziris, it
must no doubt have been mentioned by the author
in its proper place, which is here. [Bhagvanlâl
Indraji Pandit has shewn reasons however for
correcting the readings into Αβαρατικη, the Prakrit
form of A p a r â n t i k â, an old name of the western
sea board of India.—*Ind. Ant.* vol. VII., pp. 259,
263.] Regarding the name L a r i k ê, Yule has
the following note (*Travels of M. Polo* vol. II.,
p. 353) :—" L â r-D e ś a, the country of Lar," properly Lât-deśa, was an early name for the
territory of Gujrat and the northern Konkan,
embracing Saimur (the modern Chaul as I believe)
Thana, and Bharoch. It appears in Ptolemy in
the form L a r i k ê. The sea to the west of that coast
was in the early Muhammadan times called the sea
of Lâr, and the language spoken on its shores is

manufactured from Indian cotton. It has also numerous herds of cattle. The natives are men of large stature and coloured black. The metropolis of the district is M i n n a g a r, from which

---

called by M a s'u d i, L â r i. Abulfeda's authority, Ibn Said, speaks of Lâr and Gujarât as identical."

A r i a k ê (Aparântikâ), our author informs us, was the beginning or frontier of India. That part of the interior of Ariakê which bordered on Skythia was called A b e r i a or Abiria (in the MS. erroneously Ibêria). The corresponding Indian word is A b h î r a, which designated the district near the mouths of the river. Having been even in very early times a great seat of commerce, some (as Lassen) have been led to think from a certain similarity of the names that this was the O p h i r of scripture, a view opposed by Ritter. Abiria is mentioned by Ptolemy, who took it to be not a part of India but of Indoskythia. The sea-board of Ariakê was called S u r a s t r ê n ê, and is mentioned by Ptolemy, who says (VII. i. 55) it was the region about the mouths of the Indus and the Gulf of Kanthi. It answers to the Sanskrit S u r â s h-ṭ r a. Its capital was M i n n a g a r,—a city which, as its name shows, had once belonged to the Min or Skythians. It was different of course from the Minnagar already mentioned as the capital of Indo-Skythia. It was situated to the south of O z ê n ê (Ujjayinî, or Ujjain), and on the road which led from that city to the River Narmadâ, probably near where Indôr now stands. It must have been the capital only for a short time, as Ptolemy informs us (II. i. 63) that O z ê n ê was in his time the

cotton cloth is exported in great quantity to
B a r u g a z a. In this part of the country there
are preserved even to this very day memorials
of the expedition of Alexander, old temples,
foundations of camps, and large wells. The
extent of this coast, reckoned from B a r b a-
r i k o n to the promontory called P a p i k ê, near
A s t a k a p r a, which is opposite B a r u g a z a,
is 3,000 stadia.

---

capital of T i a s h a n e s [probably the Chashtana
of Coins and the Cave Temple inscriptions]. From
both places a great variety of merchandise was
sent down the Narmadâ to Barugaza.

The next place our author mentions is a promontory called P a p i k ê projecting into the Gulf
of Khambât from that part of the peninsula of
Gujarât which lies opposite to the Barugaza coast.
Its distance from Barbarikon on the middle mouth
of the Indus is correctly given at 3,000 stadia.
This promontory is said to be near A s t a k a p r a,
a place which is mentioned also by Ptolemy, and
which (*Ind. Ant.* vol. V. p. 314) has been identified by
Colonel Yule with H a s t a k a v a p r a (now H â-
t h a b near Bhaunagar), a name which occurs in
a copper-plate grant of Dhruvasena I of Valabhi.
With regard to the Greek form of this name
Dr. Bühler thinks it is not derived immediately
from the Sanskrit, but from an intermediate old
Prakrit word Hastakampra, which had been
formed by the contraction of the syllables *ava*
to *â,* and the insertion of a nasal, according to
the habits of the Gujarâtîs. The loss of the

42. After **Papikê** there is another gulf, exposed to the violence of the waves and running up to the north. Near its mouth is an island called **Baiônês**, and at its very head it receives a vast river called the **Maîs**. Those bound for **Barugaza** sail up this gulf (which has a breadth of about 300 stadia), leaving the island on the left till it is scarcely visible in the horizon, when they shape their course east for the mouth of the river that leads to Barugaza. This is called the **Namnadios**.

initial, he adds, may be explained by the difficulty which Gujarâtîs have now and probably had 1,600 years ago in pronouncing the *spirans* in its proper place. The modern name Hâthab or Hâthap may be a corruption of the shorter Sanskrit form Hastavapra.

(42) Beyond **Papikê**, we are next informed, there is another gulf running northward into the interior of the country. This is not really another Gulf but only the northern portion of the Gulf of Khambât, which the *Periplûs* calls the Gulf of Barugaza. It receives a great river, the **Maîs**, which is easily identified with the **Mahi**, and contains an island called **Baiônês** [the modern Peram], which you leave on the left hand as you cross over from Astakapra to Barugaza.

We are now conducted to **Barugaza**, the greatest seat of commerce in Western India, situated on a river called in the MS. of the *Periplûs* the **Lamnaios**, which is no doubt an erroneous reading for **Namados**, or Namnados or Namna-

43. The passage into the gulf of B a r u-
g a z a is narrow and difficult of access to those
approaching it from the sea, for they are carried
either to the right or to the left, the left being
the better passage of the two. On the right,
at the very entrance of the gulf, lies a narrow
stripe of shoal, rough and beset with rocks. It
is called H ê r ô n ê, and lies opposite the village
of K a m m ô n i. On the left side right against
this is the promontory of P a p i k ê, which lies
in front of A s t a k a p r a, where it is difficult to
anchor, from the strength of the current and
because the cables are cut through by the sharp
rocks at the bottom. But even if the passage
into the gulf is secured the mouth of the
Barugaza river is not easy to hit, since the coast
is low and there are no certain marks to be seen
until you are close upon them. Neither, if it is
discovered, is it easy to enter, from the presence
of shoals at the mouth of the river.

---

dios. This river is the N a r m a d â. It is called
by Ptolemy the Namadês.

(43) B a r u g a z a (Bharoch) which was 30
miles distant from its mouth, was both difficult and
dangerous of access; for the entrance to the Gulf
itself was, on the right, beset with a perilous stripe
(*tainia*) of rocky shoal called H e r ô n ê, and on the
left, (which was the safer course,) the violent
currents which swept round the promontory of
Papikê rendered it unsafe to approach the shore or
to cast anchor. The shoal of Herônê was opposite

44. For this reason native fishermen appointed by Government are stationed with well-
manned long boats called *trappaga* and *kotumba*
at the entrance of the river, whence they go out
as far as S u r a s t r ê n ê to meet ships, and pilot
them up to Barugaza.  At the head of the gulf
the pilot, immediately on taking charge of a ship,
with the help of his own boat's crew, shifts her
head to keep her clear of the shoals, and tows
her from one fixed station to another, moving
with the beginning of the tide, and dropping
anchor at certain roadsteads and basins when it
ebbs.  These basins occur at points where the
river is deeper than usual, all the way up to
B a r u g a z a, which is 300 stadia distant from
the mouth of the river if you sail up the
stream to reach it.

45.  India has everywhere a great abundance
of rivers, and her seas ebb and flow with tides
of extraordinary strength, which increase with

---

a village on the mainland called K a m m ô n i,
the Kamanê of Ptolemy (VII. i.), who however
places it to the north of the river's mouth.  Again,
it was not only difficult to hit the mouth of
the river, but its navigation was endangered by
sandbanks and the violence of the tides, especially
the high tide called the ' Bore,' of which our author
gives a description so particular and so vivid as
suffices to show that he was describing what he
had seen with his own eyes, and seen moreover
for the first time.  With regard to the name

the moon, both when new and when full, and
for three days after each, but fall off in the
intermediate space. About B a r u g a z a they
are more violent than elsewhere ; so that all of
a sudden you see the depths laid bare, and
portions of the land turned into sea, and the
sea, where ships were sailing but just before,
turned without warning into dry land. The
rivers, again, on the access of flood tide rushing
into their channels with the whole body of the
sea, are driven upwards against their natural
course for a great number of miles with a force
that is irresistible.

46. This is the reason why ships frequenting this emporium are exposed, both in coming
and going, to great risk, if handled by those who
are unacquainted with the navigation of the
gulf or visit it for the first time, since the impe-
tuosity of the tide when it becomes full, having
nothing to stem or slacken it, is such that

---

B a r u g a z a the following passage, which I quote
from Dr. Wilson's *Indian Castes* (vol. II. p. 113) will
elucidate its etymology :—" The B h â r g a v a s
derive their designation from B h a r g a v a, the
adjective form of B h r i g u, the name of one of
the ancient Ṛishis. Their chief habitat is the district of Bharoch, which must have got its name from
a colony of the school of Bhṛigu having been early
established in this Kshêtra, probably granted to
them by some conqueror of the district. In the
name B a r u g a z a given to it by Ptolemy, we have

anchors cannot hold against it. Large vessels,
moreover, if caught in it are driven athwart from
their course by the rapidity of the current till
they are stranded on shoals and wrecked, while
the smaller craft are capsized, and many that
have taken refuge in the side channels, being
left dry by the receding tide, turn over on
one side, and, if not set erect on props, are
filled upon the return of the tide with the very
first head of the flood, and sunk. But at new
moons, especially when they occur in conjunction
with a night tide, the flood sets in with such
extraordinary violence that on its beginning to
advance, even though the sea be calm, its roar is
heard by those living near the river's mouth,
sounding like the tumult of battle heard far off,
and soon after the sea with its hissing waves
bursts over the bare shoals.

47. Inland from B a r u g a z a the country is
inhabited by numerous races—the A r a t r i o i,

---

a Greek corruption of Bhṛigukshêtra (the territory
of Bhṛigu) or Bhṛigukachha (the tongueland of
Bhṛigu)." Speaking of the Bhârgavas Dr. Drum-
mond, in his *Grammatical Illustrations*, says:—
"These Brâhmans are indeed poor and ignorant.
Many of them, and other illiterate Gujarâtîs,
would, in attempting to articulate Bhṛigushêtra,
lose the half in coalesence, and call it Bargacha,
whence the Greeks, having no *Ch*, wrote it Barugaza."

(47) The account of the ' bore' is followed by an

and the A r a k h ô s i o i, and the G a n d a r a i o i,
and the people of P r o k l a ï s, in which is
B o u k e p h a l o s A l e x a n d r e i a. Beyond
these are the B a k t r i a n o i, a most warlike
race, governed by their own independent sovereign. It was from these parts Alexander issued
to invade India when he marched as far as the
Ganges, without, however, attacking Limurikê
and the southern parts of the country. Hence
up to the present day old *drachmai* bearing the

---

enumeration of the countries around and beyond
Barugaza with which it had commercial relations.
Inland are the A r a t r i o i, A r a k ĥ o s i o i,
G a n d a r i o i and the people of P r o k l a i s, a
province wherein is Boukephalos Alexandreia,
beyond which is the Baktrian nation. It has
been thought by some that by the A r a t r i o i are
meant the Arii, by others that they were the
A r â s t r â s of Sanskrit called Aratti in the
Prakrit, so that the A r a t r i o i of the *Periplûs*
hold an intermediate place between the Sanskrit and
Prakrit form of the name. Müller however says
"if you want a people known to the Greeks and
Romans as familiarly as the well-known names
of the Arakhosii, Gandarii, Peukelitae, you may
conjecture that the proper reading is ΔΡΑΓΓΩΝ instead of ΑΡΑΤΡΙΩΝ. It is an error of course on the
part of our author when he places B o u k e p h a l o s
(a city built by Alexander on the banks of the
Hydaspês, where he defeated Pôros), in the neighbourhood of Proklais, that is Pekhely in the neighbourhood of Peshawar. He makes a still more

P

Greek inscriptions of A p o l l o d o t o s and
M e n a n d e r are current in Barugaza.

48. In the same region eastward is a city
called O z ê n ê, formerly the capital wherein
the king resided. From it there is brought
down to Barugaza every commodity for the
supply of the country and for export to our
own markets—onyx-stones, porcelain, fine muslins, mallow-coloured muslins, and no small
quantity of ordinary cottons. At the same time
there is brought down to it from the upper
country by way of P r o k l a ï s, for transmis-
sion to the coast, Kattybourine, Patropapigic,
and Kabalitic spikenard, and another kind
which reaches it by way of the adjacent province
of Skythia; also kostus and bdellium.

49. The imports of B a r u g a z a are—

Οἶνος προηγουμένως 'Ιταλικὸς—Wine, principally
Italian.

Καὶ Λαοδικηνὸς καὶ 'Αραβικὸς—Laodikean wine
and Arabian.

Χαλκὸς καὶ κασσίτερος καὶ μόλυβδος—Brass or
Copper and Tin and Lead.

Κοράλλιον καὶ χρυσόλιθον—Coral and Gold-stone
or Yellow-stone.

---

surprising error when he states that Alexander
penetrated to the Ganges.

(48) The next place mentioned in the enumeration is O z ê n ê (Ujjain), which, receiving
nard through Proklais from the distant regions
where it was produced, passed it on to the
coast for export to the Western World. This

123

Ἱματισμὸς ἁπλοῦς καί νόθος παντοῖος—Cloth, plain and mixed, of all sorts.

Πολύμιται ζῶναι πηχυαῖαι—Variegated sashes half a yard wide.

Στύραξ—Storax.

Μελίλωτον—Sweet clover, melilot.

Ὕαλος ἀργὴ—White glass.

Σανδαράκη—Gum Sandarach.

Στίμμι—(Stibium) Tincture for the eyes,—Sûrmâ.

Δηνάριον χρυσοῦ καὶ ἀργυροῦν—Gold and Silver specie, yielding a profit when exchanged for native money.

Μύρον οὐ βαρύτιμον οὐδὲ πολὺ—Perfumes or unguents, neither costly nor in great quantity.

In those times, moreover, there were imported, *as presents* to the king, costly silver vases, instruments of music, handsome young women for concubinage, superior wine, apparel, plain but costly, and the choicest unguents. The exports from this part of the country are—

Νάρδος, κόστος, βδέλλα, ἐλέφας—Spikenard, costus, bdellium, ivory.

Ὀνυχίνη λιθία καὶ μουρρίνη—Onyx-stones and porcelain.

Λύκιον—*Ruzot*, Box-thorn.

---

aromatic was a product of three districts, whence its varieties were called respectively the *Kattybourine*, the *Patropapigic* and the *Kabolitic*. What places were indicated by the first two names cannot be ascertained, but the last points undoubtedly to the region round Kâbul, since its inhabitants are called by Ptolemy K a b o l i t a i, and Edrisi uses the term *Myrobalanos Kabolinos*

'Οθόνιον παντοῖον—Cottons of all sorts.

Σηρικὸν—Silk.

Μολόχινον—Mallow-coloured cottons.

Νῆμα—*Silk* thread.

Πέπερι μακρὸν—Long pepper and other articles supplied from the neighbouring ports.

The proper season to set sail for Barugaza from Egypt is the month of July, or Epiphi.

50. From B a r u g a z a the coast immediately adjoining stretches from the north directly to the south, and the country is therefore called D a k h i n a b a d ê s, because Dakhan in the language of the natives signifies *south*. Of this country that part which lies inland towards the east comprises a great space of desert country, and large mountains abounding with all kinds of wild animals, leopards, tigers, elephants, huge snakes, hyenas, and baboons of many different sorts, and is inhabited right across to the Ganges by many and extremely populous nations.

---

for the 'myrobolans of Kâbul.' Nard, as Edrisi also observes, has its proper soil in Thibet.

(50) B a r u g a z a had at the same time commercial relations with the Dekhan also. This part of India our author calls D a k h i n a b a d ê s, transliterating the word D a k s h i n â p a t h a—(the Dakshinâ, or the South Country). "Here," says Vincent, "the author of the *Periplûs* gives the true direction of this western coast of the Peninsula, and states in direct terms its tendency to the South, while Ptolemy stretches out the whole angle to a straight line, and places the Gulf of

51. Among the marts in this South Country there are two of more particular importance—Paithana, which lies south from Barugaza, a distance of twenty days, and Tagara, ten days east of Paithana, the greatest city in the country. Their commodities are carried down on wagons to Barugaza along roads of extreme difficulty,—that is, from Paithana a great

---

Cambay almost in the same latitude as Cape Comorin."

(51) In the interior of the Dekhan, the *Periplûs* places two great seats of commerce, Paithana, 20 days' journey to the south of Barugaza, and Tagara, 10 days' journey eastward from Paithana. Paithana, which appears in Ptolemy as Baithana, may be identified with Paithana. Tagara is more puzzling. Wilford, Vincent, Mannert, Ritter and others identify it with Dêvagiri or Deogarh, near Elurâ, about 8 miles from Aurangâbâd. The name of a place called Tagarapura occurs in a copper grant of land which was found in the island of Salsette. There is however nothing to show that this was a name of Dêvagiri. Besides, if Paithana be correctly identified, Tagara cannot be Dêvagiri unless the distances and directions are very erroneously given in the *Periplûs*. This is not improbable, and Tagara may therefore be Junnar (*i.e.* Jûna-nagar = *the old city*), which from its position must always have been an emporium, and its Buddha caves belong to about B. C. 100 to A.D. 150 (see *Archæolog. Surv. of West. India*, vol. III., and Elphinstone's *History of India*, p. 223).

quantity of onyx-stone, and from Tagara ordinary cottons in abundance, many sorts of muslins, mallow-coloured cottons, and other articles of local production brought into it from the parts along the coast. The length of the entire voyage as far as Limurikê is 700 stadia, and to reach Aigialos you must sail very many stadia further.

---

Our author introduces us next to another division of India, that called Limurikê, which begins, as he informs us, at a distance of 7,000 stadia (or nearly 900 miles) beyond Barugaza. This estimate is wide of the mark, being in fact about the distance between Barugaza and the southern or remote extremity of Limurikê. In the Indian segment of the Roman maps called from their discoverer, the *Peutinger Tables*, the portion of India to which this name is applied is called Damirikê. We can scarcely err, says Dr. Caldwell (*Dravid. Gram.* Intr. page 14), in identifying this name with the Tamil country. If so, the earliest appearance of the name Tamil in any foreign documents will be found also to be most perfectly in accordance with the native Tamil mode of spelling the name. Damirike evidently means *Damir-ike* ... In another place in the same map a district is called Scytia Dymirice; and it appears to have been this word which by a mistake of Δ for Λ Ptolemy wrote Λυμιρική. The D retains its place however in the Cosmography of the anonymous geographer of Ravenna, who repeatedly mentions Dimirica as one of the three divisions of India and the one furthest to the East.

52. The local marts which occur in order *along the coast* after B a r u g a z a are A k a-
b a r o u, S o u p p a r a, K a l l i e n a, a city which
was raised to the rank of a regular mart in the
times of the elder S a r a g a n e s, but after

---

He shows also that the Tamiḷ country must
have been meant by the name by mentioning
M o d u r a as one of the cities it contained.

(52) Reverting to B a r u g a z a our author next
enumerates the less important emporia having
merely a local trade which intervenes between it
and D i m u r i k ê. These are first A k a b a r o u,
S o u p p a r a, and K a l l i e n a — followed by
S e m u l l a, M a n d a g o r a, P a l a i p a t m a i,
M e l i g e i z a r a, B u z a n t i o n, T o p e r o n, and
T u r a n o s b o a s,—beyond which occurs a succession of islands, some of which give shelter to
pirates, and of which the last is called L e u k ê or
White Island. The actual distance from Barugaza
to Naoura, the first port of Dimurîkê, is 4,500
stadia.

To take these emporia in detail. A k a b a r o u
cannot be identified. The reading is probably corrupt. Between the mouths of the Namados and
those of the Goaris, Ptolemy interposes Nousaripa,
Poulipoula, Ariakê Sadinôn, and Soupara. N a u-
s a r i p a is N a u s a r i, about 18 miles to the
south of Surat, and S o u p a r a is S û p â r â near
Vasâï. Benfey, who takes it to be the name of a
region and not of a city, regards it as the O p h i r
of the Bible—called in the Septuagint Σωφηρά.
S ô p h i r, it may be added, is the Coptic name for
India. K a l l i e n a is now K a l y â n a near

Sandanes became its master its trade was
put under the severest restrictions; for if Greek
vessels, even by accident, enter its ports, a guard
is put on board and they are taken to Barugaza.

53.   After Kalliena other local marts oc-

Bombay [which must have been an important
place at an early date. It is named in the
Kanhêri Bauddha Cave Inscriptions].   It is
mentioned by Kosmas (p. 337), who states that
it produced copper and sesamum and other
kinds of logs, and cloth for wearing apparel.
The name Sandanes, that of the Prince who
sent Greek ships which happened to put into its
port under guard to Barugaza, is thought by
Benfey to be a territorial title which indicated
that he ruled over Ariakê of the Sandineis.
[But the elder " Saraganes" probably indicates
one of the great Sâtakarni or Ândhrabhritya
dynasty.] Ptolemy does not mention Kallienâ,
though  he supplies the name of a place omitted
in the *Periplûs*, namely Dounga (VII. i. 6)
near the mouth of the river Bênda.

(53)   Semulla (in Ptolemy Timoula and
Simulla) is identified by Yule with Chênval
or Chauî, a seaport 23 miles south of Bombay;
[but Bhagvanlâl Indraji suggests Chimûla in
Trombay island at the head of the Bombay
harbour; and this is curiously supported by one
of the Kanhêri inscriptions in which Chemûla
is mentioned, apparently as a large city, like
Supârâ and Kalyâna, in the neighbourhood].
After Simulla Ptolemy mentions Hippo-
koura [possibly, as suggested by the same,

cur—Sêmulla, Mandagora, Palaipat-
mai, Melizeigara, Buzantion, Toparon,
and Turannosboas. You come next to the
islands called Sêsekreienai and the island

---

a partial translation of Ghodabandar on
the Choda nadi in the Ṭhaṅa strait] and Balti-
patna as places still in Ariakê, but Mandagara Buzanteion, Khersonêsos, Ar-
magara, the mouths of the river Nanagouna,
and an emporium called Nitra, as belonging to
the Pirate Coast which extended to Dimurikê, of
which Tundis, he says, is the first city. Ptolemy
therefore agrees with our author in assigning the
Pirate Coast to the tract of country between
Bombay and Goa. This coast continued to be
infested with pirates till so late a period as the
year 1765, when they were finally exterminated by
the British arms. Mandagara and Palaipat-
ma may have corresponded pretty nearly in situation with the towns of Râjapur and Bankut. Yule
places them respectively at Bankut and Debal.
Melizeigara (Milizêguris or Milizigêris of
Ptolemy, VII. i. 95), Vincent identifies with Jaygadh
or Sidê Jaygadh. The same place appears in Pliny
as Sigerus (VI. xxvi. 100). Buzantium may be
referred to about Vijayadrug or Esvantgadh, Toparon may be a corrupt reading for Togaron,
and may perhaps therefore be Devagadh which
lies a little beyond Vijayadrug. Turannosboas
is not mentioned elsewhere, but it may have been,
as Yule suggests, the Bandâ or Tirakal river.
Müller placed it at Acharê. The first island on
this part of the coast is Sindhudrug near Mâlwan,

q

of the A i g i d i o i and that of the K a i n e i t a i,
near what is called the K h e r s o n ê s o s, places
in which are pirates, and after this the island
L e u k ê (or 'the White'). Then follow N a o u r a

to which succeeds a group called the Burnt Islands,
among which the Vingorla rocks are conspicuous.
These are no doubt the H e p t a n ê s i a of
Ptolemy (VII. i. 95), and probably the S ê s i-
k r i e n a i of the *Periplûs*. The island Aigidion
called that of the Aigidii may be placed at Goa,
[but Yule suggests Angediva south of Sadaśiva-
gaḍh, in lat. 14° 45′ N., which is better]. Kaineiton
may be the island of St. George.

We come next to N a o u r a in Dimurikê. This
is now H o n â v a r, written otherwise Onore,
situated on the estuary of a broad river, the
Ś a r â v a t î, on which are the falls of Gêrsappa,
one of the most magnificent and stupendous
cataracts in the world. If the N i t r a of Ptolemy
(VII. i. 7) and the N i t r i a of Pliny be the same as
N a o u r a, then these authors extend the pirate
coast a little further south than the *Periplûs* does.
But if they do not, and therefore agree in their
views as to where Dimurikê begins, the N i t r a
may be placed, Müller thinks, at Mirjan or Komta,
which is not far north from Honavar. [Yule
places it at Mangalur.] Müller regards the first
supposition however as the more probable, and
quotes at length a passage from Pliny (VI. xxvi.
104) referring thereto, which must have been ex-
cerpted from some *Periplûs* like our author's, but
not from it as some have thought. " To those
bound for India it is most convenient to depart

and T u n d i s, the first marts of L i m u rik ê,
and after these M o u z i r i s and N e l k u n d a,
the seats of Government.

54. To the kingdom under the sway of

---

from Okelis. They sail thence with the wind
Hipalus in 40 days to the first emporium of India,
Muziris, which is not a desirable place to arrive
at on account of pirates infesting the neighbourhood, who hold a place called N i t r i a s, while it is
not well supplied with merchandize. Besides,
the station for ships is at a great distance from
the shore, and cargoes have both to be landed and
to be shipped by means of little boats. There
reigned there when I wrote this C a e l o b o-
t h r a s. Another port belonging to the nation
is more convenient, N e a c y n d o n, which is
called B e c a r e (*sic. codd.*, Barace, Harduin and
Sillig). There reigned Pandion in an inland
town far distant from the emporium called M o-
d u r a. The region, however, from which they
convey pepper to Becare in boats formed from
single logs is C o t t o n a r a."

(54) With regard to the names in this extract
which occur also in the *Periplûs* the following
passages quoted from Dr. Caldwell's *Dravidian
Grammar* will throw much light. He says (Introd.
p. 97):—"M u z i r i s appears to be the M u y i r i
of Muyiri-kotta. Tyndis is T u ṇ ḍ i, and the
Kynda, of Nelkynda, or as Ptolemy has it, Mel-
kynda, *i. e.* probably Western kingdom, seems to
be K a n n e t t r i, the southern boundary of Kêrala
proper. One MS. of Pliny writes the second part
of this word not *Cyndon* but *Canidon.* The first

Kêprobotras[20] Tundis is subject, a village
of great note situate near the sea. Mouziris,
which pertains to the same realm, is a city
at the height of prosperity, frequented as it

of these places was identified by Dr. Gundert, for
the remaining two we are indebted to Dr. Burnell.

"Cottonara, Pliny; Kottonarike, *Periplûs*, the
district where the best pepper was produced. It
is singular that this district was not mentioned
by Ptolemy. Cottonara was evidently the
name of the district. κοττοναρικον the name of the
pepper for which the district was famous. Dr.
Buchanan identifies Cottonara with Kadatta-
naḍu, the name of a district in the Calicut country
celebrated for its pepper. Dr. Burnell identifies it
with Koḷatta-nâḍu, the district about Tellicherry which he says is the pepper district.
*Kadatta* in Malayâlam means 'transport, convey-
ance,' *Nâdû*, Tam.—Mal., means a district."

"The prince called Kêrobothros by Ptolemy (VII.
i. 86) is called Kêprobotros by the author of the
*Periplûs*. The insertion of π is clearly an error,
but more likely to be the error of a copyist than
that of the author, who himself had visited the
territories of the prince in question. He is called
Caëlobothras in Pliny's text, but one of the MSS.
gives it more correctly as Celobotras. The name
in Sanskrit, and in full is 'Keralaputra,' but both
*kêra* and *kêla* are Dravidian abbreviations of *kêralâ*.
They are Malayâlam however, not Tamil abbreviations, and the district over which Keralaputra ruled
is that in which the Malayâlam language is now

is by ships from A r i a k ê and Greek ships *from
Egypt.* It lies near a river at a distance from
Tundis of 500 stadia, whether this is measured
from river to river or by the length of the sea

---

spoken" (p. 95). From Ptolemy we learn that the
capital of this prince was K a r o u r a, which has
been " identified with K a r û r, an important town
in the Koimbatur district originally included in the
Chêra kingdom. Karûr means the black town . .
Ptolemy's word K a r o u r a represents the Tamil
name of the place with perfect accuracy." Nelkunda, our author informs us, was not subject to
this prince but to another called P a n d i ô n. This
name, says Dr. Caldwell, " is of Sanskrit origin,
and P a n d æ, the form which Pliny, after Megasthenes, gives in his list of the Indian nations,
comes very near the Sanskrit. The more recent
local information of Pliny himself, as well as the
notices of Ptolemy and the *Periplûs,* supply us with
the Dravidian form of the word. The Tamil sign
of the masc. sing. is *an,* and Tamil inserts *i* eupho-
nically after *ṇḍ,* consequently Pandiôn, and still
better the plural form of the word P a n d i o n e s,
faithfully represents the Tamil masc. sing. *Pâṇ-
ḍiyan."* In another passage the same scholar says :
" The Sanskrit Paṇḍya is written in Tamil Pâṇḍiya,
but the more completely tamilized form P â ṇ ḍ i
is still more commonly used all over southern
India. I derive Pâṇḍi, as native scholars always
derive the word, from the Sanskrit Pâṇḍu, the
name of the father of the Pâṇḍava brothers."
The capital of this prince, as Pliny has stated, was
M o d u r a, which is the Sanskrit Maṭhurâ pro-

voyage, and it is 20 stadia distant from the mouth of its own river. The distance of N e l-k u n d a from M o u z i r i s is also nearly 500 stadia, whether measured from river to river or

---

nounced in the Tamil manner. The corresponding city in Northern India, Maṭhurâ, is written by the Greeks M e t h o r a.

N e l k u n d a is mentioned by various authors un-der varying forms of the name. As has been already stated, it is Melkunda in Ptolemy, who places it in the country of the Aii. In the *Peutingerian Table* it is Nincylda, and in the Geographer of Ravenna, Nilcinna. At the mouth of the river on which it stands was its shipping port B a k a r e or Becare, according to Müller now represented by M a r k a r i (lat. 12° N.) Yule conjectures that it must have been between Kanetti and Kolum in Travancoré. Regarding the trade of this place we may quote a remark from Vincent. "We find," he says, "that throughout the whole which the *Periplûs* mentions of India we have a catalogue of the exports and imports only at the two ports of Barugaza and Nelcynda, and there seems to be a distinction fixed between the articles appropriate to each. Fine muslins and ordinary cottons are the principal commodities of the first; tortoise shell, precious stones, silk, and above all pepper, seem to have been procurable only at the latter. This pepper is said to be brought to this port from Cottonara, famous to this hour for producing the best pepper in the world except that of Sumatra. The pre-eminence of these two ports will account for the little that is said of the others by the author, and why he has

by the sea voyage, but it belongs to a different
kingdom, that of P a n d i ô n.  It likewise is
situate near a river and at about a distance
from the sea of 120 stadia.

55.  At the very mouth of this river lies

---

left us so few characters by which we may distinguish one from another."

Our author on concluding his account of Nelkunda interrupts his narrative to relate the incidents of the important discovery of the monsoon
made by that Columbus of antiquity Hippalus.
This account, Vincent remarks, naturally excites a
curiosity in the mind to enquire how it should
happen that the monsoon should have been noticed
by Nearkhos, and that from the time of his voyage
for 300 years no one should have attempted a
direct course till Hippalus ventured to commit
himself to the ocean.  He is of opinion that there
was a direct passage by the monsoons both in
going to and coming from India in use among
the Arabians before the Greeks adopted it, and
that Hippalus frequenting these seas as a pilot or
merchant, had met with Indian or Arabian traders
who made their voyages in a more compendious
manner than the Greeks, and that he collected
information from them which he had both the pru-
dence and courage to adopt, just as Columbus, while
owing much to his own nautical experience and
fortitude was still under obligations to the Portuguese, who had been resolving the great problems
in the art of navigation for almost a century previous to his expedition.

(55)  N e l k u n d a appears to have been the

another village, B a k a r ê, to which the ships
despatched from Nelkunda come down *empty*
and ride at anchor off shore while taking in
cargo : for the river, it may be noted, has sunken
reefs and shallows which make its navigation
difficult.   The sign by which those who come
hither by sea know they are nearing land is
their meeting with snakes, which are here of a
black colour, not so long as those already mentioned, like serpents about the head, and with
eyes the colour of blood.

56.   The ships which frequent these ports
are of a large size, on account of the great
amount and bulkiness of the pepper and betel
of which their lading consists.   The imports
here are principally—

Χρήματα πλεῖστα—Great quantities of specie.

Χρυσόλιθα—(Topaz ?)   Gold-stone, Chrysolite.

Ἱματισμὸς ἁπλοῦς οὐ πολὺς—A small assortment
of plain cloth.

Πολύμιτα—Flowered robes.

Στίμμι, κοράλλιον—Stibium, a pigment for the
eyes, coral.

῎υαλος ἀργὴ χαλκὸς—White glass, copper or
brass.

Κασσίτερος, μόλυβδος—Tin, lead.

Οἶνος οὐ πολύς, ὡσεὶ δὲ τοσοῦτον ὅσον ἐν Βαρυγάζοις
—Wine but not much, but about as much as at
Barugaza.

limit of our author's voyage along the coast of
India, for in the sequel of his narrative he defines
but vaguely the situation of the places which he

Σανδαράκη—Sandarach (*Sindúrâ*).

'Αρσενικὸν—Arsenic (Orpiment), yellow sulphuret of arsenic.

Σῖτος ὅσος ἀρκέσει τοῖς περὶ το ναυκλήριον, διὰ τὸ μὴ τοὺς ἐμπόρους αὐτῷ χρῆσθαι—Corn, only for the use of the ship's company, as the merchants do not sell it.

The following commodities are brought to it for export:—

Πέπερι μονογενῶς ἐν ἑνὶ τόπῳ τούτων τῶν ἐμπορίων γεννώμενον πολύ τῇ λεγομενῃ Κοττοναρικῇ—Pepper in great quantity, produced in only one of these marts, and called the pepper of Kottonara.

Μαργαρίτης ἱκανὸς καὶ διάφορος—Pearls in great quantity and of superior quality.

'Ελέφας—Ivory.

'Οθόνια Σηρικὰ—Fine silks.

Νάρδος ἡ Γαγγητικὴ—Spikenard from the Ganges.

Μαλάβαθρον—Betel—all brought from countries further east.

Λιθία διαφανὴς παντοία—Transparent or precious stones of all sorts.

Αδάμας—Diamonds.

'Υάκινθος—Jacinths.

Χελώνη ἥτε Χρυσονησιωτικὴ καὶ ἡ περὶ τὰς νήσους θηρευομένη τὰς προκειμένας αὐτῆς τῆς Λιμυρικῆς—Tortoise-shell from the Golden Island, and another sort which is taken in the islands which lie off the coast of Limurikê.

The proper season to set sail from Egypt for

---

notices, while his details are scanty, and sometimes grossly inaccurate. Thus he makes the Malabar Coast extend southwards beyond Cape Comorin

this part of India is about the month of July—that is, Epiphi.

57. The whole round of the voyage from K a n ê and E u d a i m ô n A r a b i a, which we have just described, used to be performed in small vessels which kept close to shore and followed its windings, but H i p p a l o s was the pilot who first, by observing the bearings of the ports and the configuration of the sea, discovered the direct course across the ocean; whence as, at the season when our own Etesians are blowing, a periodical wind from the ocean likewise blows in the Indian Sea, this wind, which is the south-west, is, it seems, called in these seas Hippalos [after the name of the pilot who first discovered the *passage by means of it*]. From the time of this discovery to the present day, merchants who sail for India either from K a n ê, or, as others do, from A r ô m a t a, if Limurikê be their destination, must often change their tack, but if they are bound for B a r u-g a z a and S k y t h i a, they are not retarded for more than three days, after which, committing themselves to the monsoon which blows right in the direction of their course, they stand far out to sea, leaving all the gulfs we have mentioned in the distance.

---

as far at least as Kolkhoi (near Tutikorin) on the Coromandel coast, and like many ancient writers, represents Ceylon as stretching westward almost as far as Africa.

58. After B a k a r ê occurs the mountain
called Pyrrhos (or the Red) towards the south,
near another district of the country called
P a r a l i a (where the pearl-fisheries are which
belong to king Pandiôn), and a city of the name
of K o l k h o i. In this tract the first place
met with is called B a l i t a, which has a good
harbour and a village on its shore. Next to
this is another place called K o m a r, where is
the cape of the same name and a haven. Those
who wish to consecrate the closing part of their
lives to religion come hither and bathe and
engage themselves to celibacy. 'This is also
done by women; since it is related that the

(58) The first place mentioned after B a k a r e
is P u r r h o s, or the Red Mountain, which extends
along a district called P a r a l i a. "There are,"
says Dr. Caldwell (Introd. p. 99), "three Paralias
mentioned by the Greeks, two by Ptolemy . . .
one by the author of the *Periplûs*. The Paralia
mentioned by the latter corresponded to Ptolemy's
country of the Ἄϊοι, and that of the Καρεοι,
that is, to South Travancore and South Tinnevelly. It commenced at the Red Cliffs south of
Quilon, and included not only Cape Comorin
but also Κόλχοι, where the pearl fishing was carried on, which belonged to King Pandion. Dr.
Burnell identifies Paralia with Parali, which
he states is an old name for Travancore, but I am
not quite able to adopt this view." " Paralia," he
adds afterwards, " may possibly have corresponded
in meaning, if not in sound, to some native word

goddess (*Kumârî*) once on a time resided at the place and bathed. From K o m a r e i (towards the south) the country extends as far as K o l k h o i, where the fishing for pearls is carried on. Condemned criminals are employed in this service. King Pandiôn is the owner of the fishery. To Kolkhoi succeeds another coast lying along a gulf having a district in the interior bearing the name of A r g a l o u. In this single place are obtained the pearls collected near the island of E p i o d ô r o s. From it are exported the muslins called *ebargareitides*.

60. Among the marts and anchorages along this shore to which merchants from Limurikê

---

meaning coast,—viz., Karei." On this coast is a place called B a l i t a, which is perhaps the B a m m a l a of Ptolemy (VII. i. 9), which Mannert identifies with Manpalli, a little north of Anjenga.

(60) We now reach the great promontory called in the *Periplûs* K o m a r and K o m a r e i, Cape Kumari. "It has derived its name," says Caldwell, " from the Sans. *Kumârî*, a virgin, one of the names of the goddess Durgâ, the presiding divinity of the place, but the shape which this word has taken is, especially in *komar*, distinctively Tamilian." In ordinary Tamil *Kumârî* becomes *Kumâri*; and in the vulgar dialect of the people residing in the neighbourhood of the Cape a virgin is neither Kumârî nor Kumâri but Kŭmăr pronounced Kŏmăr. It is remarkable that this vulgar corruption of the Sanskrit is identical with the name given to the place by the

and the north resort, the most conspicuous are
K a m a r a and P o d o u k ê and S ô p a t m a,
which occur in the order in which we have
named them. In these marts are found those
native vessels for coasting voyages which trade
as far as Limurikê, and another kind called

---

author of the *Periplûs* ... The monthly bathing in
honor of the goddess Durgâ is still continued at
Cape Comorin, but is not practised to the same
extent as in ancient times ... Through the continued encroachments of the sea, the harbour the
Greek mariners found at Cape Comorin and the
fort (if φρουριον is the correct reading for βριάριον
of the MS.) have completely disappeared ; but a
fresh water well remains in the centre of a rock, a
little way out at sea. Regarding K o l k h o i, the
next place mentioned after Komari, the same
authority as we have seen places it (*Ind. Ant.* vol.
VI. p. 80) near Tuticorin. It is mentioned by
Ptolemy and in the *Peutinger Tables*, where it is
called ' Colcis Indorum'. The Gulf of Manaar was
called by the Greeks the Colchic Gulf. The Tamil
name of the place Kolkei is almost identical with
the Greek. " The place," according to Caldwell, "is
now about three miles inland, but there are abundant traces of its having once stood on the coast, and
I have found the tradition that it was once the seat
of the pearl fishery, still surviving amongst its inhabitants. After the sea had retired from Κόλχοι...
a new emporium arose on the coast. This was
K â y a l, the Cael of Marco Polo. Kâyal in turn
became in time too far from the sea .. and Tuticorin (T û t t r u k u ḍ i) was raised instead by the

*sangara*, made by fastening together large
vessels formed each of a single timber, and also
others called *kolandiophônta*, which are of great
bulk and employed for voyages to K h r u s ê
and the G a n g e s.   These marts import all the
commodities which reach Limurikê for com-

Portuguese from the position of a fishing village
to that of the most important port on the southern
Coromandel coast.  The identification of Kolkoi
with Kolkei is one of much importance.  Being
perfectly certain it helps forward other identifica-
tions.  *Kol.* in Tamil means ' to slay.'  *Kei* is
' hand.'  It was the first capital of Pandion.

The coast beyond K o l k h o i, which has an inland district belonging to it called A r g a l o u, is
indented by a gulf called by Ptolemy the Argarik—
now Palk Bay.  Ptolemy mentions also a promontory
called Kôru and beyond it a city called A r g e i r o u
and an emporium called  S a l o u r.  This Kôru
of Ptolemy, Caldwell thinks, represents the
K ô l i s of the geographers who preceded him,
and the Ko t i of Tamil, and identifies it with
" the island promontory of R â m e s v a r a m, the
point of land from which there was always the
nearest access from Southern India to Ceylon."
An island occurs in these parts, called that of
E p i o d ô r o s, noted for its pearl fishery, on
which account Ritter would identify it with
the island of Manaar, which Ptolemy, as Mannert
thinks, speaks of as Νάνιγηρίς (VII. i. 95).  Müller
thinks, however, it may be compared with Ptolemy's K ô r u, and so be Râmêsvaram.

This coast has commercial intercourse not only

mercial purposes, absorbing likewise nearly every species of goods brought from Egypt, and most descriptions of all the goods exported from Limuriké and disposed of on this coast of India.

61. Near the region which succeeds, where

---

with the Malabar ports, but also with the Ganges and the Golden Khersonese. For the trade with the former a species of canoes was used called *Sangara*. The Malayâlam name of these, Caldwell says, is *Changâdam*, in Tuḷu *Jangâla*, compare Sanskrit *Samghâdam* a raft (*Ind. Ant.* vol. I. p. 309). The large vessels employed for the Eastern trade were called *Kolandiophonta*, a name which Caldwell confesses his inability to explain.

Three cities and ports are named in the order of their occurrence which were of great commercial importance, K a m a r a, P o d o u k e, and S o p a t - m a. K a m a r a may perhaps be, as Müller thinks, the emporium which Ptolemy calls K h a b ê r i s, situated at the mouth of the River K h a b ê r o s (now, the Kavery), perhaps, as Dr. Burnell suggests, the modern Kaveripattam. (*Ind. Ant.* vol. VII. p. 40). P ô d o u k ê appears in Ptolemy as Podoukê. It is P u d u c h c h ê r i, *i. e.* ' new town,' now well known as Pondicherry ; so Bohlen, Ritter, and Benfey. [Yule and Lassen place it at Pulikât]. S o p a t m a is not mentioned in Ptolemy, nor can it now be traced. In Sanskrit it transliterates into *Su-patna, i. e.*, fair town.

(61) The next place noticed is the Island of Ceylon, which is designated P a l a i s i m o u n - d o u, with the remark that its former name was

the course of the voyage now bends to the east, there lies out in the open sea stretching towards the west the island now called P a l a i s i- m o u n d o u, but by the ancients T a p r o- b a n ê. To cross over to the northern side of it takes a day. In the south part it gradual- ly stretches towards the west till it nearly reaches the opposite coast of A z a n i a. It pro- duces pearl, precious (*transparent*) stones, muslins, and tortoise-shell.

62. (*Returning to the coast,*) not far from the

---

T a p r o b a n ê. This is the Greek transliteration of Tâmraparnî, the name given by a band of colonists from Magadha to the place where they first landed in Ceylon, and which was afterwards ex- tended to the whole island. It is singular, Dr. Caldwell remarks, that this is also the name of the principal river in Tinnevelly on the opposite coast of India, and he infers that the colony referred to might previously have formed a settle- ment in Tinnevelly at the mouth of the Tâmra- parni river—perhaps at Kolkei, the earliest resi- dence of the Pâṇḍya kings. The passage in the *Periplûs* which refers to the island is very corrupt.

(62) Recurring to the mainland, the narra- tive notices a district called M a s a l i a, where great quantities of cotton were manufactured. This is the M a ï s ô l i a of Ptolemy, the region in which he places the mouths of a river the M a i s ô- l o s, which Benfey identifies with the Godâvarî, in opposition to others who would make it the Krishnâ, which is perhaps Ptolemy's T u n a. The

three marts we have mentioned lies M a s a l i a,
the seaboard of a country extending far inland.
Here immense quantities of fine muslins are
manufactured. From Ma s a l i a the course of
the voyage lies eastward across a neighbouring
bay to D ê s a r ê n ê, which has the breed of
elephants called Bôsarê. Leaving D ê s a r ê n ê
the course is northerly, passing a variety of
barbarous tribes, among which are the K i r r h a-
d a i, savages whose noses are flattened to the
face, and another tribe, that of the B a r g u s o i,

---

name Maisôlia is taken from the Sanskrit Mausâla,
preserved in Machhlipatana, now Masulipatam.
Beyond this, after an intervening gulf running
eastward is crossed, another district occurs, D e s-
a r ê n ê, noted for its elephants. This is not mentioned by Ptolemy, but a river with a similar name,
the D ô s a r ô n, is found in his enumeration of
the rivers which occur between the Maisôlos and
the Ganges. As it is the last in the list it may
probably be, as Lassen supposes, the Brâhmini.
Our author however places Desarênê at a much
greater distance from the Ganges, for he peoples
the intermediate space with a variety of tribes
which Ptolemy relegates to the East of the river.
The first of these tribes is that of the K i r r â d a i
(Sanskrit, Kirâtas), whose features are of the
Mongolian type. Next are the B a r g u s o i, not
mentioned by Ptolemy, but perhaps to be identified with the cannibal race he speaks of, the
B a r o u s a i thought by Yule to be possibly the
inhabitants of the Nikobar islands, and lastly the

as well as the Hîppioprosôpoi *or* Ma-
kroprosôpoi (the horse faced or long faced
men), who are reported to be cannibals.

63. After passing these the course turns
again to the east, and if you sail with the ocean
to your right and the coast far to your left, you
reach the Ganges and the extremity of the continent towards the east *called* Khrusê (the
Golden Khersonese). The river of this region
called the Ganges is the largest in India ;
it has an *annual* increase and decrease like the
Nile, and there is on it a mart called after it,
Gangê, through which passes *a considerable
traffic* consisting of betel, the Gangetic spike-

---

tribe of the long or horse-faced men who were also
cannibals.

(63) When this coast of savages and monsters
is left behind, the course lies eastward, and leads
to the Ganges, which is the greatest river of
India, and adjoins the extremity of the Eastern
continent called Khrusê, or the Golden. Near
the river, or, according to Ptolemy, on the third of
its mouths stands a great emporium of trade
called Gangê, exporting *Malabathrum* and cottons and other commodities. Its exact position
there are not sufficient data to determine. Khrusê
is not only the name of the last part of the continent, but also of an island lying out in the ocean
to eastward, not far from the Ganges. It is the
last part of the world which is said to be inhabited.
The situation of Khrusê is differently defined by
different ancient authors. It was not known to

nard, pearl, and the finest of all muslins—those
called the Gangetic. In this locality also there
is said to be a gold mine and a gold coin called
*Kaltis*. Near this river there is an island of
the ocean called K h r u s ê (or the Golden),
which lies directly under the rising sun and at
the extremity of the world towards the east.
It produces the finest tortoise-shell that is found
throughout the whole of the Erythræan Sea.

64. Beyond this region, immediately under
the north, where the sea terminates outwards,
there lies somewhere in T h î n a a very great
city,—not on the coast, but in the interior of
the country, called T h î n a,—from which silk,
whether in the raw state or spun into thread

---

the Alexandrine geographers. Pliny seems to
have preserved the most ancient report circulated
regarding it. He says (VI. xxiii. 80) : " Beyond the
mouth of the Indus are C h r y s ê and A r g y r e
abounding in metals as I believe, for I can hardly
credit what some have related that the soil consists
of gold and silver." Mela (III. 7) assigns to it a very
different position, asserting it to be near T a b i s,
the last spur of the range of Taurus. He therefore
places it where Eratosthenês places T h i n a i, to the
north of the Ganges on the confines of the Indian
and Skythian oceans. Ptolemy, in whose time the
Transgangetic world was better known, refers it
to the peninsula of Malacca, the Golden Khersonese.

(64) The last place which the *Periplûs* mentions is Thinai, an inland city of the T h i n a i or

and woven into cloth, is brought by land to
Barugaza through Baktria, or by the Ganges to
Limurikê.   To penetrate into T h î n a is not
an easy undertaking, and but few *merchants*
come from it, and that rarely.   Its situation is
under the Lesser Bear, and it is said to be con-
terminous with the remotest end of Pontos,
and that part of the Kaspian Sea which adjoins
the Maiôtic Lake, along with which it issues by
*one and* the same mouth into the ocean.

65.   On the confines, however, of T h î n a i
an annual fair is held, attended by a race of men
of squat figure, with their face very broad, but
mild in disposition, called the S ê s a t a i, who in
appearance resemble wild animals.   They come
with their wives and children to this fair, bringing heavy loads of goods wrapped up in mats
resembling in outward appearance the early
leaves of the vine.   Their place of assembly is
where their own territory borders with that of
Thinai; and here, squatted on the mats on which

S i n a i, having a large commerce in silk and
woollen stuffs.   The ancient writers are not at all
agreed as to its position,  Colonel Yule thinks it
was probably the city described by  Marco Polo
under the name of K e n j a n-f u (that is Si-
ngan-fu or Chauggan,) the most celebrated city
in Chinese history, and the capital of several of
the most potent dynasties.   It was the metropolis of Shi Hwengti of the T'Sin dynasty, properly the first emperor, and whose conquests almost

they exhibit their wares, they feast for several days, after which they return to their homes in the interior. On observing their retreat the people of Thinai, repairing to the spot, collect the mats on which they had been sitting, and taking out the fibres, which are called *petroi*, from the reeds, they put the leaves two and two together, and roll them up into slender balls, through which they pass the fibres extracted from the reeds. Three kinds of Malabathrum are thus made—that of the large ball, that of the middle, and that of the small, according to the size of the leaf of which the balls are formed. Hence there are three kinds of Malabathrum, which after being made up are forwarded to India by the manufacturers.

66. All the regions beyond this are unexplored, being difficult of access by reason of the extreme rigour of the climate and the severe frosts, or perhaps because such is the will of the divine power.

---

intersected those of his contemporary Ptolemy Euergetês—(vide Yule's *Travels of Marco Polo*, vol. II. p. 21).

THE

# VOYAGE OF NEARKHOS,

## FROM THE INDUS TO THE HEAD OF THE PERSIAN GULF,

### AS DESCRIBED IN THE SECOND PART OF THE INDIKA OF ARRIAN,

#### (FROM CHAPTER XVIII. TO THE END.)

TRANSLATED FROM MÜLLER'S EDITION
(As given in the *Geographi Græci Minores* : Paris, 1855).

WITH INTRODUCTION AND NOTES.

# THE VOYAGE OF NEARKHOS.

INTRODUCTION.

The coasting voyage from the mouth of the Indus to the head of the Persian Gulf, designed by Alexander the Great, and executed by Nearkhos, may be regarded as the most important achievement of the ancients in navigation. It opened up, as Vincent remarks, a communication between Europe and the most distant countries of Asia, and, at a later period, was the source and origin of the Portuguese discoveries, and consequently the primary cause, however remote, of the British establishments in India. A Journal of this voyage was written by Nearkhos himself, which, though not extant in its original form, has been preserved for us by Arrian, who embodied its contents in his little work on India,[1] which he wrote as a sequel to his history of the expedition of Alexander.

Nearkhos as a writer must be acknowledged to be most scrupulously honest and exact,—for the result of explorations made in modern times along the shores which he passed in the course of his voyage shows that his description of them is accurate even in the most minute particulars. His veracity was nevertheless oppugned in ancient times by Strabo, who unjustly stigmatises the whole class of the Greek writers upon India as mendacious. "Generally speaking," he says (II. i. 9), "the men who have written upon Indian

---

[1] Written in the Ionic dialect.

t

affairs were a set of liars. Deimakhos holds the
first place in the list, Megasthenês comes next,
while Onêsikritos and Nearkhos, with others of
the same class, stammer out a few words of truth."
(παραψελλίζοντες). Strabo, however, in spite of this
censure did not hesitate to use Nearkhos as one
of his chief authorities for his description of
India, and is indebted to him for many facts relating to that country, which, however extraordinary they might appear to his contemporaries,
have been all confirmed by subsequent observa-
tion. It is therefore fairly open to doubt whether
Strabo was altogether sincere in his ill opinion,
seeing it had but little, if any, influence on his practice. We know at all events that he was too much
inclined to undervalue any writer who retailed
fables, without discriminating whether the writer
set them down as facts, or merely as stories, which
he had gathered from hearsay.

In modern times, the charge of mendacity has
been repeated by Hardouin and Huet. There are,
however, no more than two passages of the Journal
which can be adduced to support this imputa-
tion. The first is that in which the excessive
breadth of 200 stadia is given to the Indus, and
the second that in which it is asserted that at
Malana (situated in 25° 17′ of N. latitude) the
shadows at noon were observed to fall southward, and this in the month of November. With
regard to the first charge, it may be supposed that
the breadth assigned to the Indus was probably
that which it was observed to have when in a
state of inundation, and with regard to the second,
it may be met by the supposition, which is quite

admissible, that Arrian may have misapprehended in some measure the import of the statement as made by Nearkhos. The passage will be afterwards examined,[2] but in the meantime we may say, with Vincent, that if the difficulty it presents admits of no satisfactory solution, the misstatement ought not, as standing alone, to be insisted upon to the invalidation of the whole work.

But another charge besides that of mendacity has been preferred against the Journal. Dodwell has denied its authenticity. His attack is based on the following passage in Pliny (VI. 23):— Onesciriti et Nearchi navigatio nec nomina habet mansionum nec spatia. *The Journal of Onesicritus and Nearchus has neither the names of the anchorages nor the measure of the distances.* From this Dodwell argues that, as the account of the voyage in Arrian contains both the names and the distances, it could not have been a transcript of the Journal of Nearkhos, which according to Pliny gave neither names nor distances. Now, in the first place, it may well be asked, why the authority of Pliny, who is by no means always a careful writer, should be set so high as to override all other testimony, for instance, that of Arrian himself, who expressly states in the outset of his narrative that he intended to give the account of the voyage which had been written by Nearkhos. In the second place, the passage in question is probably corrupt, or if not, it is in direct conflict with the passage which immediately follows it, and contains Pliny's own summary of the voyage in which little else

---

[2] See infra, note 35.

is given than the names of the anchorages and
the distances. Dodwell was aware of the inconsis-
tency of the two passages, and endeavoured to
explain it away. In this he entirely fails, and
there can therefore be no reasonable doubt, that
in Arrian's work we have a record of the voyage
as authentic as it is veracious.

Of that record we proceed to give a brief abstract, adding a few particulars gathered from other
sources.

The fleet with which Nearkhos accomplished
the voyage consisted of war-galleys and transports
which had been partly built and partly collected
on the banks of the river Hydaspes (now the
Jhelam), where Alexander had supplied them with
crews by selecting from his troops such men as
had a knowledge of seamanship. The fleet thus
manned sailed slowly down the Hydaspes, the
Akesines, and the Indus, its movements being
regulated by those of the army, which, in marching
down towards the sea, was engaged in reducing the
warlike tribes settled along the banks of these
rivers. This downward voyage occupied, according
to Strabo, ten months, but it probably did not occupy more than nine. The fleet having at length
reached the apex of the Delta formed by the Indus
remained in that neighbourhood for some time at
a place called Pattala, which has generally been
identified with Thatha—a town near to where the
western arm of the Indus bifurcates,—but which
Cunningham and others would prefer to identify
with Nirankol or Haidarâbâd.[3]     From Pattala

_____

[3] Geog. of Anc. India, p. 279 sqq.

Alexander sailed down the western stream of the
river, where some of his ships were damaged and
others destroyed by encountering the Bore, a
phenomenon as alarming as it was new to the
Greeks.⁴ He returned to Pattala, and thence made
an excursion down the Eastern stream, which he
found less difficult to navigate. On again returning
to Pattala he removed his fleet down to a station
on the Western branch of the river (at an island
called Killouta),⁵ which was at no great distance
from the sea. He then set out on his return to
Persia, leaving instructions with Nearkhos to start
on the voyage as soon as the calming of the
monsoon should render navigation safe. It was
the king's intention to march near to the coast,
and to collect at convenient stations supplies for
the victualling of the fleet, but he found that such
a route was impracticable, and he was obliged to
lead his army through the inland provinces which
lay between India and his destination, Sûsa.⁶ He
left Leonnatos, however, behind him in the country
of the Oreitai, with instructions to render every
assistance in his power to the expedition under
Nearkhos when it should reach that part of the
coast.

Nearkhos remained in the harbour at Killouta
for about a month after Alexander had departed,
and then sailed during a temporary lull in the
monsoon, as he was apprehensive of being at-

---

⁴ See Arrian's Anab. VI. 19. Καὶ τοῦτο οὔπω πρότερον
ἐγνωκόσι τοῖς ἀμφ' ᾿Αλέξανδρον ἔκπληξιν μὲν καὶ αὐτὸ
οὐ σμικρὰν παρέσχε.

⁵ See Arrian, ib.

⁶ See id. VI. 23, and Strab. xv. ii 3, 4.

tacked by the natives who had been but imperfectly
subjugated, and whose spirit was hostile.[7] The
date on which he set sail is fixed by Vincent as
the 1st of October in the year B.C. 326. He proceeded slowly down the river, and anchored first
at a place called Stoura, which was only 100 stadia
distant from the station they had quitted. Here
the fleet remained for two days, when it proceeded
to an anchorage only 30 stadia farther down the
stream at a place called Kaumana.[8] Thence
it proceeded to Koreâtis (v. l. Koreëstis)—where it
again anchored. When once more under weigh its
progress was soon arrested by a dangerous rock
or bar which obstructed the mouth of the river.[9]
After some delay this difficulty was overcome, and
the fleet was conducted in safety into the open
main, and onward to an island called Krôkala
(150 stadia distant from the bar), where it remained at anchor throughout the day following its arrival. On leaving this island Nearkhos
had Mount Eiros (now Manora) on his right hand,
and a low flat island on his left; and this, as
Cunningham remarks, is a very accurate description of the entrance to Karâchi harbour.
The fleet was conducted into this harbour, now
so well known as the great emporium of the trade
of the Indus, and here, as the monsoon was still
blowing with great violence, it remained for four
and twenty days. The harbour was so commodious
and secure that Nearkhos designated it the Port

---

[7] Strab. ib. 5.
[8] This may perhaps be represented by the modern Khâu,
the name of one of the western mouths of the Indus.
[9] See infra, p. 176, note 17.

of Alexander. It was well sheltered by an island
lying close to its mouth, called by Arrian, Bibakta,
but by Pliny, Bibaga, and by Philostratos, Biblos.

The expedition took its departure from this
station on the 3rd of November. It suffered both
from stress of weather and from shortness of provisions until it reached Kôkala on the coast of
the Oreitai, where it took on board the supplies
which had been collected for its use by the exer-
tions of Leonnatos. Here it remained for about
10 days, and by the time of its departure the
monsoon had settled in its favour, so that the
courses daily accomplished were now of much
greater length than formerly. The shores, however, of the Ikhthyophagoi, which succeeded to
those of the Oreitai, were so miserably barren
and inhospitable that provisions were scarcely procurable, and Nearkhos was apprehensive lest the
men, famished and despairing, should desert the
ships. Their sufferings were not relieved till they
approached the straits, which open into the Persian
Gulf. When within the straits, they entered the
mouth of the river Anamis (now the Minâb or Ibrahim river), and having landed, formed a dockyard
and a camp upon its banks. This place lay in Harmozeia, a most fertile and beautiful district belonging to Karmania. Nearkhos, having here learned
that Alexander was not more than a 5 days'
journey from the sea, proceeded into the interior
to meet him, and report the safety of the expedition. During his absence the ships were repaired
and provisioned, and therefore soon after his
return to the camp he gave orders for the re-
sumption of the voyage. The time spent at Har-

mozeia was one and twenty days. The fleet
again under weigh coasted the islands lying at
the mouth of the gulf, and then having shaped
its course towards the mainland, passed the
western shores of Karmania and those of Persis,
till it arrived at the mouth of the Sitakos (now the
Kara-Agach), where it was again repaired and
supplied with provisions, remaining for the same
number of days as at the Anamis. One of the
next stations at which it touched was Mesembria,
which appears to have been situated in the neighbourhood of the modern Bushire. The coast of
Persis was difficult to navigate on account of
intricate and oozy channels, and of shoals and
breakers which frequently extended far out to
sea. The coast which succeeded, that of Sousis
(from which Persis is separated by the river
Arosis or Oroâtis, now the Tâb) was equally
difficult and dangerous to navigate, and therefore the fleet no longer crept along the shore,
but stood out more into the open sea. At the
head of the gulf Sousis bends to westward,
and here are the mouths of the Tigris and
Euphrates, which appear in those days to have
entered the sea by separate channels. It was
the intention of Nearkhos to have sailed up the
former river, but he passed its mouth unawares,
and continued sailing westward till he reached
Diridôtis (or Terêdon), an emporium in Babylonia, situated on the Pallacopas branch of the
Euphrates. From Diridôtis he retraced his course,
and entering the mouth of the Tigris sailed up its
stream till he reached the lower end of a great
lake (not now existing), through which its current

flowed. At the upper end of this lake was a village called Aginis, said to have been 500 stadia distant from Sousa. Nearkhos did not, as has been erroneously supposed by some, sail up the lake to Aginis, but entered the mouth of a river which flows into its south-eastern extremity, called the Pasitigris or Eulaeus, the Ulai of the Prophet Daniel, now the Karûn. The fleet proceeded up this river, and came to a final anchor in its stream immediately below a bridge, which continued the highway from Persis to Sousa. This bridge, according to Ritter and Rawlinson, crossed the Pasitigris at a point near the modern village of Ahwaz. Here the fleet and the army were happily reunited. Alexander on his arrival embraced Nearkhos with cordial warmth, and rewarded appropriately the splendid services which he had rendered by bringing the expedition safely through so many hardships and perils to its destination. The date on which the fleet anchored at the bridge is fixed by Vincent for the 24th of February B. C. 325, so that the whole voyage was performed in 146 days, or somewhat less than 5 months.

The following tables show the names, positions, &c., of the different places which occurred on the route taken by the expedition :—

## I.

From the Station on the Indus to the Port of Alexander (Karâchi Harbour).

| Ancient name. | Modern name. | Distance in Stadia[10] | Lat. N. | Long. E. |
|---|---|---|---|---|
| 1. Station at Killouta. | Near Lari-Bandar. | ... | 24° 30' | 67° 28' |
| 2. Stoura ...... | ........ | 100 | | |
| 3. Kaumana ... | Khau ...... | 30 | | |
| 4. Koreatis ... | ......... | 20 | | |
| 5. Herma ...... | *Bar in the Indus.* | | | |
| 6. Krôkala...... | ......... | 120 | | |
| 7. *Mount Eiros.* | Manora. | | | |
| 8. *Is. unnamed.* | | | | |
| 9. The Port of Alexander. | Karâchi ... | ... | 24° 53' | 66° 57' |

[10] The Olympic stadium, which was in general use throughout Greece, contained 600 Greek feet ≐ 625 Roman feet, or 606¾ English feet. The Roman mile contained eight stadia, being about half a stadium less than an English mile. Not a few of the measurements given by Arrian are excessive, and it has therefore been conjectured that he may have used some standard different from the Olympic,—which, however, is hardly probable. See the subject discussed in Smith's Dictionary of Antiquities, S. V. *Stadium.*

## II.
### Coast of the Arabies (Sindh).

Length of the Coast from the Indus to the
Arabis R. .......................................... 1000 Stadia.
   Actual length in miles English ...    80
   Time taken in its navigation ......    38 Days.

| | Ancient name. | Modern name. | Distance in Stadia. | Lat. N. | Long.E. |
|---|---|---|---|---|---|
| 1. | Port of Alexander ...... | Karâchi ... | ... | 24° 53′ | 66o 57 |
| 2. | *Bibakta.* | | | | |
| 3. | Domai Is. ... | ......... | 60 | 24° 48′ | 66° 50′ |
| 4. | Saranga...... | ......... | 300 | 24° 44′ | 66° 34′ |
| 5. | Sakala ...... | ......... | ... | 24° 52′ | 66° 33′ |
| 6. | Morontobara | ......... | 300 | 25° 13′ | 66° 40′ |
| 7. | *Is. unnamed.* | | | | |
| 8. | Arabis R. ... | Purâli R... | 120 | 25° 28′ | 66o 35′ |

## III.
### Coast of the Oreitai (Las.)

Length of the coast (Arrian) ......... 1600 Stadia.
  Do.   do.  (Strabo) ......... 1800  ,,
Actual length in miles English ...... 100
Time taken in its navigation ........ 18 Days.

| | Ancient name. | Modern name. | Distance in Stadia. | Lat. N. | Long.E. |
|---|---|---|---|---|---|
| 1. | Pagala ...... | ......... | 200 | 25° 30′ | 66° 15′ |
| 2. | Kabana ...... | ......... | 400 | 25° 28′ | 65° 46′ |
| 3. | Kôkala ...... | Near Râs-Katchari. | 200 | 25° 21′ | 65° 36′ |
| 4. | Tomêros R. . | Maklow or HingulR. | 500 | 25° 16′ | 65° 15′ |
| 5. | Malana ...... | Râs Malan. | 300 | 25° 18′ | 65° 7′ |

## IV.

Coast of the Ikhthyophagoi (Mekran or Beluchistan).

Length of the coast (Arrian) .........10,000 Stadia.
Do.    do.    (Strabo) ......... 7,000  „
Actual length in miles English ......   480
Time taken in its navigation .........  20 Days.

| Ancient name. | Modern name. | Distance in Stadia. | Lat. N. | Long.E. |
|---|---|---|---|---|
| 1. Bagisara ... | On Arabah or Hor-maraBay | 600 | 25° 12' | 64° 31' |
| 2. *Pasira* ...... | | | | |
| 3. Cape unnamed. | RâsArabah | ... | 25° 7' | 64° 29' |
| 4. Kolta ......... | ... ...... | 200 | 25° 8' | 64° 27' |
| 5. Kalama ...... | Kalami R.. | 600 | 25° 21' | 63° 59' |
| 6. *Karbine Is.* . | Asthola or Sangâ-dîp | | | |
| 7. Kissa in *Karbis.* | ......... | 200 | 25° 22' | 63° 37' |
| 8. Cape unnamed. | C. Passence.. | ... | 25° 15' | 63° 30' |
| 9. Mosarna ... | Near do. | | | |
| 10. Balômon ... | ......... | 750 | | |
| 11. Barna......... | ......... | 400 | 25° 12' | 63° 10' |
| 12. Dendrobôsa. | Daram or Duram. | 200 | 25° 11' | 62° 45' |
| 13. Kôphas ...... | Râs Koppa | 400 | 25° 11' | 62° 29' |
| 14. Kuiza......... | Near Râs Ghunse. | 800 | 25° 10' | 61° 56' |
| 15. Town un-named. | OnGwattar Bay. | 500 | | |
| 16. Cape called Bagia. | ......... | ... | 25° 7' | 61° 28' |
| 17. Talmena ... | On Chau-bar Bay. | 1000 | 25° 24' | 60° 40' |
| 18. Kanasis...... | ......... | 400 | 25° 24' | 60° 12' |

| Ancient name. | Modern name. | Distance in Stadia. | Lat. N. | Long.E. |
|---|---|---|---|---|
| 19. Anchorage unnamed. | | | | |
| 20. Kanate ...... | Kungoun.. | 850 | 25° 25′ | 59° 15 |
| 21. Tacœi orTroïsi. | Near Sudich River. | 800 | 25° 30′ | 58° 42 |
| 22. Bagasira ... | Girishk ... | 300 | 25° 38′ | 58° 27′ |
| 23. Anchorage unnamed. | ......... | 1100 | | |

## V

Coast of Karmania (Moghistan and Laristan).
Length of the coast (Arrian and
Strabo) ........................... 3,700 Stadia.
Actual length in miles English.. 296
Time taken in its navigation ... 19 Days.

| Ancient name. | Modern name. | Distance in Stadia. | Lat. N. | Long.E. |
|---|---|---|---|---|
| 1. Anchorage unnamed. | | | | |
| 2. Badis......... | Near Cape Bombarek | ... | 25° 47′ | 57° 48 |
| 3. Anchorage unnamed. | ......... | 800 | | |
| 4. *Cape Maketa in Arabia..* | *Cape Musendom.* | | | |
| 5. Neoptana ... | Nr. Karun. | 700 | 26° 57′ | 57° 1′ |
| 6. Anamis R.... | Mînâb R.. | 100 | 27° 11′ | 57° 6′ |
| 7. *Organa Is.* . | *Ormus or Djerun.* | | | |
| 8. Oarakta Is. 2 anchorages | Kishm ... | 300 | | |

| Ancient name. | Modern name. | Distance in Stadia. | Lat. N. | Long.E. |
|---|---|---|---|---|
| 9. *Island dist. from it 40 stadia.* | *Angar or Hanjam.* | | | |
| 10. Island 300 stadia from mainland. | Tombo...... | 400 | 26° 20′ | 55° 20′ |
| 11. *Pylora Is.* ... | *Polior Is.* | ... | 26° 20′ | 54° 35′ |
| 12. Sisidônê ... | Mogos ? ... | | | |
| 13. Tarsia ...... | C. Djard... | 300 | 26° 20′ | 54° 21′ |
| 14. Kataia Is. ... | Kenn ...... | 300 | 26° 32′ | 54° |

## VI.

### Coast of Persis (Farsistan).

Length of Coast......................4,400 Stadia.
Actual length in miles English ... 382
Time taken in its navigation......... 31 Days.

| Ancient name. | Modern name. | Distance in Stadia. | Lat. N. | Long.E. |
|---|---|---|---|---|
| 1. Ila and Kaïkander Is.. | Inderabia Island. | 400 | 26° 38′ | 53° 35′ |
| 2. Island with PearlFishery. | | | | |
| 3. Another anchorage here. | ......... | 40 | | |
| 4. MountOkhos | ......... | ... | 26° 59′ | 53° 20′ |
| 5. Apostana. ... | ......... | 450 | 27° 1′ | 52° 55′ |
| 6. Bay unnamed. | On it is Nabend. | 400 | 27° 24′ | 52° 25′ |
| 7. Gogana at mouth of Areon R. | Konkan ... | 600 | 27° 48′ | 52° |

| Ancient name. | Modern name. | Distance in Stadia. | Lat. N. | Long. E. |
|---|---|---|---|---|
| 8. Sitakos ...... | Kara-Agach R. | 800 | | |
| 9. Hieratis...... | ......... | 750 | 28° 52' | 50° 45' |
| 10. HeratemisR. near it. | | | | |
| 11. Podagron, R. | | | | |
| 12. Mesambria.. | Near Bu-shire. | ... | 29° | 50° 45' |
| 13. Taökê on Granis, R. | Taaug ...... | 200 | 29° 14' | 50° 30' |
| 14. Rhogonis, R. | ......... | 200 | 29° 27' | 50° 29' |
| 15. Brizana, R.. | ......... | 400 | 29° 57' | 50° 15' |
| 16. Arosis or Oroatis, R. | River Tâb. | ... | 30° 4' | 49° 30' |

## VII.

### Coast of Sousis (Khuzistan.)

Length of the Coast...................... 2000 Stadia.

Time taken in its navigation ......... 3 Days.

| Ancient name. | Modern name. | Distance in Stadia. | Lat. N. | Long E. |
|---|---|---|---|---|
| 1. Kataderbis R. | ......... | 500 | 30° 16' | 49° |
| 2. MargastanaIs | | | | |
| 3. Anchorage unnamed. | ......... | 600 | | |
| 4. Diridôtis, the end of the sea voyage. | Near Jebel Sanâm. | 900 | 30° 12' | 47° 35' |

## TRANSLATION.

XVIII. When the fleet formed for Alexander upon the banks of the Hydaspes was now ready, he provided crews for the vessels by collecting all the Phœnikians and all the Kyprians and Egyptians who had followed him in his Eastern campaigns, and from these he selected such as were skilled in seamanship to manage the vessels and work the oars. He had besides in his army not a few islanders familiar with that kind of work, and also natives both of Ionia and of the Hellespont. The following officers he appointed as Commanders of the different galleys[11] :—

### Makedonians.

#### Citizens of Pella.

1. Hephaistiôn, son of Amyntor.
2. Leonnatos, son of Anteas.
3. Lysimakhos, son of Agathoklês.
4. Asklepiodôros, son of Timander.
5. Arkhôn, son of Kleinias.

---

[11] This list does not specify those officers who performed the voyage, but such as had a temporary command during the passage down the river. The only names which occur afterwards in the narrative are those of Arkhias and Onêsikritos. Nearkhos, by his silence, leaves it uncertain whether any other officers enumerated in his list accompanied him throughout the expedition. The following are known not to have done so : Hephaistion, Leonnatos, Lysimakhos, Ptolemy, Krateros, Attalos and Peukestas. It does not clearly appear what number of ships or men accompanied Nearkhos to the conclusion of the voyage. If we suppose the ships of war only fit for the service, 30 galleys might possibly contain from two to three thousand men, but this estimation is uncertain.
See Vincent, I. 118 sqq.

6. Demonikos, son of Athenaios.
7. Arkhias, son of Anaxidotos.
8. Ophellas, son of Seilênos.
9. Timanthês, son of Pantiadês.
Of Amphipolis.
10. Nearkhos, son of Androtîmos, who wrote a narrative of the voyage.
11. Laomedôn, son of Larikhos.
12. Androsthenês, son of Kallistratos.
Of Oresis.
13. Krateros, son of Alexander.
14. Perdikkas, son of Orontes.
Of Eördaia.
15. Ptolemaios, son of Lagos.
16. Aristonous, son of Peisaios.
Of Pydna.
17. Metrôn, son of Epikharmos.
18. Nikarkhidês, son of Simos.
Of Stymphaia.
19. Attalos, son of Andromenês.
Of Mieza.
20. Peukestas, son of Alexander.
Of Alkomenai.
21. Peithôn, son of Krateuas.
Of Aigai.
22. Leonnatos, son of Antipater.
Of Alôros.
23. Pantoukhos, son of Nikolaös.
Of Beroia.
24. Mylleas, son of Zôilos.
All these were Makedonians.
Greeks,—of Larisa :
25. Mêdios, son of Oxynthemis.
Of Kardia.

26. Eumenês, son of Hierônymos.
        Of Kôs.
27. Kritoboulos, son of Plato.
        Of Magnêsia :
28. Thoas, son of Mênodôros.
29. Maiander, son of Mandrogenês.
        Of Teos :
30. Andrôn, son of Kabêlas.
        Of Soloi in Cyprus :
31. Nikokleês, son of Pasikratês.
        Of Salamis in Cyprus :
32. Nithaphôn, son of Pnutagoras.
A Persian was also appointed as a Trierarch :
33. Bagoas, son of Pharnoukhês.

The Pilot and Master of Alexander's own ship
was Onêsikritos of Astypalaia, and the Secretary-
General of the fleet Euagoras, the son of Eukleôn,
a Corinthian. Nearkhos, the son of Androtîmos,
a Kretan by birth, but a citizen of Amphipolis on
the Strymôn was appointed as Admiral of the
expedition.

When these dispositions had been all completed,
Alexander sacrificed to his ancestral gods, and to
such as had been indicated by the oracle; also to
Poseidôn and Amphitritê and the Nêreids, and to
Okeanos himself, and to the River Hydaspês, from
which he was setting forth on his enterprise ; and
to the Akesinês into which the Hydaspês pours its
stream, and to the Indus which receives both
these rivers. He further celebrated the occasion
by holding contests in music and gymnastics,
and by distributing to the whole army, rank by
rank, the sacrificial victims.

XIX. When all the preparations for the voyage

had been made, Alexander ordered Krateros, with
a force of horse and foot, to go to one side of the
Hydaspês; while Hephaistiôn commanding a still
larger force, which included 200 elephants, should
march in a parallel line on the other side. Alexander himself had under his immediate command
the body of foot guards called the Hypaspists, and
all the archers, and what was called the companion-
cavalry,—a force consisting in all of 8,000 men.
The troops under Krateros and Hephaistiôn marching in advance of the fleet had received instructions
where they were to wait its arrival. Philip, whom
he had appointed satrap of this region, was despatched to the banks of the Akesinês with another
large division, for by this time he had a following
of 120,000 soldiers,[12] including those whom he had
himself led up from the sea-coast, as well as the
recruits enlisted by the agents whom he had
deputed to collect an army, when he admitted to
his ranks barbarous tribes of all countries in
whatever way they might be armed. Then weighing anchor, he sailed down the Hydaspês to its
point of junction with the Akesinês. The ships
numbered altogether 1800, including the long
narrow war galleys, the round-shaped roomy mer-
chantmen, and the transports for carrying horses
and provisions to feed the army. But how the
fleet sailed down the rivers, and what tribes
Alexander conquered in the course of the voyage,
and how he was in danger among the Malli,[13] and

[12] So also Plutarch in the Life of Alexander (C.66) says
that in returning from India Alexander had 120,000 foot
and 15,000 cavalry.
[13] Sansk. Malava. The name is preserved in the modern
Moultan.

how he was wounded in their country, and how
Peukestas and Leonnatos covered him with their
shields when he fell,—all these incidents have
been already related in my other work, that which
is written in the Attic dialect.[14] My present object
is to give an account of the coasting voyage which
Nearkhos accomplished with the fleet when starting from the mouths of the Indus he sailed through
the great ocean as far as the Persian Gulf, called
by some the Red Sea.

XX.  Nearkhos himself has supplied a narrative
of this voyage, which runs to this effect.   Alexander, he informs us, had set his heart on navigating
the whole circuit of the sea which extends from
India to Persia, but the length of the voyage made
him hesitate, and the possibility of the destruction
of his fleet, should it be cast on some desert
coast either quite harbourless or too barren to
furnish adequate supplies; in which case a great
stain tarnishing the splendour of his former actions
would obliterate all his good fortune.   His
ambition, however, to be always doing something new and astonishing prevailed over all his
scruples.   Then arose a difficulty as to what commander he should choose, having genius sufficient
for working out his plans, and a difficulty also
with regard to the men on ship-board how he
could overcome their fear, that in being despatched on such a service they were recklessly sent
into open peril.  Nearkhos here tells us that
Alexander consulted him on the choice of a commander, and that when the king had mentioned

---

[14] Anab. VI. 11.

one man after another, rejecting all, some because
they were not inclined to expose themselves for
his sake to danger, others because they were of a
timid temper, others because their only thought
was how to get home, making this and that
objection to each in turn, Nearkhos then proffer-
ed his own services in these terms : " I, then,
O king, engage to command the expedition, and,
under the divine protection, will conduct the fleet
and the people on board safe into Persia, if the sea
be that way navigable, and the undertaking within the power of man to perform." Alexander
made a pretence of refusing the offer, saying that he
could not think of exposing any friend of his to the
distresses and hazard of such a voyage, but Nearkhos, so far from withdrawing his proposal, only
persisted the more in pressing its acceptance upon
him. Alexander, it need not be said, warmly
appreciated the promptitude to serve him shown
by Nearkhos, and appointed him to be com-
mander-in-chief of the expedition. When this
became known, it had a great effect in calming
the minds of the troops ordered on this service
and on the minds of the sailors, since they felt
assured that Alexander would never have sent
forth Nearkhos into palpable danger unless their
lives were to be preserved. At the same time the
splendour with which the ships were equipped,
and the enthusiasm of the officers vying with
each other who should collect the best men, and
have his complement most effective, inspired even
those who had long hung back with nerve for
the work, and a good hope that success would
crown the undertaking. It added to the cheer-

fulness pervading the army that Alexander himself sailed out from both the mouths of the Indus
into the open main when he sacrificed victims to
Poseidôn and all the other sea-deities, and presented gifts of great magnificence to the sea; and
so the men trusting to the immeasurable good
fortune which had hitherto attended all the projects
of Alexander, believed there was nothing he might
not dare—nothing but would to him be feasible.

XXI.  When the Etesian winds,[15] which continue all the hot season blowing landward from
the sea, making navigation on that coast impracticable, had subsided, then the expedition
started on the voyage in the year when Kephisidôros was Archon at Athens, on the 20th
day of the month Boëdromion according to the
Athenian Kalendar, but as the Makedonians and
Asiatics reckon  *  *  in the 11th year of the
reign of Alexander.[16]  Nearkhos, before putting to

---

[15] The general effect of the monsoon Nearkhos certainly
knew; he was a native of Crete, and a resident at
Amphipolis, both which lie within the track of the annual
or Etesian winds, which commencing from the Hellespont
and probably from the Euxine sweep the Egêan sea, and
stretching quite across the Mediterranean to the coast of
Africa, entered through Egypt to Nubia or Ethiopia. Arrian
has accordingly mentioned the monsoon by the name of
the Etesian winds; his expression is remarkable, and attended with a precision that does his accuracy credit. These
Etesian winds, says he, do not blow from the north in the
summer months as with us in the Mediterranean, but from
the South. On the commencement of winter, or at latest
on the setting of the Pleiades, the sea is said to be navigable
till the winter solstice (Anab. VI. 21-1) Vincent I. 43 sq.

[16] The date here fixed by Arrian is the 2nd of October
326 B.C., but the computation now generally accepted
refers the event to the year after to suit the chronology of
Alexander's subsequent history (see Clinton's F. Hell. II.
pp. 174 and 563, 3rd ed.). There was an Archon called

# 175

sea sacrifices to Zeus the Preserver, and celebrates, as Alexander had done, gymnastic games. Then clearing out of harbour they end the first day's voyage by anchoring in the Indus at a creek called Stoura, where they remain for two days. The distance of this place from the station they had just left was 100 stadia. On the third day they resumed the voyage, but proceeded no further than 30 stadia, coming to an anchor at another creek, where the water was now salt, for the sea when filled with the tide ran up the creek, and its waters even when the tide receded commingled with the river. The name of this place was Kaumana. The next day's course, which was of 20 stadia only, brought them to Koreätis, where they once more anchored in the river. When again under weigh their progress was soon interrupted, for a bar was visible which there obstructed the mouth of the Indus; and the waves were heard breaking with furious roar upon its strand which was wild and rugged. Observing, however, that the bar at a particular part was soft, they made a cutting through this, 5 stadia long, *at low water,* and on the return of the flood-tide carried the ships through by the passage thus formed into the

Kephisidoros in office in the year B.C. 323-322; so Arrian has here either made a mistake, or perhaps an Archon of the year 326-325 may have died during his tenure of office, and a substitute called Kephisidôros been elected to fill the vacancy. The *lacuna* marked by the asterisks has been supplied by inserting the name of the Makedonian month Dius. The Ephesians adopted the names of the months used by the Makedonians, and so began their year with the month Dius, the first day of which corresponds to the 24th of September. The 20th day of Boedromion of the year B.C. 325 corresponded to the 21st of September.

open sea.[17] Then following the winding of the coast they ran a course of 120 stadia, and reach Krôkala,[18]

[17] Regarding the sunken reef encountered by the fleet after leaving Koreatis, Sir Alexander Burnes says: "Near the mouth of the river we passed a rock stretching across the stream, which is particularly mentioned by Nearchus, who calls it *a dangerous rock*, and is the more remarkable since there is not even a stone below Tatta in any other part of the Indus." The rock, he adds, is at a distance of six miles up the Pitti. "It is vain," says Captain Wood in the narrative of his *Journey to the Source of the Oxus*, "in the delta of such a river (as the Indus), to identify existing localities with descriptions handed down to us by the historians of Alexander the Great. . . . . (but) Burnes has, I think, shown that the mouth by which the Grecian fleet left the Indus was the modern P i t i. The 'dangerous rock' of Nearchus completely identifies the spot, and as it is still in existence, without any other within a circle of many miles, we can wish for no stronger evidence." With regard to the canal dug through this rock, Burnes remarks : " The Greek admiral only availed himself of the experience of the people, for it is yet customary among the natives of Sind to dig shallow canals, and leave the tides or river to deepen them ; and a distance of five stadia, or half a mile, would call for not great labour. It is not to be supposed that sandbanks will continue unaltered for centuries, but I may observe that there was a large bank contiguous to the island, between it and which a passage like that of Nearchus might have been dug with the greatest advantage." The same author thus describes the mouth of the Piti :—" Beginning from the westward we have the Pitti mouth, an embouchure of the Buggaur, that falls into what may be called the Bay of Karâchi. It has no bar, but a large sandbank, together with an island outside prevent a direct passage into it from the sea, and narrow the channel to about half a mile at its mouth."

[18] All inquirers have agreed in identifying the Kolaka of Ptolemy, and the sandy island of Krokola where Nearchus tarried with his fleet for one day, with a small island in the bay of Karâchi. Krokala is further described as lying off the mainland of the Arabii. It was 150 stadia, or 17¼ miles, from the western mouth of the Indus,—which agrees exactly with the relative positions of Karâchi and the mouth of the Ghâra river, if, as we may fairly assume, the present coast-line has advanced five or six miles during the twenty-one centuries that have elapsed since the death of Alexander. The identification is confirmed by the fact that the district in which Karâchi is situated is called K a r- k a l l a to this day. Cunningham *Geog. of An. India*, I. p. 306.

a sandy island where they anchored and remained all next day. The country adjoining was
inhabited by an Indian race called the Arabies,
whom I have mentioned in my longer work, where
it is stated that they derive their name from the
River Arabis, which flows through their country
to the sea, and parts them from the Oreitai.[19]
Weighing from Krokala they had on their right
hand a mountain which the natives called Eiros,
and on their left a flat island almost level with
the sea, and so near the mainland to which it
runs parallel that the intervening channel is
extremely narrow. Having quite cleared this passage they come to anchor in a well-sheltered harbour, which Nearkhos, finding large and commodious, designated Alexander's Haven. This
harbour is protected by an island lying about 2
stadia off from its entrance. It is called Bibakta,
and all the country round about Sangada.[20] The
existence of the harbour is due altogether to the
island which opposes a barrier to the violence of
the sea. Here heavy gales blew from seaward for
many days without intermission, and Nearkhos

---

[19] The name of the Arabii is variously written,—Arabitæ,
Arbii, Arabies, Arbies, Aribes, Arbiti. The name of their
river has also several forms,—Arabis, Arabius, Artabis,
Artabius. It is now called the Puráli, the river which
flows through the present district of Las into the bay of
Sonmiyâni. The name of the Oreitai in Curtius is Horitæ.
Cunningham identifies them with the people on the Aghor
river, whom he says the Greeks would have named Agoritæ
or Aoritæ, by the suppression of the guttural, of which a
trace still remains in the initial aspirate of 'Horitæ.' Some
would connect the name with H a u r, a town which lay on
the route to Firabaz, in Mekrân.

[20] This name Sangada, D'Anville thought, survived in
that of a race of noted pirates who infested the shores of
the gulf of Kachh, called the S a n g a d i a n s or Sangarians.

w

178

fearing lest the barbarians might, some of them,
combine to attack and plunder the camp, fortified
his position with an enclosure of stones. Here
they were obliged to remain for 24 days. The
soldiers, we learn from Nearkhos, caught mussels
and oysters, and what is called the razor-fish,
these being all of an extraordinary size as compared
with the sorts found in our own sea.[21] He adds
that they had no water to drink but what was
brackish.

XXII. As soon as the monsoon ceased they
put again to sea, and having run fully 60 stadia
came to anchor at a sandy beach under shelter of
a desert island that lay near, called Domai.[22] On
the shore itself there was no water, but 20 stadia
inland it was procured of good quality. The following day they proceeded 300 stadia to Saranga,
where they did not arrive till night. They
anchored close to the shore, and found water at a
distance of about 8 stadia from it. Weighing from
Saranga they reach Sakala, a desert place, and
anchored. On leaving it they passed two rocks so
close to each other that the oar-blades of the
galleys grazed both, and after a course of 300
stadia they came to anchor at Morontobara.[23]

---

[21] "The pearl oyster abounds in 11 or 12 fathoms of
water all along the coast of Scinde. There was a fishery in
the harbour of Kurrachee which had been of some importance in the days of the native rulers."—*Wanderings of a
Naturalist in India*, p. 36.

[22] This island is not known, but it probably lay near the
rocky headland of Irus, now called M a n o r â, which protects the port of Karâchi from the sea and bad weather.

[23] "The name of Morontobara," says Cunningham, " I
would identify with Muâri, which is now applied to the
headland of Râs Muâri or Cape Monze, the last point of
the Pab range of mountains. *Bâra*, or *Bâri*, means a

The harbour here was deep and capacious, and
well sheltered all round, and its waters quite
tranquil, but the entrance into it was narrow. In
the native language it was called Women's Haven,
because a woman had been the first sovereign of
the place. They thought it a great achievement
to have passed those two rocks in safety, for when
they were passing them the sea was boisterous
and running high. They did not remain in
Morontobara, but sailed the day after their arrival,
when they had on their left hand an island which
sheltered them from the sea, and which lay so
near to the mainland that the intervening channel
looked as if it had been artificially formed. Its
length from one end to the other was 70 stadia.[24]
The shore was woody and the island throughout
over-grown with trees of every description. They
were not able to get fairly through this passage

roadstead or haven; and Moranta is evidently connected
with the Persian *Mard* a man, of which the feminine is
still preserved in Kásmîrî as *Mahrin* a woman. From the
distances given by Arrian, I am inclined to fix it at the
mouth of the B a h a r rivulet, a small stream which falls
into the sea about midway between Cape Monze and
Sonmiyâni." *Women's Haven* is mentioned by Ptolemy
and Ammianus Marcellinus. There is in the neighbourhood a mountain now called M o r, which may be a remnant
of the name Morontobari. The channel through which the
fleet passed after leaving this place no longer exists, and
the island has of course disappeared.

[24] The coast from Karâchi to the Purâli has undergone
considerable changes, so that the position of the intermediate places cannot be precisely determined. "From Cape
Monze to Sonmiyani," says Blair, "the coast bears evident
marks of having suffered considerable alterations from the
encroachments of the sea. We found trees which had been
washed down, and which afforded us a supply of fuel. In
some parts I saw imperfect creeks in a parallel direction
with the coast. These might probably be the vestiges of
that narrow channel through which the Greek galleys
passed."

till towards daybreak, for the sea was not only
rough, but also shoal, the tide being at ebb. They
sailed on continuously, and after a course of 120
stadia anchored at the mouth of the river Arabis,
where there was a spacious and very fine haven.[25]
The water here was not fit for drinking, for the sea
ran up the mouths of the Arabis. Having gone,
however, about 40 stadia up the river, they found
a pool from which, having drawn water, they returned to the fleet. Near the harbour is an island
high and bare, but the sea around it supplied
oysters and fish of various kinds.[26] As far as
this, the country was possessed by the Arabies,

[25] Ptolemy and Marcian enumerate the following places
as lying between the Indus and the Arabis: Rhizana,
Koiamba, Women's Haven, Phagiaura, Arbis. Ptolemy
does not mention the Oreitai, but extends the Arabii to the
utmost limit of the district assigned to them in Arrian.
He makes, notwithstanding the river Arabis to be the
boundary of the Arabii. His Arabis must therefore be
identified not with the Púráli, but with the Kurmut, called
otherwise the Rumra or Kalami, where the position of
Arrian's Kalama must be fixed. Pliny (vi. 25) places a
people whom he calls the Arbii between the Oritae and
Karmania, assigning as the boundary between the Arbii
and the Oritae the river Arbis.
[26] The Arabis or Púráli discharges its waters into
the bay of Sonmiyâni. "Sonmiyâni," says Kempthrone,
"is a small town or fishing village situated at the mouth
of a creek which runs up some distance inland. It is
governed by a Sheikh, and the inhabitants appear to be
very poor, chiefly subsisting on dried fish and rice. A very
extensive bar or sandbank runs across the mouth of this
inlet, and none but vessels of small burden can get over it
even at high water, but inside the water is deep." The
inhabitants of the present day are as badly off for water
as their predecessors of old. "Everything," says one who
visited the place, "is scarce, even water, which is procured
by digging a hole five or six feet deep, and as many in
diameter, in a place which was formerly a swamp; and if
the water oozes, which sometimes it does not, it serves
them that day, and perhaps the next, when it turns quite
brackish, owing to the nitrous quality of the earth."

the last Indian people living in this direction; and the parts beyond were occupied by the Oreitai.[27]

XXIII. On weighing from the mouths of the Arabis, they coasted the shores of the Oreitai, and after running 200 stadia reached Pagala,[28] where there was a surf but nevertheless good anchorage. The crew were obliged to remain on board, a party, however, being sent on shore to procure water. They sailed next morning at sunrise, and after a course of about 430 stadia, reached Kabana[29] in the evening, where they anchored at some distance from the shore, which was a desert; the violence of the surf by which the vessels were much tossed preventing them from landing. While running the last course the fleet had been caught in a heavy gale blowing from seaward, when two galleys and a transport foundered. All the men, however, saved themselves by swimming, as the vessels at the time of the disaster were sailing close to the shore. They weighed

[27] Strabo agrees with Arrian in representing the Oreitai as non-Indian. Cunningham, however, relying on statement made by Curtius, Diodorus and the Chinese pilgrim Hwen Thsang, a most competent observer, considers them to be of Indian origin, for their customs, according to the Pilgrim, were like those of the people of Kachh, and their written characters closely resembled those of India, while their language was only slightly different. The Oreitai as early as the 6th century B.C. were tributary to Darius Hystaspes, and they were still subject to Persia nearly 12 centuries later when visited by Hwen Thsang.— *Geog. of An. Ind.* pp. 304 sqq.

[28] Another form is Pegadæ, met with in Philostratos, who wrote a work on India.

[29] To judge from the distances given, this place should be near the stream now called Agbor, on which is situated Harkânâ. It is probably the Koiamba of Ptolemy.

from Kabana about midnight, and having proceeded 200 stadia arrived at Kôkala, where the
vessels *could not be drawn on shore*, but rode at
anchor out at sea. As the men, however, had
suffered severely by confinement on board,[30] and
were very much in want of rest, Nearkhos allowed
them to go on shore, where he formed a camp, forti-
fying it in the usual manner for protection against
the barbarians. In this part of the country Leonnatos, who had been commissioned by Alexander to
reduce the Oreitai and settle their affairs, defeated
that people and their allies in a great battle,
wherein all the leaders and 6,000 men were slain,
the loss of Leonnatos, being only 15 of his horse,
besides a few foot-soldiers, and *one man of note*
Apollophanês, the satrap of the Gedrosians.[31]   A
full account, however, of these transactions is
given in my other work, where it is stated that for
this service Leonnatos had a golden crown placed
upon his head by Alexander in presence of the
Makedonian army. Agreeably to orders given
by Alexander, corn had been here collected for
the victualling of the vessels, and stores sufficient
to last for 10 days were put on board. Here
also such ships as had been damaged during the

---

[30] "In vessels like those of the Greeks, which afforded
neither space for motion, nor convenience for rest, the
continuing on board at night was always a calamity.
When a whole crew was to sleep on board, the suffering
was in proportion to the confinement."—Vincent, I.
p. 209 note.

[31] In another passage of Arrian (Anab. VI. 27, 1,) this
Apollophanês is said to have been deposed from his satrapy,
when Alexander was halting in the capital of Gedrôsia.
In the Journal Arrian follows Nearkhos, in the History,
Ptolemy or Aristobûlus.—Vincent.

voyage were repaired, while all the mariners that Nearkhos considered deficient in fortitude for the enterprise, he consigned to Leonnatos to be taken on by land, but at the same time he made good his complement of men by taking in exchange others more efficient from the troops under Leonnatos.

XXIV. From this place they bore away with a fresh breeze, and having made good a course of 500 stadia anchored near a winter torrent called the Tomêros, which at its mouth expanded into an estuary.[32] The natives lived on the marshy ground near the shore in cabins close and suffocating. Great was their astonishment when they descried the fleet approaching, but *they were not without courage*, and collecting in arms on the shore, drew up in line to attack the strangers when landing. They carried thick spears about 6 cubits long, not headed with iron, but what was as good, hardened at the point by fire. Their number was about 600, and when Nearkhos saw that they stood their ground prepared to fight, he ordered his vessels to advance, and then to anchor just within bowshot of the shore, for he had noticed that the thick spears of the barbarians were adapted only for close fight, and were by no means formidable as missiles. He then issued his directions : those men that were lightest equipped, and the most active and best at swim-

---

[32] From the distances given, the Tomêros must be identified with the M a k l o w or H i n g a l river ; some would, however, make it the B h u s â l. The form of the name in Pliny is T o m b e r u s, and in Mela—T u b e r o. These authors mention another river in connection with the Tomêros,—the A r o s a p e s or A r u s a c e s.

ming were to swim to shore at a given signal:
when any one had swum so far that he could
stand in the water he was to wait for his next
neighbour, and not advance against the barbarians
until a file could be formed of three men deep:
that done, they were to rush forward shouting the
war-cry. The men selected for this service at once
plunged into the sea, and swimming rapidly touched
ground, still keeping due order, when forming in
file, they rushed to the charge, shouting the war-
cry, which was repeated from the ships, whence all
the while arrows and missiles from engines were
launched against the enemy. Then the barbarians
terrified by the glittering arms and the rapidity
of the landing, and wounded by the arrows and
other missiles, against which they had no protection, being all but entirely naked, fled at once
without making any attempt at resistance. Some
perished in the ensuing flight, others were taken
prisoners, and some escaped to the mountains.
Those they captured had shaggy hair, not only
on their head but all over their body; their nails
resembled the claws of wild beasts, and were used,
it would seem, instead of iron for dividing fish
and splitting the softer kinds of wood. Things
of a hard consistency they cut with sharp stones,
for iron they had none. As clothing they wore
the skins of wild beasts, and occasionally also the
thick skins of the large sorts of fish.[33]

XXV. After this action they draw the ships on

---

[33] Similar statements are made regarding this savage
race by Curtius IX. 10, 9; Diodôros XVII, 105; Pliny VI.
28; Strabo p. 720; Philostratos V.Ap. III., 57. Cf. Agatharkhides passim.—*Müller*.

shore and repair all that had been damaged. On the 6th day they weighed again, and after a course of 300 stadia reached a place called Malana, the last on the coast of the Oreitai.[34] In the interior these people dress like the Indians, and use similar weapons, but differ from them in their language and their customs. The length of the coast of the Arabies, measured from the place whence the expedition had sailed, was about 1,000 stadia, and the extent of the coast of the Oreitai 1,600 stadia. Nearkhos mentions that as they sailed along the Indian coast (for the people beyond this are not Indians), their shadows did not fall in the usual direction, for when they stood out a good way to the southward, their shadows appeared to turn and fall southward.[35] Those constellations,

---

[34] Its modern representative is doubtless R â s  M a l i n, Malen or Moran.

[35] Such a phenomenon could not of course have been observed at Malana, which is about 2 degrees north of the Tropic, and Nearkhos, as has been already noticed (Introd. p. 155), has on account mainly of this statement been represented as a mendacious writer. Schmieder and Gosselin attempt to vindicate him by suggesting that Arrian in copying his journal had either missed the meaning of this passage, or altered it to bring it into accordance with his own geographical theories. Müller, however, has a better and probably the correct explanation to offer. He thinks that the text of Nearkhos which Arrian used contained passages interpolated from Onê-sikritos and writers of his stamp. The interpolations may have been inserted by the Alexandrian geographers, who, following Eratosthenes, believed that India lay between the Tropics. In support of this view it is to be noted that Arrian's account of the shadow occurs in that part of his work where he is speaking of Malana of the Oreitai, and that Pliny (VIII. 75) gives a similar account of the shadows that fall on a mountain of a somewhat similar name in the country of that very people. His words are: *In Indiae qente. Oretum Mons est Maleus nomine, juxta quem umbrae aestate in Austrum, hieme in Septemtrionem*

x

moreover, which they had been accustomed to see high in the heavens, were either not visible at all, or were seen just on the verge of the horizon, while the Polar constellations which had formerly been always visible now set and soon afterwards rose again. In this Nearkhos appears to me to assert nothing improbable, for at Syênê in Egypt they show a well in which, when the sun is at the Tropic, there is no shadow at noon. In Meroë also objects project no shadow at that particular time. Hence it is probable that the shadow is subject to the same law in India which lies to the south, and more especially in the Indian ocean, which extends still further to the southward.

XXVI. Next to the Oreitai lies Gedrosia,[36] an inland province through which Alexander led his army, but this with difficulty, for the region was so desolate that the troops in the whole course of the expedition never suffered such direful extremities as on this march. But all the particulars

---

*jaciuntur.* Now Pliny was indebted for his knowledge of Mons Maleus to Baeton, who places it however not in the country of the Oreitai but somewhere in the lower Gangetic region among the Suari and Monedes. It would thus appear that what Baeton had said of *Mount Maleus* was applied to *Malana* of the Oreitai, no doubt on account of the likeness of the two names. Add to this that the expression in the passage under consideration, *for the people beyond this (Malana) are not Indians,* is no doubt an interpolation into the text of the Journal, for it makes the Oreitai to be an Indian people, whereas the Journal had a little before made the Arabies to be the last people of Indian descent living in this direction.

[36] This country, which corresponds generally to Mekrân, was called also Kedrosia, Gadrosia, or Gadrusia. The people were an Ârianian race akin to the Arakhosii, Arii, and Drangiani.

relating to this I have set down in my larger
work (VI. 22-27). The seaboard below the Gedrosians is occupied by a people called the Ikhthyophagi, and along this country the fleet now pursued
its way. Weighing from Malana about the second
watch they ran a course of 600 stadia, and reached
Bagisâra. Here they found a commodious harbour,
and at a distance of 60 stadia from the sea a small
town called Pasira, whence the people of the neighbourhood were called Pasireës.[37] Weighing early
next morning they had to double a headland
which projected far out into the sea, and was high
and precipitous. Here having dug wells, and got
only a small supply of bad water, they rode at
anchor that day because a high surf prevented the
vessels approaching the shore. They left this
place next day, and sailed till they reached Kolta
after a course of 200 stadia.[38] Weighing thence at
daybreak they reached Kalama, after a course of

---

[37] Bagisara, says Kempthorne, "is now known by the
name of A r a b a h or H o r m a r a h Bay, and is deep and
commodious with good anchorage, sheltered from all winds
but those from the southward and eastward. The point
which forms this bay is very high and precipitous, and
runs out some distance into the sea. A rather large fishing
village is situated on a low sandy isthmus about one mile
across, which divides the bay from another. . . . . The
only articles of provision we could obtain from the inhabitants were a few fowls, some dried fish, and goats. They
grow no kind of vegetable or corn, a few water-melons
being the only thing these desolate regions bring forth.
Sandy deserts extend into the interior as far as the eye can
reach, and at the back of these rise high mountains." The
R h a p u a of Ptolemy corresponds to the Bagisara or
P a s i r a of Arrian, and evidently survives in the present
name of the bay and the headland of A r a b a.

[38] K o l t a.—A place unknown. It was situated on the
western side of the isthmus which connects R â s  A r a b a
with the main land.

600 stadia, and there anchored.[39] Near the beach
was a village around which grew a few palm-
trees, the dates on which were still green. There
was here an island called Karbinê, distant from
the shore about 100 stadia.[40] The villagers by way

---

[39] A different form is Kaluboi. Situated on the river
now called K a l a m i, or Kumra, or Kurmut, the Arabis of
Ptolemy, who was probably misled by the likeness of the
name to Karbis as the littoral district was designated here.

[40] Other forms—K a r n i n e, Karmina. The coast was
probably called Karmin, if Karmis is represented in
K u r m a t. The island lying twelve miles off the mouth
of the Kalami is now called A s t o l a or S a n g a-d i p,
which Kempthrone thus describes :—" Ashtola is a small
desolate island about four or five miles in circumference,
situated twelve miles from the coast of Mekrân. Its cliffs
rise rather abruptly from the sea to the height of about
300 feet, and it is inaccessible except in one place, which is
a sandy beach about one mile in extent on the northern
side. Great quantities of turtle frequent this island for the
purpose of depositing their eggs. Nearchus anchored off it,
and called it Karnine. He says also that he received
hospitable entertainment from its inhabitants, their presents
being cattle and fish; but not a vestige of any habitation
now remains. The Arabs come to this island, and kill
immense numbers of these turtles,—not for the purpose of
food, but they traffic with the shell to China, where it is
made into a kind of paste, and then into combs, ornaments,
&c., in imitation of tortoise-shell. The carcasses caused a
stench almost unbearable. The only land animals we could
see on the island were rats, and they were swarming.
They feed chiefly on the dead turtle. The island was
once famous as the rendezvous of the Jowassimee pirates."
Vincent quotes Blair to this effect regarding the island :—
" We were warned by the natives at Passence that it would
be dangerous to approach the island of Asthola, as it was
enchanted, and that a ship had been turned into a rock.
The superstitious story did not deter us ; we visited the
island, found plenty of excellent turtle, and saw the rock
alluded to, which at a distance had the appearance of a ship
under sail. The story was probably told to prevent our
disturbing the turtle. It has, however, some affinity to the
tale of Nearchus's transport." As the enchanted island
mentioned afterwards (chap. xxxi.), under the name of
Nosala, was 100 stadia distant from the coast, it was
probably the same as Karnine.

of showing their hospitality brought presents of sheep and fish to Nearkhos, who says that the mutton had a fishy taste like the flesh of sea birds for the sheep fed on fish, there being no grass in the place. Next day they proceeded 200 stadia, and anchored off a shore near which lay a village called Kissa, 30 stadia inland.[41] That coast was however called Karbis. There they found little boats such as might belong to miserably poor fishermen, but the men themselves they saw nothing of, for they had fled when they observed the ships dropping anchor. No corn was here procurable, but a few goats had been left, which were seized and put on board, for in the fleet provisions now ran short. On weighing they doubled a steep promontory, which projected about 150 stadia into the sea, and then put into a well-sheltered haven called Mosarna, where they anchored. Here the natives were fishermen, and here they obtained water.[42]

XXVII. From this place they took on board, Nearkhos says, as pilot of the fleet, a Gedrosian called Hydrakês, who undertook to conduct them as far as Karmania.[43] Thenceforth until they

[41] Another form of the name is Kysa.

[42] The place according to Ptolemy is 900 stadia distant from the Kalami river, but according to Marcianus 1,300 stadia. It must have been situated in the neighbourhood of Cape Passence. The distances here are so great exaggerated that the text is suspected to be corrupt or disturbed. From Mosarna to Kophas the distance is represented as 1,750 stadia, and yet the distance from Cape Passence to Râs Koppa (the Kophas of the text) is barely 500 stadia. According to Ptolemy and Marcian Karmania begins at Mosarna, but according to Arrian much further westward, at Badis near Cape Jask.

[43] "From the name given to this pilot I imagine that he was an inhabitant of Hydriakus, a town near the bay

reached the Persian Gulf, the voyage was more
practicable, and the names of the stations more
familiar. Departing from Mosarna at night,
they sailed 750 stadia, and reached the coast of
Balômon. They touched next at Barna, which
was 400 stadia distant.[44] Here grew many palm
trees, and here was a garden wherein were myrtles
and flowers from which the men wove chaplets
for their hair.[45] They saw now for the first time
cultivated trees, and met with natives in a condition above that of mere savages. Leaving this they
followed the winding of the coast, and arrived at
Dendrobosa, where they anchor in the open sea.[46]
They weighed from this about midnight, and after
a course of about 400 stadia gained the haven of

---

of Churber or Chewabad. . . . Upon the acquisition of
Hydrakes or the Hydriakan two circumstances occur,
that give a new face to the future course of the voyage,
one is the very great addition to the length of each day's
course; and the other, that they generally weighed during
the night: the former depending upon the confidence they
acquired by having a pilot on board; and the latter on the
nature of the land breeze."—Vincent I., p. 244.

[44] This place is called in Ptolemy and Marcianus Badera
or Bodera, and may have been situated near the Cape now
called Chemaul Bunder. It is mentioned under the form
Balara by Philostratos (Vit. Apoll. III. 56), whose description of the place is in close agreement with Arrian's.

[45] τῇσι κόμῃσιν. Another reading, not so good however, is, τῇσι κωμήτῃσιν for the village women, but
the Greeks were not likely to have indulged in such
gallantry. Wearing chaplets in the hair on festive occasions
was a common practice with the Greeks. Cf. our author's
Anab. V. 2. 8.

[46] In Ptolemy a place is mentioned called Derenoibila,
which may be the same as this. The old name perhaps
survives in the modern Daram or Duram, the name of a
highland on part of the coast between Cape Passence and
Cape Guadel.

Kôphas.[47] The inhabitants were fishermen possessed of small and wretched boats, which they did not manage with oars fastened to a row-lock according to the Grecian manner, but with paddles which they thrust on this side, and on that into the water, like diggers using a spade. They found at this haven plenty of good water. Weighing about the first watch they ran 800 stadia, and put into Kyiza, where was a desert shore with a high surf breaking upon it.[48] They were accordingly obliged to let the ships ride at anchor and take their meal on board. Leaving this they ran a course of 500 stadia, and came to a small town built on an eminence not far from the shore. On turning his eyes in that direction Nearkhos noticed that the land had some appearance of being cultivated, and thereupon addressing Arkhias (who was the son of Anaxidotos of Pella, and sailed in the Commander's galley, being a Makedonian of distinction) pointed out to him

---

[47] The name appears to survive in a cognominal Cape— Râs Coppa. The natives use the same kind of boat to this day ; it is a curve made of several small planks nailed or sewn together in a rude manner with cord made from the bark of date trees and called *kair*, the whole being then smeared over with dammer or pitch.—*Kempthorne*.

[48] According to Ptolemy and Marcianus this place lay 400 stadia to the west of the promontory of Alambator (now Râs Guadel). Some trace of the word may be recognized in R â s G h u n s e, which now designates a point of land situated about those parts. Arrian passes Cape Guadel without notice. "We should be reasonably surprised at this," says Vincent (I. 248), "as the doubling of a cape is always an achievement in the estimation of a Greek navigator ; but having now a native pilot on board, it is evident he took advantage of the land-breeze to give the fleet an offing. This is clearly the reason why we hear nothing in Arrian of Ptolemy's Alabagium, or Alambateir, the prominent feature of this coast."

that they must take possession of the place, as the inhabitants would not willingly supply the army with food. It could not however be taken by assault, a tedious siege would be necessary, and they were already short of provisions. But the country was one that produced corn as the thick stubble which they saw covering the fields near the shore clearly proved. This proposal being approved of by all, he ordered Arkhias to make a feint of preparing the fleet, all but one ship to sail, while he himself, pretending to be left behind with that ship, approached the town as if merely to view it.

XXVIII. When he approached the walls the inhabitants came out to meet him, bringing a present of tunny-fish broiled in pans (the first instance of cookery among the Ikhthyophagi, although these were the very last of them), accompanied with small cakes and dates. He accepted their offering with the proper acknowledgments, but said he wished to see their town, which he was accordingly allowed to enter. No sooner was he within the gates than he ordered two of his archers to seize the portal by which they had entered, while he himself with two attendants and his interpreter mounting the wall hard by, made the preconcerted signal, on seeing which the troops under Arkhias were to perform the service assigned to them. The Makedonians, on seeing the signal, immediately ran their ships towards land, and without loss of time jumped into the sea. The barbarians, alarmed at these proceedings, flew to arms. Upon this Nearkhos ordered his interpreter to proclaim that if they wished their city to be preserved from pillage they must supply his army with provisions. They replied that they had none, and proceeded to attack the wall, but were repulsed by the archers with Nearkhos, who assailed them with arrows from the summit of the wall. Accordingly, when they saw that their city was taken, and on the point of being pillaged, they at once begged Nearkhos to take whatever corn they had, and to depart without destroying the place. Nearkhos upon this orders Arkhias to possess himself of the gates and the ramparts adjoining, and sends at the same time officers to see what stores were available, and whether these would be all honestly given up. The stores were produced, consisting of a kind of meal made from fish roasted, and a little wheat and barley, for the chief diet of these people was fish with bread added as a relish. The troops having appropriated these supplies returned to the fleet, which then hauled off to a cape *in the neighbourhood* called Bagîa, which the natives regarded as sacred to the sun.[49]

XXIX. They weighed from this cape about midnight, and having made good a course of 1,000 stadia, put into Talmena, where they found a harbour with good anchorage.[50] They sailed

[49] *The little town attacked by Nearchus* lay on Gwattar Bay. The promontory in its neighbourhood called B a g i a is mentioned by Ptolemy and Marcianus, the latter of whom gives its distance from Kyiza at 250 stadia, which is but half the distance as given by Arrian. To the west of this was the river Kaudryaces or Hydriaces, the modern Baghwar Dasti or Muhani river, which falls into the Bay of Gwattar.

[50] A name not found elsewhere. To judge by the distance assigned, it must be placed on what is now called Chaubar Bay, on the shores of which are three towns, one being called T i z,—perhaps the modern representative of Tisa, a place in those parts mentioned by Ptolemy, and which may have been the Talmena of Arrian.

y

194

thence to Kanasis, a deserted town 400 stadia
distant, where they find a well ready-dug and wild
palm-trees.[51]  These they cut down, using the
tender heads to support life since provisions had
again run scarce.  They sailed all day and all
night suffering great distress from hunger, and
then came to an anchor off a desolate coast.
Nearkhos fearing lest the men, if they landed,
would in despair desert the fleet, ordered the ships
to be moved to a distance from shore.  Weighing
from this they ran a course of 850 stadia, and
came to anchor at Kanate, a place with an open
beach and some water-courses.[52]  Weighing again,
and making 800 stadia, they reach Taoi, where
they drop anchor.[53]  The place contained some
small and wretched villages, which were deserted
by the inhabitants upon the approach of the
fleet.  Here the men found a little food and dates
of the palm-tree, beside seven camels left by the
villagers which were killed for food.  Weighing
thence about daybreak they ran a course of 300
stadia, and came to anchor at Dagasira, where the
people were nomadic.[54]  Weighing again they
sailed all night and all day without intermission,
and having thus accomplished a course of 1,100

[51] The name is not found elsewhere.  It must have been
situated on a bay enclosed within the two headlands
Râs Fuggem and Râs Godem.
[52] Kanate probably stood on the site of the modern
Kungoun, which is near Râs Kalat, and not far
from the river Bunth.
[53] Another and the common form is Troisi.  The villages
of the Taoi must have been where the Sudich river enters
the sea.  Here Ptolemy places his Kommana or Nommana
and his follower Marcian his Ommana. See ante p. 104 note.
[54] The place in Ptolemy is called Agrispolis,—in Marcianus, Agrisa.  The modern name is Girishk.

stadia, left behind them the nation of the Ikhthyo-phagi, on whose shores they had suffered such severe privations. They could not approach the beach on account of the heavy surf, but rode at anchor out at sea. In navigating the Ikhthyophagi coast the distance traversed was not much short of 10,000 stadia. The people, as their name imports, live upon fish. Few of them, however, are fishermen, and what fish they obtain they owe mostly to the tide at whose reflux they catch them with nets made for this purpose. These nets are generally about 2 stadia long, and are composed of the bark (or fibres) of the palm, which they twine into cord in the same way as the fibres of flax are twined. When the sea recedes, hardly any fish are found among the dry sands, but they abound in the depressions of the surface where the water still remains. The fish are for the most part small, though some are caught of a considerable size, these being taken in the nets. The more delicate kinds they eat raw as soon as they are taken out of the water. The large and coarser kinds they dry in the sun, and when properly dried grind into a sort of meal from which they make bread. This meal is sometimes also used to bake cakes with. The cattle as well as their masters fare on dried fish, for the country has no pastures, and hardly even a blade of grass. In most parts crabs, oysters and mussels add to the means of subsistence. Natural salt is found in the country, * * * from these they make oil.[55]

---

[55] Schmieder suggests that instead of the common reading here ἀπὸ τούτων ἔλαιον ποιέουσιν Arrian may have written ἀπὸ θύννων ε. π. *they make oil from thun-nies,* i. e. use the fat for oil.

Certain of their communities inhabit deserts where
not a tree grows, and where there are not even
wild fruits. Fish is their sole means of subsistence. In some few places, however, they sow
with grain some patches of land, and eat the
produce as a viand of luxury along with the fish
which forms the staple of their diet. The better
class of the population in building their houses
use, instead of wood, the bones of whales stranded
on the coast, the broadest bones being employed
in the framework of the doors. Poor people, and
these are the great majority, construct their
dwellings with the backbones of fish.[56]

XXX. Whales of enormous size frequent the
outer ocean, besides other fish larger than those
found in the Mediterranean. Nearkhos relates that
when they were bearing away from Kyiza, the
sea early in the morning was observed to be blown
up into the air as if by the force of a whirlwind.
The men greatly alarmed enquired of the pilots
the nature and cause of this phenomenon, and
were informed that it proceeded from the blowing
of the whales as they sported in the sea. This
report did not quiet their alarm, and through
astonishment they let the oars drop from their
hands. Nearkhos, however, recalled them to duty,
and encouraged them by his presence, ordering
the prows of those vessels that were near him to
be turned as in a sea-fight towards the creatures
as they approached, while the rowers were just
then to shout as loud as they could the *alala*,

---

[56] "This description of the natives, with that of their
mode of living and the country they inhabit, is strictly
correct even to the present day."—Kempthorne.

and swell the noise by dashing the water rapidly with the oars. The men thus encouraged on seeing the preconcerted signal advanced to action. Then, as they approached the monsters, they shouted the *alala* as loud as they could bawl, sounded the trumpets, and dashed the water noisily with the oars. Thereupon the whales, which were seen ahead, plunged down terror-struck into the depths, and soon after rose astern, when they vigorously continued their blowing. The men by loud acclamations expressed their joy at this unexpected deliverance, the credit of which they gave to Nearkhos, who had shown such admirable fortitude and judgment.

We learn further, that on many parts of the coast whales are occasionally stranded, being left in shallow water at ebb-tide, and thus prevented from escaping back to sea, and that they are sometimes also cast ashore by violent storms. Thus perishing, their flesh rots away, and gradually drops off till the bones are left bare. These are used by the natives in the construction of their huts, the larger ribs making suitable bearing beams, and the smaller serving for rafters. The jaw-bones make arches for the door-ways, for whales are sometimes five and twenty *orguiœ* (fathoms) in length.[57]

XXXI. When they were sailing along the Ikhthyophagi coast, they were told about an island which was said to be about 100 stadia dis-

---

[57] Strabo (XV. ii. 12, 13) has extracted from Nearkhos the same passage regarding whales. See Nearchi fragm. 25. Cf Onesikritos (fr. 30) and Orthagoras in Aelian. N. An. XVII. 6; Diodor. XVII, 106; Curtius X. 1, 11.

tant from the mainland, and uninhabited. Its
name was Nosala, and it was according to the local
tradition sacred to the sun. No one willingly
visited this island, and if any one was carried to
it unawares, he was never more seen. Nearkhos
states that a transport of his fleet, manned with
an Egyptian crew, disappeared not far from this
island, and that the pilots accounted for their dis-
appearance by saying that they must have landed
on the island in ignorance of the danger which
they would thereby incur. Nearkhos, however,
sent a galley of 30 oars to sail round the island,
instructing the men not to land, but to approach
as near as they could to the shore, and hail the
men, shouting out the name of the captain or any
other name they had not forgotten. No one answered to the call, and Nearkhos says that he
then sailed in person to the island, and com-
pelled his company much against their will to
go on shore. He too landed, and showed that
the story about the island was nothing but an
empty fable. Concerning this same island he
heard also another story, which ran to this
effect: it had been at one time the residence
of one of the Nereids, whose name, he says, he
could not learn. It was her wont to have intercourse with any man who visited the island,
changing him thereafter into a fish, and casting him
into the sea. The sun, however, being displeased
with the Nereid, ordered her to remove from the
island. She agreed to do this, and seek a home
elsewhere, but stipulated that she should be
cured of her malady. To this condition the sun
assented, and then the Nereid, taking pity upon

the men whom she had transformed into fish, restored them to their human shape. These men were the progenitors of the Ikhthyophagi, the line of succession remaining unbroken down to the time of Alexander. Now, for my part I have no praise to bestow on Nearkhos for expending so much time and ingenuity on the not very difficult task of proving the falsehood of these stories, for, to take up antiquated fables merely with a view to prove their falsehood, I can only regard as a contemptible piece of folly.[58]

XXXII. To the Ikhthyophagi succeed the Gadrôsii, who occupy a most wretched tract of country full of sandy deserts, in penetrating which Alexander and his army were reduced to the greatest extremities, of which an account is to be found in my other work. But this is an inland region, and therefore when the expedition left the Ikhthyophagi, its course lay along Karmania.[59] Here, when they first drew towards shore,

---

[58] The story of the Nereid is evidently an Eastern version of the story of the enchantress Kirkê. The island here called Nosala is that already mentioned under the name of Karbine, now Asthola.

[59] Karmania extended from Cape Jask to Râs Nabend, and comprehended the districts now called Moghostân, Kirman, and Lâristan. Its metropolis, according to Ptolemy, was Karmana, now Kirman, which gives its name to the whole province. The first port in Karmania reached by the expedition was in the neighbourhood of Cape Jask, where the coast is described as being very rocky, and dangerous to mariners on account of shoals and rocks under water. Kempthorne says: "The cliffs along this part of the coast are very high, and in many places almost perpendicular. Some have a singular appearance, one near Jask being exactly of the shape of a quoin or wedge; and another is a very remarkable peak, being formed by three stones, as if placed by human hands, one on the top of the other. It is very high, and has the resemblance of a chimney."

they could not effect a landing, but had to remain
all night on board anchored in the deep, because
a violent surf spread along the shore and far out
to sea. Thereafter the direction of their course
changed, and they sailed no longer towards sunset,
but turned the heads of the vessels more to
the north-west. Karmania is better wooded and
produces better fruit than the country either
of the Ikhthyophagi or the Oreitai. It is also
more grassy, and better supplied with water.
They anchor next at Badis, an inhabited place in
Karmania, where grew cultivated trees of many
different kinds, with the exception of the olive, and
where also the soil favoured the growth of the
vine and of corn.[60] Weighing thence they ran
800 stadia, and came to an anchor off a barren
coast, whence they descried a headland projecting
far out into the sea, its nearest extremity being to
appearance about a day's sail distant. Persons
acquainted with those regions asserted that this
cape belonged to Arabia, and was called Maketa,
whence cinnamon and other products were exported
to the Assyrians.[61] And from this coast where

---

[60] Badis must have been near where the village of Jask
now stands, beyond which was the promontory now called
Râs Kerazi or Keroot or Bombarak, which marks the
entrance to the Straits of Ormus. This projection is the
Cape Karpella of Ptolemy. Badis may be the same as the
Kanthatis of this geographer.

[61] Maketa is now called Cape Mesandum in Omân. It is
thus described by Palgrave in the Narrative of his Travels
through Central and Eastern Arabia (Vol. II. pp. 316-7).
The afternoon was already far advanced when we reached
the headland, and saw before us the narrow sea-pass which
runs between the farthest rocks of Mesandum and the
mainland of the Cape. This strait is called the " Bab" or
" gate:" it presents an imposing spectacle, with lofty pre-
cipices on either side, and the water flowing deep and black

the fleet was now anchored, and from the headland
which they saw projecting into the sea right opposite, the gulf in my opinion (which is also that
of Nearkhos) extends up into the interior, and is
probably the Red Sea. When this headland was
now in view Onesikritos, *the chief pilot*, proposed
that they should proceed to explore it, and by so
shaping their course, escape the distressing passage
up the gulf; but Nearkhos opposed this proposal.
Onesikritos, he said, must be wanting in ordinary
judgment if he did not know with what design
Alexander had sent the fleet on this voyage. He
certainly had not sent it, because there were no
proper means of conducting the whole army safely
by land, but his express purpose was to obtain a
knowledge of the coasts they might pass on
their voyage, together with the harbours and
islets, and to have the bays that might occur
explored, and to ascertain whether there were
towns bordering on the ocean, and whether the
countries were habitable or desert. They ought
not therefore to lose sight of this object, seeing
that they were now near the end of their toils, and
especially that they were no longer in want of
the necessary supplies for prosecuting the voyage.

---

below; the cliffs are utterly bare and extremely well adapted
for shivering whatever vessels have the ill luck to come
upon them. Hence and from the ceaseless dash of the dark
waves, the name of "Mesandum" or "Anvil," a term seldom
better applied. But this is not all, for some way out at
sea rises a huge square mass of basalt of a hundred feet and
more in height sheer above the water; it bears the name
of "Salâmah" or "safety," a euphemism of good augury
for "danger." Several small jagged peaks, just projecting
above the surface, cluster in its neighbourhood; these bear
the endearing name of "Benât Salâmah," or "Daughters
of Salamah."

He feared, moreover, since the headland stretched towards the south, lest they should find the country there a parched desert destitute of water and insufferably hot. This argument prevailed, and it appears to me that by this counsel Nearkhos saved the expedition, for all accounts represent this cape and the parts adjacent as an arid waste where water cannot possibly be procured.

XXXIII. On resuming the voyage they sailed close to land, and after making about 700 stadia anchored on another shore called Neoptana.[62] From this they weighed next day at dawn, and after a course of 100 stadia anchored at the mouth of the river Anamis[63] in a country called Harmozeia.[64] Here at last they found a hospitable

[62] This place is not mentioned elsewhere, but must have been situated somewhere, in the neighbourhood of the village of Karun.

[63] The Anamis, called by Pliny the Ananis, and by Ptolemy and Mela the Andanis, is now the Minâb or Ibrahim River.

[64] Other forms—Hormazia, Armizia regio. The name was transferred from the mainland to the island now called Ormus, when the inhabitants fled thither to escape from the Moghals. It is called by Arrian Organa (chap. xxxvii.) The Arabians called it Djerun, a name which it continued to bear up to the 12th century. Pliny mentions an island called Oguris, of which perhaps Djerun is a corruption. He ascribes to it the honour of having been the birthplace of Erythres. The description, however, which he gives of it is more applicable to the island called by Arrian (chap. xxxvii.) Oârakta (now Kishm) than to Ormus. Arrian's description of Harmozia is still applicable to the region adjacent to the Minâb. " It is termed," says Kempthorne, "the Paradise of Persia. It is certainly most beautifully fertile, and abounds in orange groves, orchards containing apples, pears, peaches, and apricots, with vineyards producing a delicious grape, from which was made at one time a wine called Amber rosolia, generally considered the white wine of Kishma; but no wine is made here now." The old name of Kishma—Oârakta—is preserved in one of its modern names, Vrokt or Brokt.

region, one which was rich in every production except only the olive. Here accordingly they landed, and enjoyed a welcome respite from their many toils—heightening their pleasure by calling to remembrance what miseries they had suffered at sea and in the Ikhthyophagi country, where the shores were so sterile, and the natives so brute-like, and where they had been reduced to the last extremities of want. Here, also, some of them in scattered parties, leaving the encampment on the shore, wandered inland searching for one thing and another that might supply their several requirements. While thus engaged, they fell in with a man who wore a Greek mantle, and was otherwise attired as a Greek and spoke the Greek language. Those who first discovered him declared that tears started to their eyes, so strange did it appear, after all they had suffered, to see once more a countryman of their own, and to hear the accents of their native tongue. They asked him whence he came, and who he was. He replied that he had straggled from the army of Alexander, and that the army led by Alexander in person was not far off. On hearing this they hurry the man with shouts of tumultuous joy to the presence of Nearkhos, to whom he repeated all that he had already said, assuring him that the army and the king were not more than a 5 days' march distant from the sea. The Governor of the province, he added, was on the spot, and he would present him to Nearkhos, and he presented him accordingly. Nearkhos consulted this person regarding the route he should take in order to reach the king, and then they all went off, and made their way to the ships. Early next morning the ships by orders of Nearkhos were drawn on shore, partly for repair of the damages which some of them had suffered on the voyage, and partly because he had resolved to leave here the greater part of his army. Having this in view, he fortified the roadstead with a double palisade, and also with an earthen rampart and a deep ditch extending from the banks of the river to the dockyard where the ships were lying.

XXXIV. While Nearkhos was thus occupied, the Governor being aware that Alexander was in great anxiety about the fate of this expedition, concluded that he would receive some great advantage from Alexander should he be the first to apprize him of the safety of the fleet and of the approaching visit of Nearkhos. Accordingly he hastened to Alexander by the shortest route, and announced that Nearkhos was coming from the fleet to visit him. Alexander, though he could scarcely believe the report, nevertheless received the tidings with all the joy that might have been expected.

Day after day, however, passed without confirmation of the fact, till Alexander, on comparing the distance from the sea with the date on which the report had reached him, at last gave up all belief in its truth, the more especially as several of the parties which he had successively despatched to find Nearkhos and escort him to the camp, had returned without him, after going a short distance, and meeting no one, while others who had prosecuted the search further, and failed to find Nearkhos and his company were still absent. He therefore

ordered the Governor into confinement for having
brought delusive intelligence and rendered his
vexation more acute by the disappointment of his
hopes, and indeed his looks and perturbation of
mind plainly indicated that he was pierced to the
heart with a great grief. Meanwhile, however, one
of the parties that had been despatched in search
of Nearkhos, and his escort being furnished with
horses and waggons for their accommodation, fell
in on the way with Nearkhos and Arkhias, who
were followed by five or six attendants. At first
sight they recognized neither the admiral himself
nor Arkhias, so much changed was their appearance, their hair long and neglected, their persons
filthy, encrusted all over with brine and shrivelled,
their complexion sallow from want of sleep and
other severe privations. On their asking where
Alexander was, they were told the name of the
place. Arkhias then, perceiving who they were,
said to Nearkhos—" It strikes me, Nearkhos, these
men are traversing the desert by the route we
pursue, for no other reason than because they have
been sent to our relief. True, they did not know us,
but that is not at all surprising, for our appearance
is so wretched that we are past all recognition.
Let us tell them who we are, and ask them why they
are travelling this way." Nearkhos, thinking he
spoke with reason, asked the men whither they were
bound. They replied that they were searching for
Nearkhos and the fleet. " Well ! I am Nearkhos,"
said the admiral, " and this man here is Arkhias.
Take us under your conduct, and we will report to
Alexander the whole history of the expedition."

XXXV. They were accordingly accommodated

in the waggons, and conducted to the camp. Some
of the horsemen, however, wishing to be the first
to impart the news, hastened forward, and told
Alexander that Nearkhos himself, and Arkhias
with him, and five attendants, would soon arrive,
but to enquiries about the rest of the people in
the expedition they had no information to give.
Alexander, concluding from this that all the expedition had perished except this small band,
which had been unaccountably saved, did not so
much feel pleasure for the preservation of Nearkhos and Arkhias as distress for the loss of his
whole fleet. During this conversation Nearkhos
and Arkhias arrived. It was not without difficulty Alexander after a close scrutiny recognized
who the hirsute, ill-clad men who stood before
him were, and being confirmed by their misera-
able appearance in his belief that the expedition
had perished, he was still more overcome with
grief. At length he held out his hand to Nearkhos, and leading him apart from his attendants
and his guards he burst into tears, and wept for a
long time. Having, after a good while, recovered
some composure, "Nearkhos!" he says, "since you
and Arkhias have been restored to me alive, I can
bear more patiently the calamity of losing all my
fleet; but tell me now, in what manner did the
vessels and my people perish." "O my king!" replied Nearkhos, "the ships are safe and the people
also, and we are here to give you an account of their
preservation." Tears now fell much faster from
his eyes than before, but they were tears of joy for
the salvation of his fleet which he had given up for
lost. "And where are now my ships," he then

enquired. "They are drawn up on shore," replied Nearkhos, "on the beach of the river Anamis for repairs." Upon this Alexander, swearing by Zeus of the Greeks and Ammon of the Libyans, declared that he felt happier at receiving these tidings than in being the conqueror of all Asia, for, had the expedition been lost, the blow to his peace of mind would have been a counterpoise to all the success he had achieved.

XXXVI. But the Governor whom Alexander had put into confinement for bringing intelligence that appeared to be false, seeing Nearkhos in the camp, sunk on his knees before him, and said: "I am the man who brought to Alexander the news of your safe arrival. You see how I am situated." Nearkhos interceded with Alexander on his behalf, and he was then liberated. Alexander next proceeded to offer a solemn sacrifice in gratitude for the preservation of his fleet unto Zeus the Preserver, and Heraklês, and Apollo the Averter of Destruction, and unto Poseidôn, and every other deity of ocean. He celebrated likewise a contest in gymnastics and music, and exhibited a splendid procession wherein a foremost place was assigned to Nearkhos. Chaplets were wreathed for his head, and flowers were showered upon him by the admiring multitude. At the end of these proceedings the king said to Nearkhos, "I do not wish you, Nearkhos, either to risk your life or expose yourself again to the hardships of sea-voyaging, and I shall therefore send some other officer to conduct the expedition onward to Sousa." But Nearkhos answered, and said: "It is my duty, O king! as it is also my

desire, in all things to obey you, but if your object
is to gratify me in some way, do not take the
command from me until I complete the voyage
by bringing the ships in safety to Sousa. I have
been trusted to execute that part of the undertaking in which all its difficulty and danger lay;
transfer not, then, to another the remaining part,
which hardly requires an effort, and that, too, just
at the time when the glory of final success is
ready to be won." Alexander scarcely allowed
him to conclude his request, which he granted
with grateful acknowledgment of his services.[65]
Then he sent him down again to the coast
with only a small escort, believing that the
country through which he would pass was
friendly. He was not permitted however to
pursue his way to the coast without opposition,
for the barbarians, resenting the action of
Alexander in deposing their satrap, had gathered
in full force and seized all the strongholds
of Karmania before Tlepolemos, the newly appointed Governor, had yet succeeded in fully
establishing his authority.[66] It happened therefore that several times in the course of a day
Nearkhos encountered bands of the insurgents
with whom he had to do battle. He therefore hurried forward without lingering by the
way, and reached the coast in safety, though
not without severe toil and difficulty. On arriv-

---

[65] Diodôros (XVII. 106) gives quite a different account of
the visit of Nearkhos to Alexander.

[66] The preceding satrap was Sibyrtios, the friend of
Megasthenês. He had been transferred to govern the
Gadrosians and the Arakhotians.

ing he sacrificed to Zeus the Preserver, and celebrated gymnastic games.

XXXVII. These pious rites having been duly
performed, they again put to sea, and, after passing
a desolate and rocky island, arrived at another
island, where they anchored. This was one of
considerable size and inhabited, and 300 stadia
distant from Harmozeia, the harbour which they
had last left. The desert island was called Organa, and that where they anchored Oärakta.[67]
It produced vines, palm-trees, and corn. Its
length is 800 stadia. Mazênês, the chief of this
island, accompanied them all the way to Sousa,
having volunteered to act as pilot of the fleet. The
natives of the island professed to point out the
tomb of the very first sovereign of the country,
whose name they said was Erythrês, after whom
the sea in that part of the world was called the
Erythraean.[68] Weighing thence their course lay

[67] As stated in Note 64, Organa is now *Ormuz*, and
Oarakta, *Kishm*. Ormuz, once so renowned for its wealth
and commerce, that it was said of it by its Portuguese
occupants, that if the world were a golden ring, Ormuz
would be the diamond signet, is now in utter decay. "I
have seen," says Palgrave (II. 319), the abasement of Tyre,
the decline of Surat, the degradation of Goa: but in none
of those fallen seaports is aught resembling the utter
desolation of Ormuz." A recent traveller in Persia
(Binning) thus describes the coast: "It presents no view
but sterile, barren, and desolate chains of rocks and hills :
and the general aspect of the Gulf is dismal and forbidding.
Moore's charming allusions to Oman's sea, with its ' banks
of pearl and palmy isles' are unfortunately quite visionary;
for uglier and more unpicturesque scenery I never beheld.'
—*Two Years' Travel in Persia*, I. pp. 136, 137.

[68] For the legend of Erythres see Agatharkhides De
Mari Eryth. I. 1-4 and Strabo XVI. iv. 20. The Erythræan Sea included the Indian Ocean, the Persian Gulf, and
the Red Sea, the last being called also the Arabian Gulf,
when it was necessary to distinguish it from the Erythræan

along the island, and they anchored on its shores
at a place whence another island was visible at a
distance of about 40 stadia. They learned that it
was sacred to Poseidôn, and inaccessible.[69] Next
morning, as they were putting out to sea, the ebb-
tide caught them with such violence that three of
the galleys were stranded on the beach, and the rest
of the fleet escaped with difficulty from the surf
into deep water. The stranded vessels were however floated off at the return of the tide, and the
day after rejoined the fleet. They anchored at
another island distant from the mainland somewhere about 300 stadia, after running a course
of 400 stadia. Towards daybreak they resumed
the voyage, passing a desert island which lay on

in general. It can hardly be doubted that the epithet
*Erythræan* (which means *red*, Greek ἐρυθρὸς) first
designated the Arabian Gulf or Red Sea, and was afterwards
extended to the seas beyond the Straits by those who first
explored them. The Red Sea was so called because it
washed the shores of Arabia, called *the Red Land* (Edom),
in contradistinction to Egypt, called *the Black Land*
(Kemi), from the darkness of the soil deposited by the
Nile. Some however thought that it received its name
from the quantity of red coral found in its waters, especially along the eastern shores, and Strabo says (loc. cit.):
" Some say that the sea is red from the colour arising from
reflexion either from the sun, which is vertical, or from
the mountains, which are red by being scorched with
intense heat; for the colour it is supposed may be produced
by both of these causes. Ktesias of Knidos speaks of a
spring which discharges into the sea a red and ochrous
water."—Cf. Eustath. Comment. 38.

[69] This island is that now called A n g a r, or H a n j a m,
to the south of Kishm. It is described as being nearly
destitute of vegetation and uninhabited. Its hills, of
volcanic origin, rise to a height of 300 feet. The other
island, distant from the mainland about 300 stadia, is now
called the Great Tombo, near which is a smaller island
called Little Tombo. They are low, flat, and uninhabited.
They are 25 miles distant from the western extremity of
Kishm.

their left, called Pylôra, and anchored at Sisidônê,
a small town which could supply nothing but water
and fish.[70] Here again the natives were fish eaters,
for the soil was utterly sterile. Having taken
water on board, they weighed again, and having run
300 stadia, anchored at Tarsia, the extremity of a
cape which projects far into the sea. The next
place of anchorage was Kataia, a desert island, and
very flat.[71] It was said to be sacred to Hermês
and Aphroditê. The length of this course was
300 stadia. To this island sheep and goats are
annually sent by the people of the adjoining continent who consecrate them to Hermês and
Aphroditê. These animals were to be seen running
about in a wild state, the effect of time and the
barren soil.

XXXVIII. Karmania extends as far as this
island, but the parts beyond appertain to Persia.
The extent of the Karmanian coast was 3,700

[70] The island of P y l o r a is that now called Polior.
S i s i d o n e appears in other forms—Prosidodone, pro-
Sidodone, pros Sidone, pros Dodone. Kempthorne thought
this was the small fishing village now called M o g o s,
situated in a bay of the same name. The name may perhaps be preserved in the name of a village in the same
neighbourhood, called Dnan Tarsia—now R â s-e l-D j a r d
—described as high and rugged, and of a reddish colour.

[71] K a t a i a is now the island called K a e s or K e n n.
Its character has altered, being now covered with dwarf
trees, and growing wheat and tobacco. It supplies ships
with refreshment, chiefly goats and sheep and a few
vegetables. "At morning," says Binning (I. 137), " we
passed Polior, and at noon were running along the South
side of the Isle of Keesh, called in our maps Kenn; a
fertile and populous island about 7 miles in length. The
inhabitants of this, as well as of every other island in the
Gulf, are of Arab blood—for every true Persian appears to
hate the very sight of the sea."

stadia.[72] The people of this province live like the Persians, on whom they border, and they have similar weapons and a similar military system. When the fleet left the sacred island, its course lay along the coast of Persis, and it first drew to land at a place called Ila, where there is a harbour under cover of a small and desert island called Kaï-kander.[73] The distance run was 400 stadia. Towards daybreak they came to another island which was inhabited, and anchored thereon. Near-khos notices that there is here a fishery for pearl as there is in the Indian Sea.[74] Having sailed along the shores of the promontory in which this island terminates, a distance of about 40 stadia, they came to an anchor upon its shores. The next anchorage was in the vicinity of a lofty hill called Okhos, where the harbour was well sheltered and the inhabitants were fishermen.[75] Weighing thence they ran a course of

---

[72] The boundary between Karmania and Persis was formed by a range of mountains opposite the island of K a t a i a. Ptolemy, however, makes Karmania extend much further, to the river B a g r a d a s, now called the N a b a n or N a b e n d.

[73] K a i k a n d e r has the other forms—Kekander, Kikander, Kaskandrus, Karkundrus, Karskandrus, Sasækander. This island, which is now called I n d e r a b i a, or A n d a r a v i a, is about four or five miles from the mainland, having a small town on the north side, where is a safe and commodious harbour. The other island mentioned immediately after is probably that now called Busheab. It is, according to Kempthorne, a low, flat island, about eleven miles from the mainland, containing a small town principally inhabited by Arabs, who live on fish and dates. The harbour has good anchorage even for large vessels.

[74] The pearl oyster is found from Ras Musendom to the head of the Gulf. There are no famed banks on the Persian side, but near Bushire there are some good ones.

[75] A p o s t a n a was near a place now called S c h e v a r. It is thought that the name may be traced in D a h r a

400 stadia, which brought them to Apostana, where they anchored. At this station they saw a great many boats, and learned that at a distance of 60 stadia from the shore there was a village. From Apostana they weighed at night, and proceeded 400 stadia to a bay, on the borders of which many villages were to be seen. Here the fleet anchored under the projection of a cape which rose to a considerable height.[76] Palm-trees and other fruit-bearing trees similar to those of Greece, adorned the country round. On weighing thence they sailed in a line with the coast, and after a course of somewhere about 600 stadia reached Gôgana, which was an inhabited place, where they anchored at the mouth of a winter torrent called the Areôn. It was difficult to anchor, for the approach to the mouth of the river was by a narrow channel, since the ebbing of the tide had left shoals which lay all round in a circle.[77] Weighing thence they gained, after running as many as 800 stadia, the mouth of another river called the Sitakos, where also it was troublesome to anchor. Indeed all along the coast of Persis the fleet had to be navigated through shoals and breakers and oozy channels.

---

A h b â n, an adjacent mountain ridge of which Okhos was probably the southern extremity.

[76] This bay is that on which N a b a n or N a b e n d is now situated. It is not far from the river called by Ptolemy the Bagradas. The place abounds with palm-trees as of old.

[77] Gôgana is now K o n k a n or K o n a u n. The bay lacks depth of water ; a stream still falls into it—the Areon of the text. To the north-west of this place in the interior lay P a s a r g a d a, the ancient capital of Persia, and the burial-place of Kyros, in the neighbourhood of Murghâb, a place to the N. E. of Shiraz (30° 24' N. 56° 29' E.).

At the Sitakos they took on board a large supply
of provisions, which under orders from the king
had been collected expressly for the fleet. They
remained at this station one-and-twenty days in
all, occupied in repairing and kareening the ships,
which had been drawn on shore for the purpose.[78]

XXXIX. Weighing thence they came to an
inhabited district with a town called Hieratis,
after accomplishing a distance of 750 stadia.
They anchored in a canal which drew its waters
from a river and emptied into the sea, and was
called Heratemis.[79] Weighing next morning about
sunrise, and sailing by the shore, they reached a
winter torrent called the Padargos, where the
whole place was a peninsula, wherein were
many gardens and all kinds of trees that bear
fruit. The name of the place was Mesam-

---

[78] The Sitakos has been identified with the Kara Agach,
Mand, Mund or Kakee river, which has a course of 300
miles. Its source is near Kodiyan, which lies N. W. of
Shiraz. At a part of its course it is called the Kewar
River. The meaning of its name is *black wood*. In Pliny
it appears as the Sitioganus. *Sitakon* was probably the
name as Nearkhos heard it pronounced, as it frequently
happens that when a Greek writer comes upon a name
like an oblique case in Greek, he invents a nominative for it.
With regard to the form of the name in Pliny, 'g' is but a
phonetic change instead of 'k'. The 'i' is probably an
error in transcription for 't'. The Sitakos is probably the
Brisoana of Ptolemy, which can have no connexion with the
later-mentioned Brizana of our author. See *Report on the
Persian Gulf* by Colonel Ross, lately issued. Pliny states
that from the mouth of the Sitiogus an ascent could be
made to Pasargada, in seven days; but this is manifestly
an error.

[79] The changes which have taken place along the coast
have been so considerable that it is difficult to explain this
part of the narrative consistently with the now existing
state of things.

bria.[80] Weighing from Mesambria and running
a course of about 200 stadia, they reach Taôkê
on the river Granis, and there anchor. Inland
from this lay a royal city of the Persians, distant from the mouths of the river about 200
stadia.[81] We learn from Nearkhos that on their
way to Taôkê a stranded whale had been observed
from the fleet, and that a party of the men having
rowed alongside of it, measured it and brought
back word that it had a length of 50 cubits. Its
skin, they added, was clad with scales to a depth
of about a cubit, and thickly clustered over with
parasitic mussels, barnacles, and seaweed. The
monster, it was also noticed, was attended by a
great number of dolphins, larger than are ever
seen in the Mediterranean. Weighing from Taôkê
they proceeded to Rhogonis, a winter torrent.
where they anchored in a safe harbour.[82] The
course thither was one of 200 stadia. Weighing

[80] The peninsula, which is 10 miles in length and 3 in
breadth, lies so low that at times of high tide it is all but
submerged. The modern A b u-S h a h r or B u s h i r is
situated on it.

[81] Nearkhos, it is probable, put into the mouth of the
river now called by some the K i s h t, by others the Bosha-
vir. A town exists in the neighbourhood called G r a or
G r a n, which may have received its name from the Granis.
The royal city (or rather palace), 200 stadia distant from this
river, is mentioned by Strabo, xv. 3, 3, as being situate on
the coast. Ptolemy does not mention the Granis. He
makes Taôkê to be an inland town, and calls all the district
in this part Taôkênê. Taôkê may be the Touag mentioned
by Idrisi, which is now represented by Konar Takhta near
the Kisht.

[82] R h o g o n i s.—It is written Rhogomanis by Ammianus
Marcellinus, who mentions it as one of the four largest
rivers in Persia, the other three being the Vatrachitis,
Brisoana, and Bagrada. It is the river at the mouth of
which is Bender-Righ or Regh, which is considered now as
in the days of Nearkhos to be a day's sail from Bushire.

thence, and running 400 stadia, they arrived at
another winter torrent, called Brizana, where they
land and form an encampment.  They had here
difficulty in anchoring because of shoals and
breakers and reefs that showed their heads above
the sea.  They could therefore enter the roads
only when the tide was full; when it receded, the
ships were left high and dry.[83]  They weighed
with the next flood tide, and came to anchor at the
mouth of a river called the Arosis, the greatest,
according to Nearkhos, of all the rivers that in
the course of his voyage fell into the outer ocean.[84]

XL.  The Arosis marks the limit of the pos-
sessions of the Persians, and divides them from
the Susians.  Above the Susians occurs an independent race called the Uxians, whom I have
described in my other work (*Anab.* VII. 15, 3) as
robbers.  The length of the Persian coast is 4,400
stadia.  Persis, according to general report, has
three different climates,[85] for that part of it which
lies along the Erythraean sea, is sandy and barren

---

[83] "The measures here are neglected in the Journal,
for we have only 800 stadia specified from Mesambria to
Brizana, and none from Brizana to the Arosis; but 800
stadia are short of 50 miles, while the real distance from
Mesambria (Bushir) to the Arosis with the winding of the
coast is above 140.  In these two points we cannot be
mistaken, and therefore, besides the omission of the interval
between Brizana and the Arosis, there must be some defect
in the Journal for which it is impossible now to account."
—Vincent. I. p. 405.

[84] Another form of the name of this river is the Aroätis.
It answers to the Zarotis of Pliny, who states that the
navigation at its mouth was difficult, except to those well
acquainted with it.  It formed the boundary between
Persis and Susiana.  The form Oroâtis corresponds to the
Zend word *aurwat* ' swift.'  It is now called the Tâb.

[85] On this point compare Strabo, bk. xv. 3, 1.

from the violence of the heat, while the part which succeeds enjoys a delightful temperature, for there the mountains stretch towards the pole and the North wind, and the region is clothed with verdure and has well-watered meadows, and bears in profusion the vine and every fruit else but the olive, while it blooms with gardens and pleasure parks of all kinds, and is permeated with crystal streams and abounds with lakes, and lake and stream alike are the haunts of every variety of water-fowl, and it is also a good country for horses and other yoke cattle, being rich in pasture, while it is throughout well-wooded and well-stocked with game. The part, however, which lies still further to the North is said to be bleak and cold, and covered with snow, so that, as Near-khos tells us, certain ambassadors from the Euxine Sea, after a very brief journey, met Alexander marching forward to Persis, whereat Alexander being greatly surprised, they explained to him how very inconsiderable the distance was.[86] I have already stated that the immediate neighbours to the Susians are the Uxians, just as the Mardians, a race of robbers, are next neighbours to the Persians, and the Kossaeans to the Medes. All these tribes Alexander subdued, attacking them in the winter time when their country was, as they imagined, inaccessible. He then founded cities to reclaim them from their wandering life, and encouraged them to till their lands and devote themselves to agriculture. At the

---

[86] It has been conjectured that the text here is imperfect. Schmieder opines that the story about the ambassadors is a fiction.

*b* 2

same time he appointed magistrates armed with
the terrors of the law to prevent them having
recourse to violence in the settlement of their
quarrels. On weighing from the Arosis the expedition coasted the shores of the Susians. The
remainder of the voyage, Nearkhos says, he cannot
describe with the same precision; he can but give
the names of the stations and the length of the
courses, for the coast was full of shoals and beset
with breakers which spread far out to sea, and
made the approach to land dangerous. The navigation thereafter was of course almost entirely
restricted to the open sea. In mentioning their
departure from the mouth of the river where they
had encamped on the borders of Persis, he states
that they took there on board a five days' supply
of water, as the pilots had brought to their notice
that none could be procured on the way.

XLI. A course of 500 stadia having been
accomplished, their next anchorage was in an
estuary, which swarmed with fish, called Kataderbis, at the entrance of which lay an island
called Margastana.[87] They weighed at daybreak,
the ships sailing out in single file through shoals.
The direction of the shoal was indicated by stakes
fixed both on the right and the left side, just as posts
are erected as signals of danger in the passage
between the island of Leukadia and Akarnania to
prevent vessels grounding on the shoals. The
shoals of Leukadia, however, are of firm sand, and

---

[87] The bay of Kataderbis is that which receives the
streams of the M e n s u r e h and D o r a k; at its entrance
lie two islands, Bunah and Ḍeri, one of which is the Margastana of Arrian.

it is thus easy to float off vessels should they happen
to strand, but in this passage there is a deep mud
on both sides of such tenacity that if vessels once
touched the bottom, they could not by any ap-
pliances be got off; for, if they thrust poles into
the mud to propel the vessels, these found no
resistance or support, and the people who got over-
board to ease them off into navigable water found
no footing, but sunk in the mud higher than the
waist. The fleet proceeded 600 stadia, having
such difficulties of navigation to contend with,
and then came to an anchor, each crew remaining
in their own vessel, and taking their repast on
board. From this anchorage they weighed in the
night, sailing on in deep water till about the close
of the ensuing day, when, after completing a course
of 900 stadia, they dropped anchor at the mouth of
the Euphrates near a town in Babylonia called
Diridôtis—the emporium of the sea-borne trade in
frankincense and all the other fragrant productions of Arabia.[33] The distance from the mouth
of the Euphrates up stream to Babylon is, according to Nearkhos, 3,300 stadia.

XLII. Here intelligence having been received
that Alexander was marching towards Sousa, they
retraced their course from Diridôtis so as to join

---

[33] Diridôtis is called by other writers Terêdon, and
is said to have been founded by Nabukhodonosor. Mannert
places it on the island now called Bubian; Colonel
Chesney, however, fixes its position at Jebel Sanâm,
a gigantic mound near the Pallacopas branch of the
Euphrates, considerably to the north of the embouchure of
the present Euphrates. Nearkhos had evidently passed
unawares the stream of the Tigris and sailed too far westward. Hence he had to retrace his course, as mentioned
in the next chapter.

him by sailing up the Pasitigris. They had now
Sousis on their left hand, and were coasting the
shores of a lake into which the Tigris empties
itself, a river, which flowing from Armenia past
Nineveh, a city once of yore great and flourishing, encloses between itself and the Euphrates the
tract of country which from its position between
the two rivers is called Mesopotamia. It is a distance of 600 stadia from the entrance into the lake
up to the river's mouth at Aginis, a village in
the province of Sousis, distant from the city of
Sousa 500 stadia. The length of the voyage along
the coast of the Sousians to the mouth of the
Pasitigris was 2,000 stadia.[89] Weighing from the

---

[89] This is the Eulæus, now called the K a r û n, one arm
of which united with the Tigris, while the other fell into
the sea by an independent mouth. It is the U l a i of the
prophet Daniel. *Pas* is said to be an old Persian word,
meaning *small*. By some writers the name P a s i t i g r i s
was applied to the united stream of the Tigris and
Euphrates, now called the S h a t-e l-A r a b. The courses of
the rivers and the conformation of the country in the parts
here have all undergone great changes, and hence the
identification of localities is a matter of difficulty and
uncertainty. The following extract from Strabo will
illustrate this part of the narrative:—
Polycletus says that the C h o a s p e s, and the E u l æ u s,
and the T i g r i s also enter a lake, and thence discharge
themselves into the sea; that on the side of the lake is a
mart, as the rivers do not receive the merchandize from the
sea, nor convey it down to the sea, on account of dams in
the river, purposely constructed; and that the goods are
transported by land, a distance of 800 stadia, to Susis:
according to others, the rivers which flow through Susis
discharge themselves by the intermediate canals of the
Euphrates into the single stream of the Tigris, which on
this account has at its mouth the name of Pasitigris.
According to Nearchus, the sea-coast of Susis is swampy,
and terminates at the river Euphrates; at its mouth is a
village which receives the merchandize from Arabia, for the
coast of Arabia approaches close to the mouths of the
Euphrates and the Pasitigris; the whole intermediate space

mouth of this river they sailed up its stream
through a fertile and populous country, and
having proceeded 150 stadia dropped anchor,
awaiting the return of certain messengers whom
Nearkhos had sent off to ascertain where the
king was. Nearkhos then presented sacrifices to
the gods their preservers, and celebrated games, and
full of gladness were the hearts of all that had taken
part in the expedition. The messengers having
returned with tidings that Alexander was approaching, the fleet resumed its voyage up the river,
and anchored near the bridge by which Alexander
intended to lead his army to Sousa. In that same
place the troops were reunited, when sacrifices
were offered by Alexander for the preservation of
his ships and his men, and games were celebrated.
Nearkhos, whenever he was seen among the
troops, was decorated by them with garlands and
pelted with flowers. There also both Nearkhos
and Leonnatos were crowned by Alexander with
golden diadems—Nearkhos for the safety of the
expedition by sea, and Leonnatos for the victory
which he had gained over the O r e i t a i and the
neighbouring barbarians. It was thus that the
expedition which had begun its voyage from the
mouths of the Indus was brought in safety to
Alexander.

---

occupied by a lake which receives the Tigris. On sailing
up the Pasitigris 150 stadia is a bridge of rafts leading to
Susa from Persis, and is distant from Susa 60 (600 ?) stadia ;
the Pasitigris is distant from the Oroätis about 2,000 stadia ;
the ascent through the lake to the mouth of the Tigris is
600 stadia ; near the mouth stands the Susian village
Aginis, distant from Susa 500 stadia ; the journey by water
from the mouth of the Euphrates up to Babylon, through
a well-inhabited tract of country, is a distance of more
than 3,000 stadia."—Book xv. 3, *Bohn's trans.*

XLIII. Now[90] the parts which lie to the right
of the E r y t h r æ n[91] S e a beyond the realms of
Babylonia belong principally to A r a b i a, which
extends in one direction as far as the sea that washes
the shores of P h œ n i k i a and S y r i a n P a l e s-
t i n e, while towards sunset it borders on the Egyptians in the direction of the M e d i t e r r a n e a n
S e a. Egypt is penetrated by a gulf which extends up from the great ocean, and as this ocean is
connected with the E r y t h r æ a n S e a, this fact
proves that a voyage could be made all the way
from B a b y l o n to E g y p t by means of this
gulf. But, owing to the heat and utter sterility
of the coast, no one has ever made this voyage,
except, it may be, some chance navigator. For
the troops belonging to the army of K a m b y s ê s,
which escaped from E g y p t, and reached S o u s a
in safety, and the troops sent by P t o l e m y, the
son of Lagos, to S e l e u k o s N i k a t ô r to
B a b y l o n, traversed the Arabian isthmus in
eight days altogether.[92] It was a waterless and
sterile region, and they had to cross it mounted
on swift camels carrying water, travelling only by
night, the heat by day being so fierce that they
could not expose themselves in the open air. So
far are the parts lying beyond this region, which
we have spoken of as an isthmus extending from
the A r a b i a n G u l f to the E r y t h r æ a n S e a

---

[90] The 3rd part of the *Indika*, the purport of which is
to prove that the southern parts of the world are uninhabit-
able, begins with this chapter.

[91] Here and subsequently meaning the Persian Gulf.

[92] It is not known when or wherefore Ptolemy sent
troops on this expedition.

from being inhabited, that even the parts which run up further to the north are a desert of sand. Moreover, men setting forth from the A r a b i a n G u l f in E g y p t, after having sailed round the greater part of A r a b i a to reach the sea which washes the shores of P e r s i s and S o u s a, have returned, after sailing as far along the coast of Arabia as the water they had on board lasted them, and no further. The exploring party again which A l e x a n d e r sent from B a b y l o n with instructions to sail as far as they could along the right-hand coast of the E r y t h r æ a n S e a, with a view to examine the regions lying in that direction, discovered some islands lying in their route, and touched also at certain points of the mainland of A r a b i a. But as for that cape which Nearkhos states to have been seen by the expedition projecting into the sea right opposite to K a r m a n i a, there is no one who has been able to double it and gain the other side. But if the place could possibly be passed, either by sea or by land, it seems to me that Alexander, being so inquisitive and enterprising, would have proved that it could be passed in both these ways. But again H a n n o the L i b y a n, setting out from C a r t h a g e, sailed out into the ocean beyond the Pillars of H e r c u l e s, having L i b y a on his left hand, and the time until his course was shaped towards the rising sun was five-and-thirty days; but when he steered southward he encountered many difficulties from the want of water, from the scorching heat, and from streams of fire that fell into the sea. K y r ê n ê, no doubt, which is situated in a some-

what barren part of L i b y a, is verdant, possessed
of a genial climate, and well watered, has groves
and meadows, and yields abundantly all kinds of
useful animals and vegetable products.   But this
is only the case up to the limits of the area within
which the fennel-plant can grow, while beyond
this area the interior of Kyrênê is but a desert of
sand.

So ends my narrative relating to A l e x a n d e r,
the son of Philip the Makedonian.

# INDEX.

## CHIEFLY GEOGRAPHICAL.

*Abbreviations.*—B. Bay, C. Cape, G. Gulf, Is. Island or Islands, M. Mountain, R. River.

Common names are printed in Italics. Many proper names which in the usual orthography begin with C, will be found under K.

c 2

# ANCIENT INDIA AS DESCRIBED
# BY
# KTESIAS THE KNIDIAN

# ANCIENT INDIA

AS DESCRIBED BY

# KTÊSIAS THE KNIDIAN;

BEING

A TRANSLATION OF THE ABRIDGEMENT OF HIS "INDIKA"
BY PHÔTIOS, AND OF THE FRAGMENTS OF THAT
WORK PRESERVED IN OTHER WRITERS.

BY

## J. W. McCRINDLE, M.A., M.R.A.S.,

LATE PRINCIPAL OF THE GOVERNMENT COLLEGE, PATNA,
LATE FELLOW OF THE UNIVERSITY OF CALCUTTA,
MEMBER OF THE GENERAL COUNCIL OF THE UNIVERSITY
OF EDINBURGH.

WITH INTRODUCTION, NOTES, AND INDEX.

*Reprinted (with additions)*
*from the " Indian Antiquary," 1881.*

# PREFACE.

THIS little book forms the third volume
of the series of Annotated Translations of
those works of the Classical writers which
relate to Ancient India. The volumes already
issued contain Translations of the Fragments
of Megasthenês—of the Indika of Arrian—
and of the Periplûs of the Erythræan Sea;
and in those which are to follow will be
rendered the Geography of India as given
by Strabo and by Ptolemy, and the accounts
of the Makedonian Invasion as given by
Arrian and by Curtius—and these works
will complete the series.

*Upper Norwood : December*, 1881.

# CONTENTS.

# ANCIENT INDIA,

## AS DESCRIBED BY KTÊSIAS.

---

### INTRODUCTION.

#### The Life and Writings of Ktêsias.

To Ktêsias belongs the distinction of having
been the first writer who gave to the Greeks a
special treatise on India—a region concerning
which they had, before his time, no further knowledge than what was supplied by the few and
meagre notices of it which had appeared in the
*Geography* of Hêkataios of Milêtos, and in
the History of Herodotos. This Ktêsias was
a native of Knidos, an important Lakedemo-
nian colony situate on the sea coast of Karia, and
was the son of Ktêsiokhos (or Ktêsiarkhos).[1]
His family, as we learn from Galen,[2] was a branch
of the Asklêpiadai, a caste of priests settled
principally in Kôs and Knidos, with whom medicine
was an hereditary profession. He was contemporary with Hippokratês, who like himself
was an Asklêpiad; but he was very much younger
than his illustrious kinsman, though by how
many years we know not, as the date of his birth
cannot be ascertained. We may conclude, however,

---

[1] V. Tzetz. *Chil.* I. 1; Suidas, *Eudoc.* p. 268; Plutarch. *Artaxerxes*; Lucian. *Ver. Hist.* I. 3.
[2] Tom. V. p. 652, l. 51 ed. Basil.

1

that he must have risen to eminence by the
practice of his art before the year 416 B.C., for
about that time he repaired to Persia, probably on
the invitation of the king who appointed him
physician to the royal court. Here he remained
for 17 years, of which the first eleven were spent
under D a r i u s II, and the remaining six under
his successor A r t a x e r x ê s M n ê m ô n.[3] He
accompanied the latter when he took the field
against Cyrus, and, as we learn from Xenophon,
cured the wound which his royal master received
in the battle of Kunaxa.[4] Soon after this he
appears to have left Persia and returned to his
own country. This was in the year 398, after
which we know nothing of his career.

K t ê s i a s diversified his professional with literary pursuits and was the author of several works,
of which the most important was his history of
Persia. This was written in 23 books, of which
the first six contained the history of the Assyrian
monarchy down to the foundation of the kingdom
of Persia. The next seven contained the history of
Persia down to the end of the reign of Xerxes,
and the remaining ten carried the history down
to the time when the author left the Persian
Court. This great work, whatever may have been
its other merits, possessed this especial value, that
the facts which it recorded were derived principally

[3] Diodôros (I., 1) followed by Tzetzes (Chil. I. i, 82),
writes that Ktêsias fighting with his countrymen on behalf of Cyrus was taken prisoner at the battle of
Kunaxa, and was thereafter on account of his skill in
medicine taken into the king's service, in which he
remained for 17 years. A comparison however of well
ascertained facts discredits this statement.
[4] V. Anab. I. viii, 27.

from the Persian state-records⁵ which Ktêsias was
permitted by the king to consult. His statements, as might be expected, are frequently at
variance with those of Herodotos whose sources of
information were different. He is also in a few
instances at variance with his contemporary Xenophon. The work unfortunately no longer exists,
but we possess a brief abstract of its contents
made by P h ô t i o s, and some fragments which
have been preserved by Diodôros and other writers.

Besides the History and the Treatise on India,
Ktêsias appears to have composed several minor
works. These consisted, so far as is known, of
treatise on the Revenues of the Persian Empire, two treatises of a geographical nature—one
being on Mountains, and the other on Rivers, and
some books of voyages entitled *Periploi*.

The *Indika* of Ktêsias, like his other works,
has been lost, but, like his great work on the
History of Persia, it has been abridged by P h ô-
t i o s, while several fragments of it have been preserved in the pages of other writers, as for instance
Ælian. It was comprised in a single book, and embodied the information which Ktêsias had gathered
about I n d i a, partly from the reports of Persian
officials who had visited that country on the king's
service, and partly also perhaps from the reports
of Indians themselves, who in those days were
occasionally to be seen at the Persian Court,
whither they resorted, either as merchants, or as
envoys bringing presents and tribute from the

⁵ ἐκ τῶν βασιλικῶν διφθερῶν ἐν αἷς οἱ Πέρσαι τὰς
παλαιὰς πράξεις κατά τινα νόμον εἶχον συντεταγμέας.
Diod. II. 32.

princes of Northern India, which was then subject to Persian rule. Ktêsias unfortunately was
not only a great lover of the marvellous, but also
singularly deficient, for one of his profession, in
critical acumen. He took, therefore, no pains to
sift the accounts which were communicated to
him, and the book which he gave to the world,
instead of being, what a careful enquirer with his
advantages might have made it—a valuable reper-
tory of facts concerning India and its people,
seemed to be little else than a tissue of fables and
of absurd perversions or exaggerations of the
truth, and was condemned as such, not only by
the consentient voice of antiquity, but also by the
generality of the learned in modern times. The
work was nevertheless popular, and in spite of its
infirm credit, was frequently cited by subsequent
writers. Its 'tales of wonder' fascinated the
credulous, while its style, which was remarkable
alike for its ease, sweetness, and perspicuity,
recommended it to readers of every stamp.[6] It
was the only systematic account of India the
Greeks possessed till the time of the Makedonian
invasion.

We must notice in conclusion the fact, that, as
the knowledge of India, and especially of Indian
antiquity, has increased, scholars have been led
to question the justice of the traditional verdict
which condemns K t ê s i a s as a writer of unscru-

---

[6] Ktêsias, though a Dorian, used many Ionic forms and
modes of expression, and these more in the *Indika* than in
the *Persika*. His style is praised for the qualities mentioned in the text by Phôtios, Dion. Halicarn, and Demet.
Phaler, who does not hesitate to speak of him as a poet,
the very demiurge of perspicuity (ἐναργείας δημιουργός),

pulous mendacity. They do not indeed wholly exculpate him, but they have shown that many of his statements, which were once taken to be pure falsehoods, have either certain elements of truth underlying them, or that they originated in misconceptions which were perhaps less wilful than unavoidable. The fabulous races for instance which he has described are found, so far from being fictions of his own invention, to have their exact analogues in monstrous races which are mentioned in the two great national epics and other Brahmanical writings, and which, though therein depicted with every attribute of deformity, were nevertheless, not purely fictitious, but misrepresentations of such aboriginal tribes as offered a stout resistance to their Aryan invaders while still engaged in the task of conquering India.

These moderate views, which have been advocated by such authorities as Heeren, Bähr, C. Müller, Lassen, and others, will no doubt come eventually to be very generally accepted.

### Notice of Phôtios.

Phôtios, to whom we are indebted for the abridgments of Ktêsias, was the Patriarch of Constantinople, an office to which he was elected, though previously a layman, in the year A. D. 858. Soon after the accession of Leo VI. as emperor (886) he was accused of having conspired against his life, and was in consequence banished to a monastery in Armenia, where he ended his days. He was not only a scholar of wonderful erudition and sound judgment, but was the author of many

works, the most important of which was that entitled *Myriobiblion* or *Bibliothêkê*—which was a
review on an extensive scale of ancient Greek
literature. It contained abstracts of the contents of
280 volumes, many of which are now known only
from the account which he has given of them.
His abridgment of the Persian history of our
author is much more concise than that of his
*Indika.* The latter is however a careless and unsatisfactory performance, for the passages summar-
ized are chiefly those for which Ktêsias was
stigmatized as a fabulist and a liar.

As Lassen has devoted one of the leading
sections[7] of his great work on Indian Antiquity
to an examination of the reports which are yet
extant of K t ê s i a s upon India, and as his review
is all but exhaustive, and reflects nearly all the
light that learned research has yet been able to
throw upon the subject, I have for this reason, as
well as with a view to obviate the need which
would otherwise occur, of having constant recourse to long foot-notes, thought it advisable to
append to the translation of the Greek text a
translation of this review. I have appended also
a translation of some passages from Indiko-
pleustês, which will serve to illustrate the descriptions given by Ktêsias of certain Indian animals
and plants.

---

[7] In vol. II., pp. 641 ff. 2nd ed. 1874.

# THE INDIKA OF KTÊSIAS.

## FRAGMENT I.

Ecloga in Photii, *Bibl.* LXXII, p. 144 seqq.

1. Another work was read—the *Indika* of Ktêsias, contained in a single book wherein the author has made more frequent use of Ionic forms. He reports of the river I n d u s that, where narrowest, it has a breadth of forty stadia, and where widest of two hundred;[1] and of the Indians themselves that they almost outnumber all other men taken together.[2] He mentions the *skôlex*,[3] a kind of worm bred in the river, this being indeed the only living creature which is found in it. He states that there are no men who live beyond the Indians,[4] and that no rain falls in India[5] but that the country is watered by its river.

2. He notices the *pantarba*,[6] a kind of

---

[1] This differs from what Arrian states on the authority of Ktêsias, (see Frag. ii.) Probably Arrian has quoted the sentence more correctly than Photios. And 100 stadia is far enough from the truth. With Ktêsias Conf. Philostratus, *Vit. Apoll.* II, 18: τόν μὲν δὴ Ἰνδὸν ὧδε ἐπεραιώθησαν, σταδίους μάλιστα τεσσαράκοντα τὸ γὰρ πλώιμον αὐτοῦ τοσοῦτον. See Mannert, *Geogr. d. Gr. u. Rom.* Bd. V, i, p. 74.

[2] Conf. Herodot. III, 94; Strabo II, v. 32.

[3] Conf. § 27, and Frag. xxvi.

[4] Conf. Herodot. III, 98, 105; Strabo II, v, 1, 32.

[5] But conf. Strabo XV, i, 1, 13, 17, 18; Arrian, *Indika*, VI, 4; Philost. *Vit. Apoll.* II, 19; Diodor. II, 36.

[6] Count Weltheim (*Sammlung von Aufsätzen*, &c. Bd. II, p. 168ff.) regards this as the *Hydrophanes* or the changing stone, sun agate, a kind of opal, remarkable for the variety of colours it displays when thrown into water.

8

sealstone, and relates that when sealstones and
other costly gems to the number of 477[7] which
belonged to the Baktrian merchant, had been
flung into the river, this *pantarba* drew them
up to itself, all adhering together.

3. He notices also the elephants[8] that demolish walls; the kind of small apes[9] that have
tails four cubits long; the cocks that are of
extraordinary size;[10] the kind of bird called the
parrot[11] and which he thus describes: it has a
tongue and voice like the human, is of the size
of a hawk, has a red bill, is adorned with a
beard of a black colour, while the neck is red
like cinnabar, it talks like a man in Indian, but
if taught Greek can talk in Greek also.

4. He notices the fountain[12] which is filled
every year with liquid gold, out of which are

---

[7] So Müller's text, the common reading is 77.
[8] With this compare Frag. iv. below.
[9] This is reconcilable with the accounts of others if for
μικρῶν we read μακρῶν. For Megasthenês also speaks of
Indian apes not smaller than large dogs and which have
tails of *five* cubits length which answer to the *Mandi* ape
or *Simia Faunus*, with the hair on the forehead projecting
over the eyes, and the beard white, the body being dark.
Vid. Æliani, *Nat. An.* XVII, 39; conf. XVI, 10, and Strabo
XV, i, 37:—" The monkeys are larger than the largest dogs
. . . .their tails are more than two cubits in length."
[10] Conf. Frag. v.c.
[11] Βιττακός: Reland *De Ophir*, p. 184, compares this
with the Persian تدك *tedek*. In Arrian, *Ind.* XV, 8
and Ælian, *Nat. An.* XVI, 2 and 15, the bird is called
σιττακος. Ælian however elsewhere calls it ψιττακός
and so also Diodôros and Pausanias. A feminine form
ψιττακή occurs in Arist. *H. An.* VIII, 12. The form in
Pliny is *Psittacus*.
[12] Conf. Philostrat. *Vit. Apoll.* III, 45.

annually drawn a hundred earthen pitchers
filled with the metal. The pitchers must be
earthen since the gold when drawn becomes
solid, and to get it out the containing vessel
must needs be broken in pieces. The fountain
is of a square shape, eleven cubits in circumference, and a fathom in depth. Each pitcherful
of gold weighs a talent. He notices[13] also the
iron found at the bottom of this fountain, adding
that he had in his own possession two swords
made from this iron, one given to him by the king
of Persia,[14] and the other by P a r y s a t i s, the
mother of that same king. This iron, he says,
if fixed in the earth, averts clouds and hail and
thunderstorms, and he avers that he had himself
twice seen the iron do this, the king on both
occasions performing the experiment.[15]

5. We learn further that the dogs of India[16]
are of very great size, so that they fight even
with the lion;[17] that there are certain high
mountains having mines which yield the sar-

---

[13] The Munich MS. 287, makes this a separate fountain :
ἔστι δὲ ἕτερα κρίνη (read κρήνη) ἥτις ἐξάγει σίδηρον.
Conf. Philost. *Vit. Apoll.* III, 45.

[14] Artaxerxes Mnêmôn.

[15] Baehr thinks that Ktêsias here refers to the magnet,
the properties of which were not at that time so well
known as now.

[16] Conf. Ælian. *Nat. An.* IV, 19; VIII, 1, 9; and
Frag. vi, below.

[17] Compare what Ælian (Frag. vi.) says of the dogs of
the Kynamolgoi ; compare also Strabo, quoting Megasthenes
XV, p. 1029, and the account in Curtius (*de Reb. Alex.*
IX, i, 31) of an Indian dog attacking a lion.

dine-stone, and onyxes, and other seal stones ;[18] that the heat is excessive, and that the sun appears in India to be ten times larger[19] than in other countries; and that many of the inhabitants are suffocated to death by the heat. Of the sea in India, he says, that it is not less than the sea in Hellas ; its surface however for four finger-breadths downward is hot, so that fish cannot live that go near the heated surface, but must confine themselves always to the depths below.

6. He states that the river I n d u s flows through the level country, and through between the mountains, and that what is called the Indian reed[20] grows along its course, this being so thick that two men could scarcely encompass its stem with their arms, and of a height to equal the mast of a merchant ship of the heaviest burden.[21] Some are of a greater size even than this, though some are of less, as might be expected when the mountain it grows on is of vast range. The reeds are distinguished by sex, some being male,

[18] These mountains have been variously identified with Taurus, with Imaus, with Paropamisus, and with the mountains of Great and Little Bukharia, which stretch through Tibet, and Kaśmîr, but Count Weltheim takes them to be the Bala Ghâts near Bharoch. The Periplûs states that onyxes and other precious stones were found in Ozênê (now Ujjain) and thence sent to Barygaza (Bharûch) for export. The well known Khambay stones come from a neighbouring district.

[19] Strabo III, p. 202, contests this.

[20] Conf. Frag. vii, below.

[21] Lit. of 10,000 talents : or μυριαμφόρου (Lobeck, ad. Phyrn. p. 662) 60,000 amphoræ. Conf. Frag. vii.

others female. The male reed has no pith, and is exceedingly strong, but the female has a pith.[22]

7. He describes an animal called the *martikhora*,[23] found in India. Its face is like a man's — it is about as big as a lion, and in colour red like cinnabar. It has three rows of teeth—ears like the human—eyes of a pale-blue like the human and a tail like that of the land scorpion, armed with a sting and more than a cubit long.[24] It has be,ides stings on each side of its tail, and, like the scorpion, is armed with an additional sting on the crown of its head, wherewith it stings any one who goes near it, the wound in all cases proving mortal. If attacked from a distance it defends itself both in front and in rear—in front with its tail, by up-lifting it and darting out the stings, like shafts shot from a bow, and in rear by straightening it out. It can strike to the distance of a hundred feet, and no creature can survive the wound it inflicts save only the elephant. The stings are about a foot in length, and not thicker than the finest thread. The

---

[22] Cf. Theophrastos, *Plant. Histor.* IV, ii, where he states that the male reed is solid, and the female, hollow. Cf. also Pliny, *Hist. Nat.* XVI, 36. Sprengel identifies this reed of Ktêsias with the *Bambusa* and *Calamus Rotang* of Linnæus. The same reed is mentioned by Herodotus (III, 98).

[23] See Frags. viii—xi, below.

[24] μείζω ὑπάρχουσαν πήχεος. Baehr rightly amends the reading here to μείζον ὑπάρχον ἂν, which refers the measure to the sting instead of to the tail.

name *martikhora*[25] means in Greek ἀνθρωποφάγος (*i.e.* man-eater), and it is so called because it carries off men and devours them, though it no doubt preys upon other animals as well. In fighting it uses not only its stings but also its claws. Fresh stings grow up to replace those shot away in fighting. These animals are numerous in India, and are killed by the natives who hunt them with elephants, from the backs of which they attack them with darts.

8. He describes the Indians as extremely just, and gives an account of their manners and customs. He mentions the sacred spot in the midst of an uninhabited region which they venerate in the name of the Sun and the Moon.[26] It takes one a fifteen days' journey to reach this place from Mount Sardous. Here for the space of five and thirty days the Sun every year cools down to allow his worshippers to celebrate his rites, and return home unscorched by his

---

[25] Tychsen says—This is the Persian مرد خور from *mard*, a man and *khorden* to eat : *khor*, the eater, is an abbreviated form of the participle *khordeh*, which is still on use . . . if the final be viewed as a component part of the Persian word, we have only to substitute the participial form مرد خورا *mardikhorâ*, (abbreviated from *mardikhorân*) as Reland has already done (p. 223), and we obtain precisely the same signification. Conf. Frags. viii—xi ; also Philostratus, *Vit. Apoll.* IV, 45.

[26] Weltheim, rejecting the opinion of some that this uninhabited region was the desert of Cobi, takes it to be rather the great desert east of the Indus where the worship of the sun flourished in early times. This desert also was in reality about a fifteen days' journey distant from the mountains which produced the onyx and sardine stones. Lassen has however assigned the locality to the Vindhyas.

burning rays.[27] He observes that in India
there is neither thunder nor lightning nor rain,
but that storms of wind and violent hurricanes
which sweep everything before them, are of
frequent occurrence. The morning sun produces coolness for one half of the day, but an
excessive heat during the other half, and this
holds good for most parts of India.[28]

9. It is not, however, by exposure to the
sun that the people are swarthy,[29] but by
nature, for among the Indians there are both
men and women who are as fair as any in
the world, though such are no doubt in a
minority. He adds that he had himself seen
two Indian women and five men of such a fair
complexion.[30]

10. Wishing to assure us of the truth of his
statement that the sun makes the temperature
cool for five and thirty days, he mentions several
facts that are equally strange—that the streams
of fire which issue from Ætna[31] leave unscathed
amidst the surrounding havoc those lands which

---

[27] ἵνα μὴ ἄφλεκτοι αὐτὴν τελέσωσι, lit. *that they may
not celebrate his rites unscorched.* As the writer must
have meant the opposite of this, φλεκτοὶ must be read
instead of ἄφλεκτοι.

[28] Conf. Herodot. III, 104.

[29] Conf. Herodot. III, 101 ; Arrian. *Exp. Alex.* V, 4, 8;
but on the contrary, Aristot. *Hist. Anim.* III, 22 ; *Gener.
Anim.* II, 2 ; Strabo, XV, i, 13, 24.

[30] Possibly from Kâśmir.—J. B.

[31] Conf. Pausan. X, 28, 2 ; Strabo, VI, 2 ; Valer. Max.
V, 4.

belong to just men[32]—that in Zakynthos there
are fountains with fish whence pitch is taken
out[33]—that in Naxos is a fountain which at times
discharges a wine of great sweetness,[34] and that
the water of the river Phasis likewise, if kept in
a vessel for a night and a day, changes into a
wine which is also of great sweetness[35]—that
near Phasêlis in Lykia there is a perpetual
volcano,[36] always flaming on the summit of the
rock both by night and by day, and this is not
quenched by water, which rather augments the

---

[32] The reference is to *the field of the pious*, εὐσεβῶν
χώρα, near Catana, the scene of the story regarding the two
brothers Amphinomos and Anapos, who saved their parents
during an eruption by carrying them off on their shoulders.
Vid. Pausan. X. xxviii, 2; Strabo, VI, 2; and Valer.
Max. V, 4.

[33] Herodotus (IV. 195) states that he had himself seen
this bituminous fountain. It is mentioned by Antigonos;
*Hist. Mirabil.* 169; by Dioskor. I, 99; by Vitruv. VIII, 3;
and Pliny, XXXV, 15. Their accounts have been verified
by modern travellers.

[34] This fountain is mentioned by Stephan. Byz. *s. v.*
Naxos, and a similar one by Pliny (*Hist. Nat.* II, ciii,
106)—in the island of Andros; Cf. idem. XXXI, ii; and
also Philostrat. *Icon.* I, 25.

[35] The waters of the Phasis, according to modern accounts, are lead-coloured, possessed of a healing virtue and
held as sacred, perhaps because they were thought by the
ancients to have sprung from the gates of the morning
sun, and therefore to have formed the dividing line between day and night. Arrian in the *Peripl. Pont. Eux.*, no
doubt with an eye to this passage of Ktêsias, says that
the water of the Phasis if kept in certain vessels acquired
a pleasant vinous taste. V. Ritter, *Erdk.* II. pp. 817 and 915.
Conf. Pliny (*H. N.* II. ciii, 106) who says that the water of
the Lyncestis in Epirus is somewhat acid, and intoxicates
like wine those who drink it.

[36] See Frag. xii, below.

blaze, but by casting rubbish into it[37]—and in like manner, the volcanoes of Ætna and of Prusa keep always burning.[38]

11. He writes that in the middle of India are found the swarthy men called P y g m i e s,[39] who speak the same language as the other Indians. They are very diminutive, the tallest of them being but two cubits in height, while the majority are only one and a half. They let their hair grow very long—down to their knees, and even lower. They have the largest beards anywhere to be seen, and when these have grown sufficiently long and copious, they no longer wear clothing, but, instead, let the hair of the head fall down their backs far below the knee, while in front are their beards trailing down to their very feet. When their hair has thus thickly enveloped their whole body, they bind it round them with a zone, and so make it serve for a garment. Their privates are thick,

[37] Conf. Frag. xii, A. and B. Beaufort, an English traveller, confirms this statement. He reports that while travelling in the regions nearest the country of the Phaselitae he came upon a place where there was to be seen an ever-burning flame which like the fire of a volcano was inextinguishable. V. Beaufort's *Caramania*, p. 44.

[38] There is a Prusa in Bithynia and another in Mysia, each near a mountain. Strabo, (XII, p. 844 seqq.) mentions both; but as he says nothing of a volcanic mountain in connexion with either, Baehr inclines to think that the reference is to Prusa in the vicinity of Mount Olympus, formerly called Cios, famous for miraculous fountains and things of that sort.

[39] Conf. Homer, *Il.* III, 6; Aristot. *Hist. An.* VIII, 12 and 14; Philostrat. *Vit. Apollon.* III, 47; Plin. *Hist. Nat.* VII, 2; Strabo, *Geog.* XV, i, 57; Aulus Gellius, *Noct. Att.* IX, 4.

and so large that they depend even to their
ancles. They are moreover snubnosed, and
otherwise ill-favoured. Their sheep are of the
size of our lambs, and their oxen and asses
rather smaller than our rams, which again are
as big as their horses and mules and other
cattle.[40] Of the Pygmies three thousand men
attend the king of the Indians, on account of
their great skill in archery. They are eminently
just, and have the same laws as the Indians.
They hunt hares and foxes not with dogs but
with ravens and kites and crows and vultures.[41]
In their country is a lake eight hundred stadia
in circumference, which produces an oil like
our own. If the wind be not blowing, this oil
floats upon the surface, and the Pygmies going
upon the lake in little boats collect it from
amidst the waters in small tubs for *household* use.[42]
They use also oil of sêsamum[43] and nut oil, but
the lake-oil[44] is the best. The lake has also fish.

12. There is much silver in their part of
the country, and the silver-mines though not
deep are deeper than those in Baktria. Gold
also is a product of India.[45] It is not found

---

[40] See Frag. xii, c.
[41] See Frag. xiii below.
[42] Conf. Frag. xxvii.
[43] See Salmas, *Exerc. Plin.* p. 1033; Sprengel, *Histor. Botan.* vol. I, p. 79; Reynier, *de l'Economie publique des Perses*, p. 283.

[44] Antigon, c, 165, in Frag. xxvii, below.
[45] On metals in India, see Heeren, *Asiat. Nat.* vol. II, p. 268.

in rivers and washed *from the sands* the like gold of the river Paktôlos, but is found on those many high-towering mountains which are inhabited by the G r i ffi n s,[46] a race of four-footed birds, about as large as wolves, having legs and claws like those of the lion, and cover-ed all over the body with black feathers except only on the breast where they are red. On account of those birds the gold with which the mountains abound is difficult to be got.

13. The sheep and the goats of the Indians[47] are bigger than asses, and generally produce young by four and by six at a time. The tails grow to such a size that those of the dams must be cut off before the rams can get at them. India does not however produce the pig, either the tame sort or the wild.[48] Palm-trees and their dates are in India[49] thrice the size of those in Babylon,[50] and we learn that there is a certain river flowing with honey out of a rock, like the one we have in our own country.

14. The justice of the Indians, their devo-tion to their king and their contempt of death

---

[46] Γρὺψ, in Persian گرفتن *giriften*, means to gripe or seize and گرف *girif* corresponds well enough with γρὺψ. See Frag. xiv, below, where a fuller account of the *gryphons* is given.

[47] See Frag. xii, below.

[48] See Frag. xv, below; also Frag. xxix, D. Swine, wild and tame, are common enough now in India.

[49] Conf. Palladius *De Brachman*, p. 4.

[50] Regarding the Babylonian palms, vid. Herodot. I, 193; and Diodor. II, 53.

3

are themes on which he loves to expatiate. He notices a fountain having this peculiarity, that when any one draws water from it, the water coagulates like cheese, and should you then detach from the solid lump a piece weighing about three obols, and having triturated this, put the powder into common water, he to whom you give this potion blabs out whatever he has done, for he becomes delirious, and raves like a madman all that day.[51] The king avails himself of this property when he wishes to discover the guilt or innocence of accused persons. Whoever incriminates himself *when undergoing the ordeal* is sentenced to starve himself to death, while he who does not confess to any crime is acquitted.[52]

15. The Indians are not afflicted with headache, or toothache, or ophthalmia, nor have they mouthsores or ulcers in any part of their body. The age to which they live is 120, 130, and 150 years, though the very old live to 200.[53]

16. In their country is a serpent a span long, in appearance like the most beautiful purple with a head perfectly white but without any teeth.[54] The creature is caught on those very hot mountains whose mines yield the sardine-stone. It does not sting, but on whatever part of the body it casts its vomit, that place invariably putrifies.

---

[51] Antigonus Caryst. *Histor. Mirab.* C. 160; Sotion, C. 17; Strabo, XVI, iv, 20.     [52] Conf. Frag. xv, G.
[53] Arrian, *Ind.* 15, 12, and Frag. xxii, C.
[54] See Frag. xvii.

If suspended by the tail, it emits two kinds of
poison, one like amber which oozes from it
while living, and the other black, which oozes
from its carcase. Should about a sesame-seed's
bulk of the former be administered to any one,
he dies the instant he swallows it, for his brain
runs out through his nostrils. If the black sort
be given it induces consumption, but operates
so slowly that death scarcely ensues in less than
a year's time.[55]

17. He mentions an Indian bird called
the *Dikairon*,[56] a name equivalent in Greek to
δίκαιον (*i.e.* just). It is about the size of a
partridge's egg. It buries its dung under the
earth to prevent its being found. Should it be
found notwithstanding, and should a person at
morning tide swallow so much of it as would
about equal a grain of sêsamum, he falls into a
deep unconscious sleep from which he never
awakes, but dies at the going down of the
sun.[57]

18. In the same country grows what is called

---

[55] Conf. Frag. xvii, also Strabo, XV, i, 37, where, quoting Megasthenes, he speaks of flying serpents that let fall drops which raise putrid sores on the skin.

[56] Δίκαιρος : Tychsen compares the word with دی
*di*, good, the good principle, and کر *kar*, doing, a participle
of the verb کردن *kerden*; the whole then means *benefactor*, and might be supposed to allude to the custom of the bird here mentioned. Bekker reads δίκερον here. See Frag. xviii.

[57] For fuller particulars vide Frag. xviii.

the *Parébon*,[58] a plant about the size of the olive, found only in the royal gardens, producing neither flower nor fruit, but having merely fifteen roots, which grow down into the earth, and are of considerable thickness, the very slenderest being about as thick as one's arm. If a span's length of this root be taken, it attracts to itself all objects brought near it—gold, silver, copper, stones and all things else except amber. If however a cubit's length of it be taken, it attracts lambs and birds, and it is in fact with this root that most kinds of birds are caught. Should you wish to turn water solid, even a whole gallon of it, you have but to throw into the water not more than an obol's weight of this root, and the thing is done. Its effect is the same upon wine which, when condensed by it, can be held in your hand like a piece of wax, though it melts the next day. It is found beneficial in the cure of bowel disorders.

19. Through India there flows a certain river, not of any great size, but only about two stadia in breadth, called in the Indian tongue H y-p a r k h o s,[59] which means in Greek φέρων πάντα

---

[58] Πάρηβον (in Apollonius παρύβος,) may be compared with the Persian بار *bâr*, weight, burthen, and آور *âver*, bearing, drawing. This comparison however is rather defective.—Tychsen. See Frag. xix.

[59] Ὕπαρχος: Tychsen adduces the Persian *âver*, bringing, carrying, and خوش *khosh*, good : consequently *âver-khosh*, bringing good, which exactly corresponds with the

τα ἀγαθὰ (*i.e.* the bearer of all things good).
This river for thirty days in every year floats
down amber, for in the upper part of its course
where it flows among the mountains there are
said to be trees overhanging its current which
for thirty days at a particular season in every
year continue dropping tears like the almond-tree
and the pine-tree and other trees. These tears on
dropping into the water harden into gum. The
Indian name for the tree is siptakhora,[60] which
means when rendered into Greek γλυκύ, ἡδὺ (*i.e.*
sweet). These trees then supply the Indians
with their amber.[61] And not only so but they are
said to yield also berries, which grow in clusters
like the grapes of the vine, and have stones as
large as the filbert-nuts of Pontos.[62]

20. He writes that on the mountains just
spoken of there live men having heads like

signification pointed out by Ktêsias. We might also compare برخوش *berkhosh*, good, so that the initial letter in
ὕπαρχος would be merely euphonic, but then the participle
φέρων would not be expressed. The river is called by
Pliny the Hypobarus, vide Frag. xx.

[60] Σιπταχόρα : Compare this with the Persian شیفتهخور
شیفتهخور *shiftehkhor*, 'agreeable to eat.' The Persians call an
apricot شیفتهرنگ *shifteh-reng*, 'agreeable colour.'
Pliny (*Hist. Nat.* xxxvii. 2) has 'arbores eas Aphytacoras
vocare,' where the word is disfigured.—Tychsen.

[61] India however does not produce amber, and the tree of
which it is here said to be the gum, cannot be satisfactorily
identified. Baehr quotes Pliny XII, ix, 19, as a passage of
no small importance for settling the question.

[62] Pliny (*Hist. Nat.* XV, xxii, 24), explains why *Pontic
nuts* were so called.

those of dogs, who wear the skins of wild
beasts, and do not use articulate speech, but
bark like dogs, and thus converse so as to be
understood by each other.[63] They have larger
teeth than dogs, and claws like those of dogs,
only larger and more rounded. They inhabit
the mountains, and extend as far as the river
Indus. They are swarthy, and like all the other
Indians extremely just men. With the Indians
they can hold intercourse, for they understand
what they say, though they cannot, it is true,
reply to them in words, still by barking and
by making signs with their hands and their
fingers like the deaf and the dumb, they can
make themselves understood. They are called
by the Indians *Kalystrioi*, which means in
Greek Κυνοκέφαλοι[64] (*i. e.*, dog-headed). Their
food is raw flesh. The whole tribe numbers
not less than 120,000 men.

21. Near the sources of this river[65] there
grows a certain purple flower, which is used for
dying purple, and is not inferior to the Greek
sort, but even imparts a far more florid hue.

---

[63] See Frags. xxi and xxii.

[64] Tychsen compares the word with the Persian كلك
*kelek* or *keluk*, a wolf, and سر *ser*, the head, *i.e. kelu
kser*, 'wolf-headed.' Another word more exactly answering
the sound of the Greek would be *Kalusterin*, the super-
lative of *kalus*, stupid, which would convert the doghead-
ed people into ' blockheads,' but this is not consonant with
the translation of the name.—Heeren, *Asiat. Nat.* vol. II.
p. 364. Vide Frags. xxi, xxii, xxxi.

[65] The Hyparkhos.

In the same parts there is a wild insect about
the size of a beetle, red like cinnabar, with legs
excessively long. It is as soft as the worm called
*skôlex* and is found on the trees which produce
amber, eating the fruits of those trees and
destroying them, as in Greece the wood-louse
ravages the vine-trees. The Indians grind
these insects to a powder and therewith dye such
robes, tunics, and other vestments as they want
to be of a purple hue.[66] Their dye-stuffs are
superior to those used by the Persians.

22. The Kynokephaloi living on the
mountains do not practise any of the arts but
subsist by the produce of the chase. They
slaughter the prey, and roast the flesh in the
sun. They rear however great numbers of sheep
and goats and asses. They drink the milk of the
sheep and the whey which is made therefrom.
They eat moreover the fruit of the *Siptakhora*—
the tree which produces amber, for it is sweet.
They also dry this fruit, and pack it in hampers
as the Greeks do raisins. The same people
construct rafts, and freight them with the
hampers as well as with the flowers of the purple
plant, after cleansing it, and with 260 talents
weight of amber, and a like weight of the
pigment which dyes purple, and 1000 talents
more of amber. All this cargo, which is the

[66] It is generally agreed that the cochineal insect is that
to which Ktêsias refers, though his description of it is not
quite accurate. For fuller particulars vide **Frag. xxiii.**

season's produce, they convey annually *as tribute*
to the King of the Indians.   They take also additional quantities of the same commodities for sale
to the Indians, from whom they receive in exchange loaves of bread and flour and cloth which
is made from a tree-grown stuff (cotton).[67]   They
sell also swords such as they use in hunting wild
beasts, and bows and javelins, for they are fell
marksmen both in shooting with the bow and
in hurling the javelin.   As they inhabit steep
and pathless mountains they cannot possibly
be conquered in war, and the king moreover
once every five years sends them as presents
300,000 arrows and as many javelins, 120,000
shields and 50,000 swords.

23.   These Kynokephaloi have no
houses but live in caves.   They hunt wild beasts
with the bow and the spear, and run so fast that
they can overtake them in the chase.   Their
women bathe once a month at the time of men-
struation, and then only.   The men do not bathe
at all, but merely wash their hands.   Thrice a
month, however, they anoint themselves with an
oil made from milk,[68] and wipe themselves with
skins.   Skins denuded of the hair, and made
thin and soft, constitute the dress both of
the men and their wives.   Their richest men

[67] See Larcher's Note on Herodot. III, 47; Plin. *Nat.
Hist.* XIX, 1; and Frag. xxiv.
[68] Butter; conf. Polyæn. *Strateg.* IV, 3, 32; cf. also
*Peripl. Ær. Mar.* § 41, where the same expression
occurs.

however use cotton raiment,[69] but the number of such men is small. They have no bed but sleep on a litter of straw or leaves. That man is considered the richest who possesses most sheep, and in property of this sort consists all their wealth. Both men and women have, like dogs, tails above their buttocks but larger and more hairy.[70] They copulate like quadrupeds in dog-fashion, and to copulate otherwise is thought shameful. They are just, and of all men are the longest-lived, attaining the age of 170, and some even of 200 years.

24. Beyond these again are other men who inhabit the country above the sources of the river, who are swarthy like the other Indians, do no work, and neither eat grain nor drink water, but rear a good many cows and goats and sheep, and drink their milk as their sole sustenance. Children are born among them with the anus closed up, and the contents of the bowels are therefore voided, it is said, as urine, this being something like curds, though not at all thick but feculent. When they drink milk in the morning and take another draught at noon, and then immediately after eat a certain sweet-tasted root of indigenous growth which is said to prevent milk from coagulating in the

---

[69] Curtius, VIII, 9, 21.
[70] Conf. Frag. i, section appended to § 33. Malte-Brun considered that this statement had reference to the Ourang-Outang of the Island of Borneo, or perhaps of the Andaman islands.

4

stomach, this root towards evening acts as an
emetic, and they vomit up everything quite
readily.

25. Among the Indians, he proceeds, there
are wild asses as large as horses, some being
even larger.[71] Their head is of a dark red
colour, their eyes blue, and the rest of their
body white. They have a horn on their forehead, a cubit in length [the filings of this horn,
if given in a potion, are an antidote to poison-
ous drugs]. This horn for about two palm-
breadths upwards from the base is of the purest
white, where it tapers to a sharp point of a
flaming crimson, and, in the middle, is black.[72]
These horns are made into drinking cups, and
such as drink from them are attacked neither
by convulsions nor by the sacred disease
(epilepsy). Nay, they are not even affected by
poisons, if either before or after swallowing
them they drink from these cups wine, water, or
anything else. While other asses moreover,
whether wild or tame, and indeed all other
solid-hoofed animals have neither huckle-bones,[73]
nor gall in the liver, these *one-horned* asses[74]
have both. Their huckle-bone is the most
beautiful of all I have ever seen, and is, in ap-

[71] See Frag. xxv.
[72] Conf. Bruce's account (*Travels*, vol. V, p. 93) who
describes its surface as of a reddish-brown.
[73] Ἀστραγάλους, conf. Aristot. *Hist. An.* II, 2, 9.
[74] Tychsen thinks the rhinoceros is here meant, but the
colour and other details do not quite agree with that
animal. Heeren, *As. Nat.* vol. II, pp. 364 ff.

pearance and size, like that of the ox. It is as
heavy as lead, and of the colour of cinnabar[75]
both on the surface, and all throughout. It is
exceedingly fleet and strong, and no creature that
pursues it, not even the horse, can overtake it.

26. On first starting it scampers off somewhat leisurely, but the longer it runs, it gallops
faster and faster till the pace becomes most
furious.[76] These animals therefore can only be
caught at one particular time—that is when
they lead out their little foals to the pastures
in which they roam. They are then hemmed
in on all sides by a vast number of hunters
mounted on horseback, and being unwilling
to escape while leaving their young to perish,
stand their ground and fight, and by butting
with their horns and kicking and biting kill
many horses and men. But they are in the
end taken, pierced to death with arrows and
spears, for to take them alive is in no way
possible. Their flesh being bitter[77] is unfit for
food, and they are hunted merely for the sake
of their horns and their huckle-bones.[78]

27. He states that there is bred in the

---

[75] That is, vermilion.
[76] This is what Bruce relates of the rhinoceros.—*Travels,*
vol. V, pp. 97 and 105.
[77] Bruce says it has a disagreeable musky flavour.
[78] Cf. Frag. xxv, and the account of the unicorn
in Kosmas Indikopl.; conf. also Aristotle, *de Part. An.*
III, 2, and *Hist. Anim.* II, 1; and also Philostrat.
*Vit. Apoll.* III, 2 and 3. Ælian's account in the above
Frag. of the wild ass may be compared with his account
of the Kartazôn,—*Ind. Ant.,* vol. VI, p. 128.

Indian river a worm[79] like in appearance to that
which is found in the fig, but seven cubits more
or less in length, while its thickness is such
that a boy ten years old could hardly clasp it
within the circuit of his arms. These worms
have two teeth—an upper and a lower, with
which they seize and devour their prey. In
the daytime they remain in the mud at the
bottom of the river, but at night they come
ashore, and should they fall in with any prey
as a cow or a camel, they seize it with their
teeth, and having dragged it to the river, there
devour it. For catching this worm a large hook is
employed, to which a kid or a lamb is fastened
by chains of iron. The worm being landed, the
captors hang up its carcase, and placing vessels
underneath it leave it thus for thirty days. All
this time oil drops from it, as much being got
as would fill ten Attic *kotylai*. At the end of
the thirty days they throw away the worm, and
preserving the oil they take it to the king of
the Indians, and to him alone, for no subject is
allowed to get a drop of it. This oil [like fire]
sets everything ablaze over which it is poured
and it consumes not alone wood but even animals.
The flames can be quenched only by throwing
over them a great quantity of clay, and that of a
thick consistency.[80]

---

[79] See § 1, and Frag. xxvi.    [80] Cf. Frag. xxvi, where
Ælian gives fuller particulars.  A somewhat similar creature is mentioned by Palladius (*de Brachman.* 10) as
belonging to the Ganges. He calls it the *Odontotyrranos*.

28. But again there are certain trees in India as tall as the cedar or the cypress, having leaves like those of the date palm, only somewhat broader, but having no shoots sprouting from the stems. They produce a flower like the male laurel, but no fruit. In the Indian language they are called *karpion*, but in Greek μυρορόδα (unguent-roses[31]). These trees are scarce.

---

[31] Baehr thinks this may be the Chetak (*Pandanu odoratisima*), Kaiḍa, or Kyura. Regarding the word *karpion* Dr. Caldwell in the Introduction to his *Dravidian Grammar* thus writes : The earliest Dravidian word in Greek of which we know the date is κάρπιον, Ktêsias's name for cinnamon. Herodotus describes cinnamon as the κάρφεα, which we, after the Phœnicians, call Κιννάμωμον. Liddell and Scott say "this word bears a curious likeness to its Arabic name *kerfat, kirfah*." This resemblance must, I think, be accidental, seeing that Herodotus considered 'cinnamon' alone as a foreign word. The word mentioned by Ktêsias seems however to have a real resemblance to the Arabic word and also to a Dravidian one. Ktesias describes an odorous oil produced from an Indian tree having flowers like the laurel, which the Greeks called μυρορόδα, but which in India was called κάρπιον. From Ktêsias's description (making allowance for its exaggerations) it is evident that cinnamon oil was meant, and in this opinion Wahl agrees. Uranius, a writer, quoted by Stephen of Byzantium, mentions κέρπαθον as one of the productions of the Abaseni, the Arabian Abyssinians, by which we are doubtless to understand, not so much the products of their country as the articles in which they traded. From the connexion in which it is found κέρπαθον would appear to be cinnamon, and we can scarcely err in identifying it with *kerfat* or more properly *kirfah*, one of the names which cinnamon has received in Arabia. Some Arabian scholars derive *kirfah* from *karafa* 'decortavit,' but Mr. Hassoun does not admit this derivation, and considers *kirfah* a foreign word. We are thus brought back to Ktêsias's κάρπιον, or the Indian word which κάρπιον represented. As this is a word of which we know the antiquity, the supposition that the Greeks or the Indians borrowed it from the Arabs is quite inadmissible. What then is the Indian word Ktesias referred to ? Not, as has been supposed, *kurundhu*, the Singhalese

There oozes from them an oil in drops, which are wiped off from the stem with wool, from which they are afterwards wrung out and received into alabaster boxes of stone. The oil is in colour of a faint red, and of a somewhat thick consistency. Its smell is the sweetest in all the world, and is said to diffuse itself to a distance of five stadia around. The privilege of possessing this perfume belongs only to the king and the members of the royal family. A present of it was sent by the king of the Indians to the king of the Persians, and Ktêsias alleges that he saw it himself, and that it was of such an exquisite fragrance as he could not describe, and he knew nothing whereunto he could liken it.

29. He states that the cheese and the wines of the Indians are the sweetest in the world, adding that he knew this from his own experience, since he had tasted both.

---

name for cinnamon derived from the Sanskrit *kuruṇṭa*, but the Tamil-Malayâlam word *karuppu* or *kârppu*, e. g. *karappa-(t)tailam*, Mal. oil of cinnamon. Other forms of this word are *karappu*, *karuva* and *karuvâ*, the last of which is the most common form in modern Tamil. Rheede refers to this form of the word when he says that "in his time in Malabar oils in high medical estimation were made from both the root and the leaves of the *karua* or wild cinnamon of that country." There are two meanings of *karu* in Tamil-Malayâlam, 'black,' and 'pungent', and the latter doubtless supplies us with the explanation of *karuppu* 'cinnamon'. . . . . I have little doubt that the Sanskrit *karpûra*, 'camphor,' is substantially the same as the Tamil-Malayâlam *karuppu*, and Ktêsias's κάρπιον, seeing that it does not seem to have any root in Sanskrit and that camphor and cinnamon are nearly related. The camphor of commerce is from a cinnamon tree, the *camphora officinarum*.

30. There is a fountain[32] among the Indians of a square shape and of about five ells in circumference. The water lodges in a rock. The depth downward till you reach the water is three cubits and the depth of the water itself three *orguiai*. Herein the Indians of highest distinction bathe [both for purification and the averting of diseases] along with their wives and children ; they throw themselves into the well foot foremost, and when they leap in the water casts them up again, and not only does it throw up human beings to the surface, but it casts out upon dry land any kind of animal, whether living or dead, and in fact anything else that is cast into it except iron and silver and gold and copper, which all sink to the bottom. The water is intensely cold and sweet to drink. It makes a loud bubbling noise like water boiling in a caldron. Its waters are a cure for leprosy, and scab.[33] In the Indian tongue it is called *Balladé*[34] and in Greek ὠφελίμη (*i. e.* useful).

31. On those Indian mountains where the Indian reed grows, there is a race of men whose number is not less than 30,000, and whose wives bear offspring only once in their whole life-time. Their children have teeth of perfect

[32] Conf. frag. xxxvii.
[33] Conf. Frag. xxvii.
[34] *Balada* in Sank. means ' giving strength' ; and is applied to a bullock, and a medical plant : *baladâ* is the *Physalis flexuosa.*—ED.

whiteness, both the upper set and the under,
and the hair both of their head and of their
eyebrows is from their very infancy quite hoary,
and this whether they be boys or girls.  Indeed
every man among them till he reaches his
thirtieth year has all the hair on his body white,
but from that time forward it begins to turn
black, and by the time they are sixty, there is
not a hair to be seen upon them but what is
black.  These people, both men and women alike,
have eight fingers on each hand, and eight toes
on each foot.  They are a very warlike people,
and five thousand of them armed with bows
and spears follow the banners of the King of
the Indians.  Their ears, he says, are so large
that they cover their arms as far as the elbows
while at the same time they cover all the back
and the one ear touches the other.[85]

32.  There is in Ethiopia an animal called
properly the *Krokottas*, but vulgarly the *Kyno-
lykos*.  It is of prodigious strength, and is said
to imitate the human voice, and by night to
call out men by their names, and when they
come forth at their call, to *fall upon them* and
devour them.  This animal has the courage of
the lion, the speed of the horse, and the strength
of the bull, and cannot be encountered success-

[85] For an account of the various fabulous Indian races
mentioned by the classical writers, and for their identification with the races mentioned in Sanskrit writings. see
*Ind. Ant.*, vol. VI, pp. 133-135, and footnotes.

fully with weapons of steel.[86] In Eubœa about Khalkis the sheep have no gall,[87] and their flesh is so extremely bitter that dogs even will not eat it. They say also that in the parts beyond the Maurusian Straits[88] rain falls in the summer-time, while the same regions are in winter-time scorched with heat. In the country of the Kyônians[89] there is, according to his account, a certain fountain, which instead of water has springs of oil—this oil being used by the people in the neighbourhood for all kinds of food. In the region also called Metadrida there is another fountain, this being at no great distance from the sea. At midnight it swells with the utmost violence, and in receding casts forth fish upon dry land in such quantities that the people of the place cannot gather them, and are obliged to leave them lying rotting on the ground.[90]

33. Ktêsias thus writing and romancing professes that his narrative is all perfect truth,

[86] Regarding the *Krokotta*, a sort of hyæna, vide Diodor. III, 34; Ælian, *Hist. Nat.* VII, 22; Pliny. *H. N.* VIII, 31; Porphyr. *De Abstin.* III, p. 223. Conf. Hesych. s. h. voc.; Bruce's *Travels*, vol. V, p. 113.

[87] Conf. Theophr. *H. Plant.* IX, 18, and Arist. *Hist. An.* I, 27.

[88] Μαυρουσίων πυλῶν—understand of the Pillars of Hercules. We have Maurusios in Pliny, *Hist. Nat.* V, 2; Strabo, *Geog.* XVII, iii, 2.

[89] Ἐν τῶν Κυωνίων χώρα appears to be corrupt. We might suggest Cio in Mysia. The same thing is told of the fountain ἐν Σικάνων χώρα at the city Κυτίστρατον thus commonly for Μυτίστρατον (Antigon. *Mirab.* 154). Conf. also Aristot. *Mir. ausc.* c. 123.

[90] This section is found only in the MS. of Müniah and perhaps does not belong to Ktesias.

5

and, to assure us of this, asseverates that he has recorded nothing but what he either saw with his own eyes, or learned from the testimony of credible eye-witnesses. He adds moreover that he has left unnoticed many things far more marvellous than any he has related, lest any one who had not a previous knowledge of the facts might look upon him as an arrant story-teller.

The[91] S ê r e s[92] and the natives of Upper India are said to be men of huge stature, so that among them are found some who are 13 cubits in height and who also live till they are above 200 years old.  There are besides somewhere in the river called the Gaïtês[93] men of a brute-like appearance who have a hide like that of a rhinoceros being quite impervious to darts,[94] while in India itself in the central parts of an island of the ocean the inhabitants are said to have tails of extraordinary length such as satyrs are represented with in pictures.[95]

## Frag. II.
### From Arrian, *Anab*. Book V. 4, 2.

And Ktêsias (if any one considers him a competent authority) asserts that the distance from the one bank of the Indus to the other where the stream is narrowest is 40 stadia, and

---

[91] This fragment in the Münich MS. forms a part of the 15th Section of the text of Photios.
[92] Cf. Lucian *Macrob*. c. 5.
[93] Var. lect.—Gaitres.
[94] Cf. Ptolemy, *Geog.* VII, iii, where the same words are used.
[95] Cf. same chapter of same Book p. 178.

where it is widest, so much even as 100 stadia, though its breadth in general is the mean between these two extremes.

### FRAG. III.

#### Strabo, *Geog.* Book XV.

From this we can see how greatly the opinions of the others differ, Ktêsias asserting that India is not less than all the rest of Asia, and Onesikritos that, &c.

#### From the *Indika* of Arrian, 30.

Ktêsias the Knidian states that India is equal to the rest of Asia, but he is wrong.

### FRAG. IV.

#### Ælian, *De Nat. Anim.* Book XVII, 29.

When the King of the Indians goes on a campaign, one hundred thousand war-elephants go on before him, while three thousand more, that are of superior size and strength, march, I am told, behind him, these being trained to demolish the walls of the enemy. This they effect by rushing against them at the King's signal, and throwing them down by the overwhelming force with which they press their breasts against them. Ktêsias reports this from hearsay, but adds that with his own eyes he had seen elephants tear up palm trees, roots and all, with like furious violence ; and this they do whenever they are instigated to the act by their drivers.[96]

---

[96] Conf. Diodor. II., 17 ; Strabo, XV, I, 41 ff. ; Curtius, VIII, 9, 17 ; Kosmos Indikopleustes, XI, p. 339.

## Frag. V.

### (A)   Aristotle, *De Gener. Anim.* II, 2.

What Ktêsias has said regarding the seed of
the elephant is plainly false, for he asserts that
when dry it turns hard so as to become like
amber; and this it does not.[97]

### (B)   From the same, towards the end of the 3rd Book of his *History of Animals*.

What Ktêsias has written regarding the seed
of the elephant is false.

### (C)   Ælian, *De Animal*. XVI, 2.

Cocks [in India] are of immense size, and
their crests are not red like the crests of our
own cocks, but many-hued, like a floral garland;
their rump feathers are neither curved nor
wreathed, but broad, and these they trail after
them in the way the peacock drags his tail when
he does not make it stand erect. The feathers
of the Indian cocks are partly golden, and
partly of a gleaming azure like the smaragdus
stone.[98]

## Frag. VI.

### (A)   Ælian, *De Animal. Nat.* XVI, 31.

Ktêsias in his account of India says that the
people called the Kynamolgoi rear many
dogs as big as the Hyrkanian breed, and this
Knidian writer tells us also why they keep so
many dogs, and this is the reason: From the
time of the summer solstice on to mid-winter

---

[97] Ktêsias, however, probably referred to the matter
which issued from the orifice in the temples.
[98] A kind of pheasant is meant—the *Impeyanum Lophop.*

they are incessantly attacked by herds of wild
oxen, coming like a swarm of bees or a flight
of angry wasps, only that the oxen are more
numerous by far. They are ferocious withal
and proudly defiant, and butt most viciously
with their horns. The K y n a m o l g o i, unable
to withstand them otherwise, let loose their
dogs upon them, which are bred for this express
purpose, and these dogs easily overpower the
oxen and worry them to death. Then come
the masters, and appropriate to their own use
such parts of the carcases as they deem fit for
food, but they set apart for their dogs all the
rest, and gratitude prompts them to give this
share cheerfully. During the season when
they are left unmolested by the oxen, they
employ their dogs in hunting other animals.
They milk the bitches, and this is why they
are called Kynamolgoi (dog-milkers). They
drink this milk just as we drink that of the
sheep or the goat.

(B) Polydeukês (Pollux), *Onomastic.* V, 5, 41, p. 497.

The K y n a m o l g o i are dogs living about
the lakes in the south of India and subsisting
upon cows' milk. They are attacked in the
hot season by the oxen of India, but they fight
these assailants and overcome them, as Ktêsias
relates.[99]

[99] Conf. Diod. III, 31 ; Megasthenes in Strabo, XV,
37 ; Plin. *Hist. Nat.* VII, 2 ; Curtius, IX, i. 31.

(B) Ælian, *De Animal. Nat.* IV, 32.

It is worth while learning what like are the
cattle of the Indians. Their goats and their
sheep are, from what I hear, bigger than the
biggest asses, and they produce four young ones
at a time, and never fewer than three. The tails
of the sheep reach down to their feet, and the
tails of the goats are so long that they almost
touch the ground. The shepherds cut off the
tails of those ewes that are good for breeding
to let them be mounted by the rams, and these
tails yield an oil which is squeezed out from
their fat. They cut also the tails of the rams,
and having extracted the fat, sew them up
again so carefully that no trace of the incision
is afterwards seen.

### Frag. VII.

Tzetzês, *Chil.* VII, v. 739, from the Third Book of the
Ἀραβικιον of Uranius.

If any one thinks that the size of the Arabian
reeds has been exaggerated, who, asks Tzetzês,
would believe what Ktêsias says of the Indian
reeds—that they are two *orguiai* in breadth, and
that a couple of cargo-boats could be made from
a single joint of one of these reeds.[100]

### Frag. VIII.

Aristotle, *De Hist. Anim.* II, 1.

No animals of these species have a double
row of teeth, though, if we are to believe

[100] Conf. Pliny, *Hist. Nat.* XVI, 36 ; VII, 2 ; Theo-
phrast. *Plant. Hist.* IX. 11 ; Herodot. III. 98 ; Strabo,
XV, 21.

Ktêsias, there is one exception to the rule, for
he asserts that the Indian beast called the
Martikhora has a triple row of teeth in each of
its jaws. He describes the animal as being
equal in size to the lion, which it also resembles
in its claws and in having shaggy hair, though
its face and its ears are like those of a human
being. Its eyes are blue and its hair is of the
colour of cinnabar.[101] Its tail, which resembles
that of the land scorpion, contains the sting, and
is furnished with a growth of prickles which it
has the power of discharging *like shafts shot from
a bow*. Its voice is like the sound of the pipe
and the trumpet blended together. It runs fast,
being as nimble as a deer. It is very ferocious
and has a great avidity for human flesh.

### FRAG. IX.

Pausanias (*Boiôt.* IX. xxi. 4) quoting Ktêsias, thus
describes the same animal.

The animal mentioned by Ktêsias in his
*Indika*, called by the Indians the *Martikhora*,
but by the Greeks, it is said, ἀνδροφάγον (man-
eater) is, I am convinced, the tiger. It is described as having three rows of teeth in each of
its jaws and as having stings at the end of its
tail, wherewith it defends itself against its
assailants whether fighting at close quarters or
at a distance. In the latter case it shoots its
stings clean away from its tail like shafts shot
from a bow-string.

---

[101] *i. e.* vermilion.

[The Indians appear to me to have accepted this account, which is not true, through their excessive dread of this creature.]

## Frag. X.

Pliny, *H. N.* VIII, 21 (al. 30.)

Ktêsias states that the animal which he calls the *Martikhora* is found among these people [the Indians or rather the Aethiopians]. According to his description, it has a triple row of teeth, ranged together like the teeth of a comb; its face and its ears are like those of a human being, while its eyes are blue and its hair of a blood-red colour. It has the body of a lion and its tail is armed with stings, with which it smites like the scorpion. Its voice is like the commingled sound of the pipe and the trumpet. It runs very fast, and is very fond of human flesh.

## Frag. XI.

From Ælian, *De Animal.* IV. 21 ; respecting the Indian Martikhora.

In India is found a wild animal called in the native tongue the *Martikhora.* . It is of great strength and ferocity, being about as big as a lion, of a red colour like cinnabar, and covered with shaggy hair like a dog. Its face, however, is not bestial, but resembles that of a human being. It has both in the upper and the lower jaw a double row of teeth which are extremely sharp at the points and larger than the canine.

Its ears in their conformation are like the
human, but they are larger and covered with
shaggy hair. Its eyes also are like the human,
and of a blue colour. It has the feet and the claws
of a lion, but its tail, which may be more than
a cubit long, is not only furnished at the tip
with a scorpion's sting but is armed on both
sides with a row of stings. With the sting at
the tip it smites any one who comes near it, and
kills him therewith instantaneously, but if it is
pursued it uses the side stings, discharging
them like arrows against the pursuer, whom it
can hit even though he be at a good distance
off. When it fights, having the enemy in front,
it bends the tail upward, but when, like the
Sakians, it fights while retreating, it straightens
it out to the fullest length. The stings, which
are a foot long and as slender as a rush (or a
fine thread), kill every animal they hit, with
the exception of the elephant only. Ktêsias
says that he had been assured by the Indians
that those stings that are expended in fighting
are replaced by a growth of new ones as if to
perpetuate this accursed plague. Its favourite
food, according to the same author, is human
flesh, and to satisfy this lust, it kills a great many
men, caring not to spring from its ambush
upon a solitary traveller, but rather upon a band
of two or three for which it is singly more than
a match. All the beasts of the forest yield to
its prowess, save only the lion, which it is im-

6

potent to subdue. That it loves above all
things to gorge itself with human flesh, is
clearly shown by its name—for the Indian
word *Martikhora* means *man-eater*—and it has
its name from this particular habit. It runs
with all the nimbleness of a deer. The Indians
hunt the young ones before the stings appear
on their tails, and break the tails themselves
in pieces on the rocks to prevent stings growing upon them. Its voice has a most striking
resemblance to the sound of a trumpet. Ktêsias
says that he had seen in Persia one of these
animals, which had been sent from India as a
gift to the Persian king. Such are the peculiarities of the Martikhora as described by
Ktêsias, and if any one thinks this Knidian
writer a competent authority on such subjects,
he must be content with the account which he
has given.

## FRAG. XII.

(A) Antigonos, *Mirab. Nar. Cong. Hist.* c. 182.

He says that Ktêsias gives an account of an
undying fire burning on Mount Chimaera
in the country of the Phasêlitai. Should
the flame be cast into water, this but sets it
into a greater blaze, and so if you wish to put
it out you must cast some solid substance
into it.

(B) Pliny, *Hist. Nat.* II, 106.

Mount Chimaera in Phasêlis is volcanic, and burns night and day with a perpetual

flame.[102] According to Ktêsias the Knidian, the fire is augmented by water, but extinguished by earth or hay.[103]

C. Ælian, *De Anim.* XVI. 37.

Among the Indian P s y l l o i (who are so called to distinguish them from the Libyan Psylloi) the horses are no bigger than rams, while the sheep look as small as lambs. The asses are likewise correspondingly small and so are the mules and the oxen, and in short all cattle of whatever kind.[104]

### FRAG. XIII.

Ælian, *Nat. An.* IV, 26.

Hares and foxes are hunted by the Indians in the manner following. They do not require dogs for the purpose, but taking the young of eagles, of ravens and of kites, they rear and train them to pursue these animals by subjecting them to this course of instruction. Taking a pet hare and a tame fox, they fasten on to each a gobbet of flesh, and then making them run away, at the same time dismiss the birds to give them instant chase, and catch the alluring bait. The birds eagerly pursue, and catching up either the hare or the fox, pounce upon the flesh, with which they are allowed to glut their maw in recompense for their activity in having

[102] Conf. *Ind. Ant.*, vol. IX, p. 109, and Beaufort's *Travels.*
[103] *Foeno*, for which perhaps *fimo* should be read.
[104] See Frag. xv. From this it appears that Ktêsias calls the same race both Psylli and Pygmies.

captured it. When they have thus become
adepts in hunting, they are taken out to pursue mountain hares and wild foxes, when, on
sighting the quarry, they at once give it chase
in hope of earning the customary dainty, and
having quickly caught it bring it to their masters,
as Ktêsias acquaints us. From the same
source we further learn that the entrails of
the quarry are given them instead of the gob-
bets of flesh to which they had been formerly
treated.

### FRAG. XIV.

#### (A) Ælian *Nat. Anim*. IV, 27.

The *gryphon*, an Indian animal, is, so far as I
can learn, four-footed like the lion and has
claws of enormous strength closely resembling
his. It is described as having feathers on its
back, and these black, while the breast feathers
are red and those of the wing white. According to Ktêsias its neck is variegated with
feathers of a bright blue; its beak is like an
eagle's; and its head like the representations
which artists give of it in paintings and sculp-
tures. Its eyes are said to be fiery red, and it
builds its nest upon the mountains, and, as it
is impossible to catch these birds when full
grown, they are caught when quite young. The
B a k t r i a n s who are next neighbours to the
Indians give out that these birds guard the gold
found in the regions which they haunt, and
that they dig it out of the ground and build

their nests with it, and that the Indians carry
off as much of it as falls to the ground. The
Indians however deny that the gryphons guard
the gold, alleging, what I think is highly
probable, that gold is a thing gryphons have no
use for; but they admit that when these birds
see them coming to gather the gold, they become
alarmed for their young and attack the in-
truders. Nor do they resist man only, but beasts
of whatever kind, gaining an easy victory over
all except only the elephant and the lion, for
which they are no match. The gryphons, then,
being so formidable, the natives of these
countries go not to gather gold in the day time,
but set out under cover of night when they are
least likely to be detected. Now the auriferous
region which the gryphons inhabit is a fright-
ful desert,[105] and those who make a raid upon
the gold, select a moonless night, and set out
armed, the expedition being a thousand or even
two thousand strong. They take with them
mattocks for digging the gold and sacks in
which to carry it away. If they are unobserved by
the gryphons they have a double share of good
luck, for they not only escape with their lives
but bear a freight of gold in triumph home, where,
the metal having been purified by those who
are skilful in smelting ores, they are recom-
pensed with overflowing wealth for all the

---

[105] Perhaps the Desert of Cobi.

hazards of the enterprise. Should they on the other hand be detected in the act of theft, certain death would be their fate. I have learned by enquiry that they do not return home till after an absence of three or four years.[106]

## FRAG. XV.

### (A) Ælian, *Nat. An.* XVI, 37.

It is said that neither the wild nor the tame swine is found in India, and that the Indians so much abhor the flesh of this animal that they would as soon taste human flesh as taste pork.

### (B) Ælian, *De Nat. Anim.* III, 4.

The following also are peculiarities in the nature of animals. The swine, according to Ktêsias, whether wild or tame, is not found in India, and he somewhere states that Indian sheep have tails a cubit in breadth.

### (C) Arist., *De Hist. Anim.* VIII, 28.

In India, as Ktêsias, a writer not to be depended on, tells us, the swine is not found either wild or tame.

[The animals of that country however which are bloodless and those that lie in holes are all large.]

### (D) Palladius, *De Brachman*, p. 5.

For the swine of the Thebâïd, on account of the excessive heat, is no longer found either in the parts of India or of Æthiopia.

---

[106] The same is related from Ælian by Philo, *De animall. propriett.* 2, pp. 15 seq. ; conf. Herodot. III. 116 ; IV. 13, 27. Baehr has a very long note on the Gryphons.

(E)  Pallad., *De Brach.*, p. 4.

It (India) has also palms and the largest of nuts, the Indian as well as the small nut which is aromatic.

(F)  Antig. *Mirab. Nar.* 160.

Ktêsias, he says, informs us that in Æthiopia there is a fountain whose waters are red like cinnabar, and make those who drink them mad.

(G)  From the work of Sôtiôn.

Ktêsias relates that in Æthiopia there is a fountain of water resembling cinnabar in colour which deprives those who drink it of their reason, so that they confess all the misdeeds which they have secretly committed.

(H)  Pliny, XXXI, 2.

In drinking this water due moderation must be observed lest it make you mad like those persons who drink of that red fountain in Æthiopia whereof Ktêsias writes.

(I)  Michael. Apostol. *Proverb,* XX, 6.[107]

*A swine among the roses,* a proverb applied by Kratês to the intractable and uneducated. Ktêsias asserts that the swine is not bred in India, either the wild or the tame kind, and he somewhere mentions that the sheep have tails a cubit in breadth.

## Frag. XVI.

Pliny, *Hist. Nat.* XVII, 2.

Onesikritus says that in those parts of India where no shadows are cast there are men who are 5 cubits and 2 palms in stature and who

---

[107] This is given as frag. 29 by Lion, but not by Müller.

live 130 years without becoming old, for if
they die then they are cut off as it were in
mid-life. Krates of Pergamus calls the Indians
who live over a hundred years Gymnetae, but
many writers call them Makrobii. Ktêsias
asserts that a tribe of them called Pandarae
inhabiting the valleys live for 200 years, and
have in their youth white hair, which turns
black when they grow old.

FRAG. XVII.

*Ælian, Nat. An.* IV, 36.

Writers on India inform us that that country
produces many drugs, and is astonishingly pro-
lific of those plants that yield them. Many of
these drugs are medicinal and cure snake-bites,
which are so dangerous to life, but others are
deleterious and quickly destroy life. Among
these may be reckoned the poison of a particular kind of serpent, one which to appearance
is about a span long. Its colour is purple of
the deepest dye, but not on the head, which
so far from being purple, is extraordinarily white,
whiter even than snow or than milk. It is
found in those parts of India which are most
scorched by the sun. It has no teeth, and does
not at all incline to bite, and hence one would
think it to be of a tame and gentle nature, but
nevertheless, wherever it casts its vomit, be it
upon the limb of a man or of a beast, nothing
can prevent the whole of that limb from morti-
fying. It is sought after for the sake of this

poison, and is, when caught, suspended from a
tree by the tail, so that the head may look downward to the ground. Below its mouth they
place a casket made of brass, to receive the
drops of poison as they fall. The matter thus
discharged condenses and becomes a solid mass
which might be mistaken for the gum which
oozes from the almond-tree. When the snake is
dead the vessel is replaced by another, which
is also of brass, for the carcase then discharges
a serous humour like water, which, after being
allowed to stand for three days, takes also a solid
form. The two masses differ from each other
in colour, the one being jet-black and the other
the colour of amber. If you take of the latter
no more than what would equal the bulk of a
sesame seed, and administer this to one either
in his food or his drink, he is first of all seized
with violent spasms, and his eyes in the next
place become distorted, and his brain, forcing its
way through his nostrils, runs out, when death
ensues after a short but sharp agony. If a
smaller dose is taken, death does not immediately ensue, but does so eventually. The
black poison, again, which has oozed from the
snake when dead, operates but slowly, for if one
swallows the same bulk of it as of the other, it
corrupts his blood and he falls into a consumption, of which he dies in a year's time. Many,
however, survive for two years, dying inch
by inch.

7

## Frag. XVIII.

Ælian, *De Nat. An.* IV, 41.

There is a species of Indian bird of very
diminutive size which may be thus described.
It builds its nests on high and precipitous mountains, and is about as big as a partridge egg,
and of a bright red colour like realgar. The
Indians call it in their tongue *dikairon*, and the
Greeks in theirs, as I am informed, *dikaion* (*i. e.*
just). Its dung has a peculiar property, for if
a quantity of it no bigger than a grain of millet
be dissolved into a potion, it would be enough to
kill a man by the fall of evening. But the
death that comes thereby resembles a sleep,
and is most pleasant withal and pangless, being
like that death which the poets are wont to call
*lusimelês* (limb-relaxing) and *ablêkhros* (easy),
for such a death is painless, and is therefore to
those who wish to be rid of life, the sweetest
of all deaths. The Indians accordingly spare
no pains to procure this substance, which they
regard as a genuine anodyne for all human
ills. Hence it is included among the costly
presents sent by the king of the Indians to
the Persian king, by whom it is prized more
than aught else, and who treasures it up as a
sure defence in case of necessity against ills
that are past all other remedy. No one in all
Persia possesses it save only the king himself
and the king's mother. Let us here then
compare this Indian drug with the Egyptian

so as to determine which is superior. The Egyptian we saw, had the effect throughout the day it was taken of restraining and checking tears, whereas the Indian induced an unending oblivion of all ills. The former was the gift of a woman, and the latter the gift of a bird, or rather of Nature, which, through the agency of this bird, unfetters man from the sternest bondage. And the Indians, they say, are happy in the possession of this, since they can by its means whenever they please, escape from their prison-house here below.

### Frag. XIX.

Apollonios (Dyskolos), *Hist. Mirab.* XVII.

Ktêsias says that in India is found a tree called the *parybon*. This draws to itself everything that comes near, as gold, silver, tin, copper and all other metals. Nay, it even attracts sparrows when they alight in its neighbourhood. Should it be of large size, it would attract even goats and sheep and similar animals.

### Frag. XX.

Pliny, *Hist. Nat.* XXXVII, 2.

Ktêsias says that in India is a river, the Hypobarus, and that the meaning of its name is *the bearer of all good things*. It flows from the north into the Eastern Ocean near a mountain well-wooded with trees that produce amber. These trees are called *aphytacorae*, a name which means *luscious sweetness*.

## Frag. XXI.
### Tzetzês, *Chil.* VII, v, 714.

Ktêsias says that in India are the trees that produce amber, and the men called the Kyno-kephaloi, who, according to his account, are very just men living by produce of the chase.

## Frag. XXII.
### Pliny, *Hist. Nat.* VII, 2.

On many mountains (of India) is found a race of men with heads like those of dogs, who are dressed with the skins of wild beasts, who bark instead of speaking, and who, being armed with claws, live by hunting and fowling. Ktêsias says that in his time the number of these men was 120,000.

## Frag. XXIII.
### Ælian, IV, 46.

Among the Indians are found certain insects about the size of beetles and of a colour so red that at first sight one might mistake them for cinnabar. Their legs are of extraordinary length and soft to the touch. They grow upon the trees which produce amber, and subsist upon their fruit. The Indians collect them for the sake of the purple dye, which they yield when crushed. This dye is used for tinting with purple not only their outer and their under-garments, but also any other substance where a purple hue is required. Robes tinted with this purple are sent to the Persian king, for the Indian purple is thought by the Persians to be marvellously beautiful and far

superior to their own. This we learn from
Ktêsias, who says well, for this dye is in fact
deeper and more brilliant than the renowned
Lydian purple.

In that part of India where the beetles
(κανθάροι) are met with, live the Kynokephaloi,
who are so called from their being like dogs in
the shape of their head and in their general
appearance. In other respects, however, they
resemble mankind, and go about clad in the
skins of wild beasts. They are moreover very
just, and do no sort of injury to any man.
They cannot speak, but utter a kind of howl.
Notwithstanding this they comprehend the
language of the Indians. They subsist upon wild
animals, which their great fleetness of foot en-
ables them to capture with the utmost ease.
Having killed the prey they cut it into pieces, and
roast it by the heat of the sun and not by fire.
They keep goats however and sheep, whose milk
supplies them with drink, as the chase with food.
I have mentioned them among the brutes, and
with good reason, for they do not possess articulate and intelligible speech like mankind.[108]

### Frag. XXIV.

Servius the Commentator on Virgil ; *Æneid*, I, v, 653.

*Acantho*—*i. e.* with a flexible twig in imitation of which a robe is artificially adorned

---

[108] Herodotus mentions Kynokephaloi in Africa (IV,
192) ; conf. Diodor. III, 34 ; Augustine, *C. D.* XVI, 8 ;
Aristot. *Hist. Anim.* 11, 8 ; Strabo, XVI, iv, 15 ; Philost.
*Vit. Apollon.* VI, 1.

and wrought. Varius makes this statement.
Ktêsias says that there are trees in India which
grow wool.

## Frag. XXV.
### (A) Ælian, *Hist. An.* IV, 52.

I have ascertained by enquiry that wild
asses are found in India as big as horses. The
animal is entirely white, except about the head,
which is of a reddish colour, while the eye
gleams with azure. It has a horn upon its
forehead about a cubit and a half long. This
horn is white at the base, crimson at the tip, and
jet black in the middle. These particoloured
horns are used, I understand, as drinking cups
by the Indians, not indeed by people of all
ranks, but only by the magnates, who rim
them at intervals with circlets of gold just
as they would adorn with bracelets the arm of
some beautiful statue. They say that whoever
drinks out of this horn is protected against all
incurable diseases, for he can neither be seized
by convulsions nor by what is called the sacred
disease (epilepsy),[109] and neither can he be cut
off by poison; nay if before drinking from it he
should have swallowed anything deleterious, he
vomits this, and escapes scatheless from all ill
effects, and while, as has been believed, all
other asses, wherever found, and whether wild
or tame, and even all solid-hoofed animals, have
neither a huckle-bone (ἀστραγαλος) nor a gall in

[109] Cf. Herod. III, 33.

the liver, the Indian horned asses have according
to Ktêsias both a huckle-bone and a gall in
the liver. The huckle-bones are said to be black,
not only on the surface but all throughout as
may be proved by breaking one to pieces. They
are fleeter not only than other asses but even
than horses and deer. On first starting they run
leisurely, but they gradually strengthen their
pace, and then to overtake them, is, to use a
poetic expression, the unattainable ($\tau a$ '$a\kappa i\chi\eta\tau a$).[110]
When the dams have brought forth and begin to
lead out their young ones to the pastures, the
males are in close attendance, and guard their
offspring with devoted care. They roam about
in the most desolate tracts of the Indian plain,
and when the hunters come to attack them, they
relegate their foals, being as yet but young and
tender, to graze in the rear, while in front they
fight to defend them. Their mode of attack is
to charge the horsemen, using the horn as the
weapon of assault, and this is so powerful, that
nothing can withstand the blow it gives, but
yields and snaps in two, or is perhaps shivered
to pieces and spoiled for further use. They
sometimes even fall upon the horses, and so
cruelly rip up their sides with the horn that
their very entrails gush out. The riders, it
may well be imagined, dread to encounter them
at close quarters, since the penalty of approach-

---

[110] Used by Homer.

ing them is a miserable death both to man and horse. And not only do they butt, but they also kick most viciously and bite; and their bite is much to be dreaded, for they tear away all the flesh they grasp with their teeth. It is accordingly impossible to take them alive if they be full-grown; and hence they must be despatched with such missiles as the spear or the arrow. This done, the Indians despoil them of their horns, which they ornament in the manner already described. The flesh is so very bitter that the Indians cannot use it for food.[111]

(B) Ælian, III, 41.

India, he says, produces unicorn horses and breeds likewise unicorn asses. Drinking cups are made from these horns. Should one who plots against another's life put a deadly poison into these cups no harm is done to the man who drinks therefrom. The horn of the horse and the ass, it would appear, is an antidote against evil.

FRAG. XXVI.

Ælian, *Nat. An.* V, 3.

The river Indus has no living creature in it except, they say, the Skôlêx, a kind of worm which to appearance is very like the worms that are generated and nurtured in trees. It differs however in size, being in general seven cubits in length and of such a thickness that a child of

---

[111] Conf. Ælian III, 41; XVI, 20; Aristot. *De partt. Anim.* III, 2; Philostrat. *Vit. Apoll.* III, 2.

ten could scarcely clasp it round in his arms. It has a single tooth in each of its jaws, quadrangular in shape and above four feet long. These teeth are so strong that they tear in pieces with ease whatever they clutch, be it a stone or be it a beast, whether wild or tame. In the daytime these worms remain hidden at the bottom of the river, wallowing with delight in its mud and sediment, but by night they come ashore in search of prey, and whatever animal they pounce upon—horse, cow, or ass, they drag down to the bottom of the river, where they devour it limb by limb, all except the entrails. Should they be pressed by hunger they come ashore even in the daytime, and should a camel then or a cow come to the brink of the river to quench its thirst, they creep stealthily up to it, and having with a violent spring secured their victim by fastening their fangs in its upper lip, they drag it by sheer force into the water, where they make a sumptuous repast of it. The hide of the *skôlêx* is two finger-breadths thick. The natives have devised the following method for catching it. To a hook of great strength and thickness they attach an iron chain, which they bind with a rope made of a broad piece of white cotton. Then they wrap wool round the hook and the rope, to prevent them being gnawed through by the worm, and having baited the hook with a kid, the line is thereupon lowered into the stream. As many as thirty men, each of whom

8

is equipped with a sword and a spear fitted
with a thong, hold on to the rope, having also
stout cudgels of cornel lying ready to hand, in
case it should be necessary to fell the monster
with blows. As soon as it is hooked and swallows
the bait, it is hauled ashore and despatched by
the fishermen, who suspend its carcase till it has
been exposed for 30 days to the heat of the
sun. An oil all this time oozes out from it, and
falls by drops into earthen vessels. A single
worm yields ten *kotulai* (about five pints). The
vessels having been sealed up, the oil is despatched to the king of the Indians, for no one
else is allowed to have so much as one drop of
it. The rest of the carcase is useless. Now this
oil possesses this singular virtue, that if you
wish to burn to ashes a pile of any kind of wood,
you have only to pour upon it half a pint of the
oil, and it ignites without your applying a
spark of fire to kindle it, while if it is a man or a
beast you want to burn, you pour out the oil, and
in an instant the victim is consumed. By means
of this oil also the king of the Indians, it is
said, captures hostile cities without the help of
rams or testudos or other siege apparatus, for
he has merely to set them on fire with the oil,
and they fall into his hands. How he proceeds
is this. Having filled with the oil a certain
number of earthen vessels which hold each
about half a pint, he closes up their mouths, and
aims them at the uppermost parts of the gates;

and if they strike there and break, the oil runs
down the woodwork, wrapping it in flames
which cannot be put out, but with insatiable
fury burn the enemy, arms and all. The only
way to smother and extinguish this fire is to
cast rubbish into it. This account is given by
Ktêsias the Knidian.

### Frag. XXVII.

(A) From Antigonos, *Mirab. Nar. Cong. Hist.* 165.

It is said that Ktêsias mentions certain lakes in
India, one of which, like the lakes in Sicily and
Media made everything that was cast into it
sink down [float] except gold, copper, and iron.
Moreover, should anything fall into it aslant, it is
thrown up standing erect. It is said to cure the
disease called the white leprosy. Another lake
at certain seasons yields an oil which is found
floating on the surface.

(B) From Sôtiôn in scattered passages where he relates
marvels about rivers, fountains and lakes.

There is a fountain in India which throws
out upon its banks as if shot from an engine those
who dive into its waters, as Ktêsias relates.[112]

(C) Strabo, *Geog.* XVI, 4.

Ktêsias the Knidian mentions a fountain
which discharges into the sea water of a red
colour and full of minium (red-lead).

### Frag. XXVIII.

Pliny, *Hist. Nat.* XXXI, 2.

Ktêsias records that in India is a pool of

---

[112] Conf. Aristot. *Mir. Ausc.* c. 122; Plin. *Hist. Nat.*
II, 103.

water called S i d e[113] in which nothing will float,
but everything sinks to the bottom.

FRAG. XXIX.

(A) Antigonos, Mirab. Nar. Cong. Hist. c. 182.

Ktêsias mentions the water which falls from
a rock in Armenia, and which casts out black
fish which cause the death of the eater.

(B) Pliny, Hist. Nat. XXXI, 2.

Ktêsias writes that in Armenia there is a
fountain with black fish which, if taken as food,
produce instantaneous death, and I heard the
same said of the Danube, that where it rises,
the same kind of black fish is found in it till
you come to a fountain adjoining its channel,
and that this fountain is therefore commonly
believed to be the head of the river. They
tell the same thing of the Nymph's pool in
Lydia.

FRAG. XXX.

(A) Tzetzês, Chil. VII, v, 638.

This Skylax (of Karyanda) writes other such
stories by the myriads, stories of one-eyed men,
and of men that sleep in their ears, and
thousands of other wonderful creatures, all which
he speaks of as really existing, and not fictitious ;
but for my part, as I have never met with any
of them, I do not believe in them, although there
are multitudes, such as Ktêsias, Iamboulos,

---

[113] Isidor. *Origg.* xiii, 13 ; Conf. Antigon. c. 161;
Diodorus, II, 36, 7 ; Arrian, *Ind.* c. 6 ; Strabo, XV, i,
38; and *Ind. Ant.* vol. V, pp. 333, 334, and vol. VI,
pp. 121, 130.

Hêsigonos, Rhêginos, who not only believe
that these, but that still greater monstrosities,
are to be found in the world.

(B) Pliny, *Hist. Nat.* VII, 2.

And he affirms that there is a tribe of Indians
whose women bear offspring once only in their
lifetime, and whose hair turns white in the
very childhood. He mentions also a race of
men called Monosceli (one-legged), who, though
they had but a single leg, could hop upon it
with wonderful agility, and that they were
also called Sciopodae, because that when they
lay on their back in very hot weather, they
shaded themselves from the sun with their feet.
They lived not very far from the Troglodytes
(cave-dwellers). To the west of these, he adds,
lived men without a neck, and who had their
eyes placed in their shoulders.

(C) From the same.

According to Ktêsias the Indian people which
is called P a n d o r e and occupies the valleys,
live for 200 years, and have in early youth
hoary hair which turns black as they become
old. There is a people on the other hand
whose life-time does not exceed forty years.
They are next neighbours to the Makrobii, and
their women produce offspring once only. Aga-
tharchidês asserts the same, and adds that they
live upon locusts and are fleet of foot. [To
these Klitarchus gave the name of M a n d i,
and Megasthenês reckons the number of their

villages at 300. Their women bear children
when they are seven years old, and they are
in their old age at forty.]

FRAG. XXXI.

Gellius, Noct. Attic. IX. c, 4.

When we were returning from Greece into
Italy, and had made our way to Brundusium,
and having disembarked, were walking about
in that famous seaport which Ennius, using a
somewhat far-fetched but sufficiently well-
known word, called the fortunate (praepes),
we saw a number of bundles of books lying
exposed for sale. I lost not a moment, but
pounced with the utmost avidity upon these
books. Now, they were all in Greek and full
of wonders and fables—containing relations of
things unheard of and incredible, but written
by authors of no small authority—Aristeas of
Proconnêsos and Isigonos of Nicaea, and Ktêsias, and Onêsikritos and Polystephanos and
Hegesias. The volumes themselves however
were musty with accumulated mould, and their
whole condition and appearance showed that
they were going fast to decay. I went up to
the stall however, and enquired the prices, and
being induced by the wonderful and unexpected cheapness, I bought a great lot of the books
for a few coppers; and occupied myself for the
next two days in glancing over the contents.
As I read I made some extracts, noting the
wonderful stories which none of our writers

have as yet aimed at composing, and inter-
spersing them with these comments of my
own, so that whoever reads these books may
not be found quite a novice in stories of the
sort like one who has never even heard of
them before. [Gellius now goes on to record
many particulars regarding the Skythians, Arimaspians, Sauromatae and others of whom
Pliny has written at length in his Natural
History. These particulars have been evidently extracted from the Indika of Ktêsias and
are here subjoined] :—" On the mountains of
India are men who have the heads of dogs, and
bark, and who live by hunting and fowling.
There are besides in the remotest regions of
the East other strange creatures—men who are
called Monocoli (one-legged), who run hopping
upon their one leg with wonderful agility ;
others who have no necks but have eyes in their
shoulders." All unbounded however is his astonishment on his learning from these writers
about a race of men in the uttermost parts of
India having shaggy bodies and plumage like
that of birds, who live not upon food, but on
the perfume of flowers inhaled through the nostrils. Not far from these live the Pygmies, the
tallest of whom do not exceed $2\frac{1}{4}$ feet. The books
contained these and many similar absurd stories,
and as we perused them we felt how wearisome
a task it is to read worthless books which
conduce neither to adorn nor to improve life.

64

## Frag. XXXII.

Frag. IV.  From Athênaios, lib. X. [c. 9.][114]

Ktêsias says that in India the king is not allowed to make himself drunk, but that the Persian king is allowed to do so on one particular day —that on which sacrifice is offered to Mithras.

## Frag. XXXIII.

Tzetzês, *Chil.* VIII, v, 987.[115]

Herodotus, Diodôros, Ktêsias and all others agree that the Happy Arabia, like the Indian land, is most odoriferous, exhales a spicy fragrance, so that the very soil of the former, and the stones of the latter, if cut, emit a delicious perfume, while the people there, when made languid and faint by the rich odours, recover from the stupor by inhaling the smoke of certain bones and horns and strong-smelling substances.

## Frag. XXXV.

Lucian, *Ver. Hist.* I, 3.[116]

Ktêsias the son of Ktêsiokhos, the Knidian, wrote about India and its inhabitants what he neither himself saw nor heard from the report of others.

## Frag. XXXVI.

Strabo, *Geog.* I. 2.[117]

Theopompos professes in express terms that in his history he will tell fables better than such as have been related by Herodotus, and Ktêsias and Hellanikos and those who wrote about India.

[114] Müller places this as frag. 55 of the *Persica*.
[115] Müller places this among the fragments of the *Periplus* or *Periegesis.*
[116] This belongs to the life of Ktêsias ; conf. Müller, p. 8.
[117] This is Lion's 49th frag., but can hardly be regarded as one.

## LASSEN'S REVIEW
### OF THE REPORTS OF KTÉSIAS
### CONCERNING INDIA.[1]

In proceeding to examine the reports concerning Indian matters which yet survive from
the work of Ktesias, I call to mind what I previously
remarked, that on account of the unsatisfactory
state in which we possess the fragments, as well
as on account of the predilection of the author
for the marvellous, it is difficult to separate what
is exaggerated from what is true, and to give a
satisfactory explanation of his statements, while
further, I have shown in several examples that his
descriptions, as far as they have been examined,
have been found to be true in material points, though
they cannot be absolved from the reproach that the
facts have been purposely disfigured by being
magnified. In judging of his work, two especial
points are to be taken into account. The first is,
that he resided at the Court of A r t a x e r x ê s
M n ê m ô n as his physician, and thereby enjoyed
the best opportunity of questioning the Persians
about all the information they had acquired regarding India. He could question even Indians
themselves about their native country, because he
testifies that he had seen such men, these being
white, *i.e.* Aryans.[2]  The second is that the
extract from his work was made by a Byzantine
of far later date, the Patriarch P h o t i u s, who

---

[1] Translated from his *Ind. Alterthum*. vol. II, pp. 641 ff.
2nd edition, 1874.

[2] Ctesiae, *Fragm.* ed. C. Müller, p. 81a.

9

lived about the middle of the ninth century of our æra, and who had such a predilection for the wonderful and did the work so negligently, that it can offer no suitable scale whereby to measure the true value of the original. Most of the quotations, besides, concern the fabulous Indian races and the wonderful products of the country. Regarding several of his statements the advancing knowledge of Indian archæology has sufficed to show that they had not been invented by the author, but that they originated in fictions current among the Indians. Accordingly, the accusations of mendacity heaped upon him by the ancients, with reference to his book on India, have been generally withdrawn; but it would be going too far to absolve him entirely from lying, although in most cases his corruptions of the truth originate in his desire to tell unheard of stories.

He composed his work, which consisted of one book, after his return to his own country in the year 398 B.C.,[3] but how long afterwards cannot be determined. He did not consult Herodotus or any other of his predecessors. Whether his coincidence with Skylax about the fabulous peoples is a plagiarism is dubious.[4] Besides what I shall presently have to say about his Indian reports, it will suffice to mention only what is of essential importance, as it would be unsuitable in this place to enter into detailed researches on as yet unexplainable reports, while, as regards the fabulous nations, it will suffice to point out their Indian origin.

---

[3] Müller, p. 16.
[4] Schwanbeck's *Megasth. Ind.*, p. 8.

According to Ktêsias, India was not smaller than all the rest of Asia[5]—which is a palpable exaggeration. Like Herodotus he considered the Indians to be the greatest of nations and the outermost, beyond whom there lived no other.[6] Of the Indian rivers he knows strictly speaking only the Indus, for it must remain undecided whether the Hyparkhos be the Ganges.[7] As the Persians had obtained exact information only of the Indus region, we must expect to find that his more accurate communications have reference to that region exclusively. Of the former river he assumed the breadth where it was smallest at forty, and where it was widest at one hundred stadia, while in most parts it was a mean between these two extremes.[8] These figures are, however, without doubt excessive, but one need not be surprised thereat, since at that time no measurement had been made. On the other hand it is correctly stated that it flows through the mountains as well as through the plains.[9] Of the Indian sea Ktêsias had learned that it is larger than the Grecian, but it must be considered as an invention that to the depth of four finger breadths, the surface is so hot that fish on that account do not approach it, but live in the deep below.

It must also be ascribed to fiction that in India the sun appears ten times larger than in other countries, and that the heat there is so powerful that it suffocates many persons ; that there are neither storms nor rain in India, but that the

---

[5] Frag. iii.         [6] Frag. i, 1, 2.
[7] Lassen, *Ind. Alt.* vol. II, p. 563.
[8] Frag. ii and i, 1.        [9] Frag. i. 6.

country is watered by the river; there are on the
other hand violent hurricanes which carry away
everything that stands in their course.[10]   The
last remark may be considered as correct, but
the assertion that India has no rain is on the
contrary false, for it is known to possess regular
rainy seasons, whereby the soil is watered.  The
Indus region is inundated by the river only in the
Delta and, to a slight extent, in the upper country,
while in the north under the mountains it has
heavy rains, and lower down is not unvisited by
slight showers.   On the other hand, it is correctly
remarked that in most parts of India the sun
at his rising brings coolness, while during the rest
of the day he causes vehement heat.[11]

His statements about the precious stones have
already been elucidated.[12]  Concerning the iron
taken from the bottom of a well, of which iron
swords were manufactured possessing the property
of turning off hail, clouds and lightning, I have
already remarked that they were probably lightning
conductors.  As to the method of obtaining it there
is no information, but there is somehow gold was
obtained.[13]   Every year a spring filled itself with
fluid gold which was drawn from it in one hundred
earthen pitchers.  It was necessary that they
should be of clay, because the gold afterwards
congealed, and the pitchers had to be broken
in order to get it out.  The spring was quadrangular, eleven ells in circumference, and about two
yards deep.  Each pitcher contained one talent of
gold.  The sense of this passage can only be that

[10] Frag. i, 2, 5, 8.   [11] Frag. i, 8.
[12] Frag. i, 5 and 2.   [13] Frag. i, 4.

auriferous ores were melted, and that the gold
obtained from them was drawn out in a fluid state.
That there was a spring, must be a misapprehen-
sion, and we must imagine instead that there was
a cistern prepared to receive the gold. As a
pitcher need not be very large to contain one
talent (which is only somewhat more than fifty-
three pounds) of gold, this particular may be considered as correct, but no stress need be placed
on the statement that this operation was repeated
every year. If this supposition is right, it follows
that the Indians knew how to extract gold from
the ore by melting.

Of the gold it is said also, that it is not obtained
from rivers by washing, (which, however, is a mistake), but that it was met with on mountains that
stretched far away, and was there guarded by
griffins.[14] This, as has already been remarked, is
the fiction which had reached the ears of Ktêsias,
whereas according to the account given by others
it was dug out of the ground by the ants. Of
silver-mines, it is said that there are many of
them, although not as deep as those in Baktriana.
This agrees with the reality, because in India
silver mines seem to occur only in U d a y a p û r a
in Ajmîr: on the other hand Badakshan, in the
upper Oxus valley, is rich in silver.[15] His report
would accordingly refer to a more eastern country
than the Indus region.

On the seal-ring, *Pantarba*, which is said to have
had the property when thrown into the water of
attracting other seal-rings and precious stones, so

[14] Frag. i. 12.
[15] Yule's *Marco Polo*, vol. I, p. 166; *Cathay*, p. 595.

that they became connected with each other, the
remark may suffice that an altogether satisfactory
solution of this story does not seem to have been
found.[16]  It must also be left undecided what we
are to understand by the *elektron* (amber) which
during thirty days of the year exuded like sweat
from the trees on the mountains into the river
Hyparkhos, and which turned hard in its
waters.[17]  Of this much only can we be certain,
that it was a gum exuding from trees, of which
there are several kinds in India, especially towards
the east—the likeliest quarter wherein to seek for
this river.

The mention of this tree leads us to the reports
concerning Indian plants, and the products of the
vegetable kingdom.  The trees producing the oil
called *Karpion* have been already treated of [18]
Of the Indian palms it is said that their fruits,
which are called nuts, are three times as large as
the Babylonian.[19]  It is evident that it was some
other than the date-palm, and was no doubt the
cocoa-palm, which has a nut of the size indicated.

Of the Indian reed Ktêsias has reported that it
grows in the mountain regions on the Indus, and
is so thick that two men with outstretched hands
cannot span it round, and that it is as high as the
mast of a large ship.[20]  This report agrees with
that of Herodotus, only that it gives a more exact
description, which may be considered as true, since
the bamboo can grow to the height of sixty feet,

---

[16] Frag. ii. and note.
[17] Frag. i. 15, and note.
[18] Lassen, *Ind. Alt.*, vol. II, p. 564.
[19] Frag. i, 13, and xv.
[20] Frag. i, 6, and vii.

and may be two feet in diameter. Ktêsias was
the first who brought to notice that there are male
and female reeds ; that the latter only had a pith,
and the former none; and that the former were
more strong and compact, and the latter broader.
He mentions also the fact that small boats were
made of them, which could hold not more than three
men, provided, as is probable, this statement really
does belong to him.[21]

The expression, *garments produced by trees*, can
only mean cotton garments.[22] Ktêsias has without
doubt stated that the Indians from preference use
oil of sesame, and it can only be the fault of the
author of the extract if the use of this oil, together
with that of the oil expressed from nuts, is ascribed
to the pygmies.[23]  His other statements with regard to the obtaining of oils are evidently fictions.[24]
Among these products of the exuberant fancy of the
Indians, there may here be appropriately mentioned
the story that those living near the Indus obtained a
kind of oil from the worms living in that river, said
to have possessed the property of setting everything
on fire.   Some have supposed from this that the
ancient Indians were acquainted with fire-arms,[25]
but the report must on the contrary be used to show
that poetical ideas peculiar to the Indians had
already in the time of Ktêsias become known to the
Persians.   There can scarcely be a doubt that the
report of Ktêsias now in question is the corruption
of the ancient Indian idea that the possession of

[21] Plin. *Hist. Nat.* XVII, 3.
[22] Frag. i, 22, and xxiv.
[23] Frag. i, 11.
[24] Frag. i, 11, and xxvii, &c.
[25] P. von Bohlen, *Altes Indien*, vol. II, p. 64.

supernatural arms, which they might at times
entrust to mortals, was one of the special preroga-
tives of the gods.[26] The worship of snakes was
particularly current in the north-western frontier
countries,[27] to which the report of Ktêsias regarding the oil specially relates. It will accordingly
be a fire-weapon lent to man by one of the serpent-
gods then worshipped, but which was represented
to Ktêsias as one that really existed.

For the sake of continuity of subject, I have
anticipated what is to be remarked about the reports
of Ktêsias concerning Indian animals. Of the
products of the vegetable kingdom he had mentioned a *very sweet wine*,[28] by which expression
probably must be understood only an intoxicating
liquor prepared from sugar and palm-juice, since we
know that grapes do not grow in India. Lastly,
according to our author, there existed also a tree
*Parêbos*, or *Parybos*, which was found only in the
gardens of the king, the root whereof attracted
everything to itself, such as metals, and birds
also, and sheep; birds for the most part being
caught by it. The root served also as a medicine
against bowel disorders.[29] With this conception
may be suitably compared that of divining-rods, by
the aid whereof metals were sought to be discovered. What Indian tree is meant is not certain.

Whoever is aware of the great vegetable riches
of India cannot fail to remark that the reports of
Ktêsias concerning them are extremely scanty.

[26] Lassen, *Ind. Alt.* vol. I, p. 674, n. 1.
[27] Lassen, vol. II, p. 468.
[28] Frag. i, 29.
[29] Frag. i, 18, and xix.

Possibly the reason for this defect may be partly
that the regions best known to the Persians, and
consequently to him, are less rich in vegetable
products than those of inner India, but the principal reason is to be sought in the negligence
and incompleteness of the whole extract, wherein
the various subjects follow each other without a
proper connexion, as well as in the circumstance
that quotations from his book are by accident
pretty copious on some subjects and not on others.
Thus the extracts are meagre which describe
ordinary things, whereas about the extraordinary,
much richer extracts have come down to us.
Accordingly we cannot absolve the classic writers
who have preserved for us passages from the
work of Ktêsias from the reproach of having
selected precisely those that relate what is extraordinary and wonderful.

This reproach attaches also to his statements
about Indian animals—some of those most valued
and praised by the Indians, as cows and lions, are
not even mentioned in the extracts, but on the
contrary those only that are extraordinary and
fictitious. It can scarcely be denied that Ktêsias
treated of the former. About other animals he had
been misinformed. The knowledge of the Indian
animal kingdom which was communicated by him
to his countrymen is doubly significant for the
history of zoology. Firstly, it is certain that
Aristotle, the founder of this science, had made use
of his reports about Indian animals, and his book
therefore contributed, though but slightly, to the
materials whereon that eminent genius founded
his observations. Secondly, through him several

10

Indian animals first became known to the Greeks,
and he has therefore co-operated so far to pro-
pagate zoological knowledge among his countrymen.  To represent this addition to science is the
business of zoology; for a history of Greek knowledge about India it is sufficient to enumerate the
animals which he has mentioned—an exception
being allowable only when an animal through some
real or imaginary peculiarity appears pre-eminent
over others, or when the form of the representation is characteristic of the way the author views
things.

Concerning the animal most remarkable to
foreigners on account of its size, docility and
multifarious uses, the elephant I mean, he had been
misled by the Persians into making the exaggerated statement that in war the king of the Indians
was preceded by one hundred thousand of them,
whilst three thousand of the strongest and most
valiant followed him.[30]  It can just as little be
true that these animals were used to demolish the
walls of hostile towns.  On the other hand, he
truthfully reports what he had seen with his own
eyes, that in Babylon, elephants pulled up palm-
trees, roots and all.  He is the first Greek who
mentioned the peculiarity of the female elephants
that when they were in heat a strongly smelling
fluid issued out from an orifice in their temples.[31]
Of the parrots he remarked with charming simplicity that they spoke Indian, but also spoke
Greek if they had been taught to do so.  The

[30] Frag. i, 3, iv, and v.
[31] Frag. i, 3, and v.

75

Indian name of the jackal he was the first to communicate to the Greeks under the form, *Krokottos,* and it follows from what he says, as well as from the fables current about this animal, that the Æthiopian kind cannot be meant.[32] The qualities attributed to it, such as that it imitates the human voice, has the strength of the lion, and the swiftness of the horse, show that the jackal already at that time played a prominent part in animal fables, and that such were generally current in India, if there were any need of such an argument.

Of the four yet remaining animals, two must be considered as real, though it is not easy to identify them. The other two have on the contrary been invented but not by the Indians themselves. The wild ass was specially distinguished by his horn, because, of the horns cups were manufactured which protected those who drank out of them from certain kinds of diseases and from poison.[33] He was further distinguished from solid-hoofed animals by the gall on his liver and by his anklebone. The first mark suits the rhinoceros, as it possesses a large gall bladder, but not the second, because all quadrupeds have ankle-bones. This, however, may only be an error of the author, though one that is surprising since he was a physician and had himself seen such ankle-bones. According to him, they were red, which is likewise false. The great strength attributed to the animal points to the rhinoceros, but not the great swiftness. At the same time the name, *kartazonon,* does

[32] Schwanbeck, *Megasth. Ind.* p. 3. The Greek is a form of *kotthâraka* from *kroshṭuka,* a jackal.
[33] Frag. i, 25, 26, and xxv.

not furnish us with any certain means of identification. The explanation of this word from new Persian is not tenable—we might rather think that Ktêsias had altered the Indian name of the rhinoceros, *Kadga* (which can be easily changed to *Kharga*) to *Karta*, in order to assimilate the sound to that of Greek words whose significations are very suitable to the animal.[34]

By piecing these remarks together it would appear most probable that by the wild ass is to be understood the rhinoceros, because there is no other Indian animal which the description suits better. If Ktêsias attributes to it a red head and a white body, whilst its colour is really grey-brown, he had perhaps been so informed. With reference to this so-called Indian unicorn, and also to the two fabulous animals, the griffin and the martikhoras, I have already remarked that it is incorrect either to recognize them in the wonderful animals of Persepolis, or to attribute to them a Baktro-Indian origin. In opposing this view, I have shown that the similarity of the sculptured animals to those described by Ktêsias is only general—that in both cases the animals have been composed from parts of such as were real, and further that an ethico-religious symbolism through miraculous animals was unknown to the Indians. The conjecture there thrown out that the old Persian miraculous animals are of Babylonic-Assyrian origin, have been confirmed by the recent discoveries at Nineveh.

About the bird, *Dikairos*, which was not larger

---

[34] καρτα strong, and ζῶον animal.

than the egg of a partridge, the dung of which was dug up, and first produced sleep and afterwards death,[35] I can say nothing more satisfactory than others. That it is not fictitious appears from the fact that the King of India had sent some of it to the King of Persia, who preserved it as something very precious, because it was a remedy against incurable diseases. That opium, as has been suggested, cannot be meant by it, is certain, since the cultivation of that drug was introduced much later into India. It would be futile to try to explain the name because it is explained by the word *just*, and has been altered to assimilate its sound to that of a Greek word.

If the *griffins* have been indicated as Indian animals,[36] there is no confirmation of this discoverable in the Indian writings—and so the griffins must be classed along with the Issedonians,[37] the Arimaspians, and other fictions of the more northern peoples, which had found admission also among the Persians, where they survived till later. Just as foreign to the Indians is the *Martikhoras*, whose name is correctly explained as *the man-eater*,[38] but in old Iranian, because *Martija-qâra* has this meaning, but the second part is foreign to the Indian language. If Ktêsias has reported that he had seen such an animal with the Persian King to whom it had been presented by the Indian king, he cannot in this instance be acquitted of mendacity.

[35] Frag. i, 17, and xviii ; the name is also written *Dikeros*.
[36] Frag. i, 12, and xiv.
[37] Lassen, *Ind. Alt.*, vol. II, p. 609.
[38] Frag. i, 7, and viii—xi ; Herodot. III, 116 ; IV, 13, 27.

Since he has specified a pretty large number of
Indian animals without exhausting the list, and
has also described some of them minutely, if we
may judge from the details which have been preserved, we may conclude that he had also treated
at large of the manners and customs of the
Indians. From this portion of the work which,
had it been preserved, would have interested us
most of all, we cannot expect to have learned anything about those subjects which we do not already
know, but light would have been thrown upon
the communications which had at that time reached the Persians from India, and upon the
nature of the ideas they had conceived regarding
the inhabitants of India. But unfortunately we
possess only very scanty extracts on such topics,
while, on the other hand, there are tolerably complete repetitions of his reports of fabulous peoples.

Of the Indians he correctly asserted that they
had their black colour not from the sun, but from
nature.[39] As a proof he adduced the fact that he
had with his own eyes seen white Indians, viz.
two women and five men. He mentioned their
great justice, their laws and customs, their love
for their sovereigns, and their scorn of death.
Nothing shows so plainly how little the way in
which the extracts have been made is to be relied
on, as the omission of these very subjects, with the
exception of four of the less important usages.
The first is that the Indians went on pilgrimage to
a holy place distant fifteen days from the Sard
mountains, situated in an uninhabited region where

---

[39] Frag. i, 9.

they worshipped the sun and the moon. During
the festival the sun is said to have afforded them
coolness for thirty-five days, so that they might
be able to perform all the rites and return to their
homes unscorched by his heat. There can be no
doubt as to where this place lay. It was among
the V i n d h y a s, one of whose off-shoots are the
S a r d i a n mountains. It is self-evident that
this can only have been an isolated worship of
the two luminaries,[40] probably by a barbarous tribe,
to which also the legend of the cooling down of
the temperature may have belonged.

The second custom mentioned is connected
with the idea formed by Ktêsias of the bodily
constitution of the Indians. They attained an
age of 130 or 140 years, and the oldest of 200.
None of them suffered from headache, eye diseases,
toothache, sore mouths, or putrid ulcers. In
India there was a quadrangular well, enclosed by
rocks, wherein the Indians of high rank bathed
along with their wives and children. It had the
property of throwing out again upon the bank
not only the bathers, but everything else, except
gold, silver, iron and copper. It is called in
India *balladê*, which meant *useful*. This word is
really Indian, for in Sanskrit *balada* means *strength-
giving*. From this report we learn the unimpor-
tant fact that the Indians had discovered the
healing power of *mineral* wells.

Another well had the peculiarity that the water
drawn from it congealed to the thickness of
cheese.[41] If three obols weight of this was tri-

---

[40] Frag. i. 8.                    [41] Frag. i, 14.

turated to a powder and being put in water was given
as a dose to an inculpated person, he confessed all
his transgressions. The king used this as a means
to bring the accused to a confession. Those found
guilty under the ordeal were condemned to die
of starvation, and the innocent were dismissed.
This particular is remarkable, because the Chinese
pilgrim, Fah-hian, relates something similar regarding U d y â n a, a country west of the Indus
and to the north of Peshawar. He says it was the
custom there, if a doubt existed about the guilt of
an accused person, to remove the doubt by admi-
nistering to him a medicinal drink; those guilty
of a capital offence were banished. Pliny had much
earlier reported something similar of an Indian
plant.[42] Guilty persons who had swallowed pills
prepared from its roots and administered in wine,
were during the night tormented by visions, and
confessed all their transgressions. Although the
origin of the drink mentioned by Ktêsias may be incorrect, there can be no doubt but that it was used
for judicial purposes, as it is confirmed by the other
two witnesses. Of such ordeals, called *divya* and
*pariksha*, several are adduced in the codes of law.[43]
Among these, poison also occurs. If the accused,
after swallowing the dose, felt no hurtful effects
ensuing, he was declared innocent, so that the report
of Ktêsias is justified by the Indians themselves.[44]

This, however, cannot be said of the fourth custom mentioned in the fragments of the work; that in

---

[42] *Hist. Nat.* xxiv, 102.
[43] Manu, *Dharmaś.* VII, 114-116; Yâjn. *Dharmaś.* II, 95ff.
[44] See Stenzler, *Zeitschrift d. D. Morg. Ges.* vol. IX, p.
661.

hunting hares and foxes, the Indians did not use dogs, but eagles, crows, and vultures, which they trained for that purpose.[45] For this practice the Indian writings afford no confirmation, though it by no means follows that the report is untrue. It is only doubtful whether eagles can be so tamed. It would be important to know whether from an oversight on the part of Aelian, who alone has preserved this report, vultures have not been substituted for falcons; in that case this custom would be one which the Indians had in common with the Thrakians and the ancient Germans.

With regard to the Aryan Indians we learn nothing from the extracts from the work of Ktêsias, but the fact already noticed, that they were white. He invariably speaks of but one king of India[46]; but from this we must not conclude that at that time Western India formed a single state. It would rather appear that Ktêsias did not care to treat of the separate kingdoms.

The fabulous peoples are divided into two classes, one purely fictitious, and the other embracing the aboriginal tribes that have obtained their name from some one peculiarity, and in one particular instance this name is Greek. Of the first class Skylax had already mentioned several. There is but this one fact with reference to these tribes which is significant, that since the fictions regarding them had been propagated to foreign nations so early as the time of Skylax, they must have been still earlier widely current among the Indians. It will therefore be sufficient, if, without

---

[45] Frag. xiii.

[46] Frag. i, 14, 28, 31, &c.

11

treating of them specially, I content myself with
merely establishing their claim to be of Indian
origin.[47] When Ktêsias, following no doubt the
precedent of the Persians, reported of one of these
tribes that it was a very brave nation, and that five
thousand men of them followed the king of the
Indians as archers and lancers, so far from seeing
in this circumstance a reason to consider them a
real nation, as in the great epic the one-footed
men brought gifts to a king, we shall only find a

[47] The Ἐνοτίκτοντες—the *once-bearing*—seeTzetzes, *Chil·*
vii. 636, Frag. i. and xxx, are called in Sanskrit *Ekagarbha*,
and inhabit the eight *varshas* or divisions of the terrestrial
heavens: *Bhâg. Purâna* v, 17, 12. According to an earlier
opinion the *varshas* were parts of the world. Whether
Ktêsias also mentioned the one-eyed *Ekalochana*, who
appear in the great epic, is doubtful. Conf. Tzetzes, *Chil.*
ibid. and *Mahâb.* III, 297, v, 16137. But both do mention
the Indian *Karnaprâvarana*, or those who used their ears
as a covering, and who dwelt in the southern region. By
Skylax they are called Ὠτόλικνοι, *i.e.* having shovel-sized
ears, Tzetzes, *Chil.* vii, 631, 638. Ktêsias (frag. i, 31) does
not seem to have known their name, but he says they had
eight fingers on each hand, and eight toes on each foot, a
feature wanting in the Indian accounts, but which is certainly an Indian idea. Megasthenes had translated the
Indian name by Ἐνωτοκοῖται, *i.e.* such as slept in their
ears: (see *Ind. Ant.* vol. VI, pp. 133-4). The Σκιάποδες
are mentioned by Skylax, Hekataios, and Ktesias,—by the
second as in Ethiopia, with the frequent attribution of
Indian fictions to Ethiopia: Tzetzes, *Chil.* vii, 629 f.;
Philostrat. *Vit. Appolon.* vii, 14; Ktês. frag. xxvii, or
Müller, *Ctes. Frag.* 89, p. 106. They have not yet been
identified in Indian writings: their name must have been
*Chhâyâpâda.* Possibly they were considered to have feet
large enough to overshadow them. The predecessors of
Ktêsias had not mentioned the one-footed race called *Eka-
pâda*, who were able nevertheless to run fast—frag. xxx.
The passage relating to them in the *Mahâbhârata*, accord-
ing to which they lived in the north, is cited by Lassen,
*Ind. Alt.* vol. I, p. 1026n., and that from the *Râmâyana*
in the *Zeitschrift f. d. k. d. Morg.* vol. II. p. 40. Pliny
(*Hist. Nat.* VII, 2.) incorrectly considers them to have been
the same as the *Sciapodes.*

new proof of the wide dissemination of such fictions at that early period.

It will be suitable here to mention that Ktêsias was the first Greek who had received intelligence of the holy country of the U t t a r a  K u r u, although considering the incomplete state in which his work lies before us, this can only be shown by the help of the native writings. He had, to wit, stated that there existed a fountain called S i l a s, in whose waters even the lightest substances that were thrown in sank to the bottom.[48] Now, this is the river Ś i l â or Ś a i l o d â which one must cross before he can reach that country. It was believed that nothing would float or swim in its waters because by contact with them everything was transmuted into stone. It was only possible to effect a passage by means of the K î c h a k a-reed which grew there. The Greek representation offers itself as an inversion of the Indian fiction; if anything that came into contact with the water was changed into stone, it must have become as heavy as stone and sunk to the bottom. The Greeks accordingly supposed that the lightness of the water was the cause of its being innavigable.

In the extant excerpts there is no mention of the Hyperboreans, who, as we shall afterwards show, answer to the Indian U t t a r a  k u r u. According to Megasthenes, they lived one thousand years, but according to the Indian view one thousand

[48] Frag. xxviii. Megasthenês also mentions a river Silas flowing from a source of the same name through the country of the Sileoi, and so light that everything sank in it. The Śilâ is mentioned also in the *Mahâbh.* VI, 6, v. 219, but north of Meru.

and even ten thousand years.[49] Accordingly it is not at all impossible but that Ktêsias has mentioned them under the name of M a k r o b i o i, who lived four hundred years. These are attributed also to Ethiopia by Herodotus[50] and other writers of later date, but are probably of Indian origin.

The accounts given of the real tribes deserve more consideration, because from them several particulars appear which shed over the aborigines and their contact with the Arian Indians a light all the more unexpected, as it has been the common practice to deny all value to the statements advanced by Ktêsias in this connection.

Among the real tribes was one that was black, and dwelt above the river H y p a r k h o s, probably the Ganges.[51] They spent their days in idleness, ate no corn, but lived only on the milk of kine, goats and sheep which they maintained in great numbers. This notice is interesting, in so far as it shows that on the upper Ganges, or more correctly in the Himalaya, there still existed in those days black aborigines, as the great Epos also knows them there. It must be considered as an exaggeration that they drank no water, and that though not agriculturists, they subsisted also upon fruits. The fullest reports are those relating to the K y n a m o l g o i or K y n o k e p h a l o i, the dog-headed,[52] who must on account of this peculiarity being attributed to them have particularly

---

[49] Frag. xxx ; Pliny, *H. N.* VII, 2, has confounded the Pandore with the Mandi of Kleitarkhos and Ktêsias. See Schwanbeck's *Megasth. Ind.* p. 71 ; *Ind. Alter.* vol. I, p. 797.

[50] Herodot. III, 17.          [51] Frag. i, 24.

[52] Frag. i, 20, 22, 23, and xxi, xxii, xxiii.

attracted the attention of the classical authors. They were widely propagated, because they dwelt near the sources of the Hyparkbos, as well as in Southern India; their number is stated to have amounted to one hundred and twenty thousand. They were black, and the teeth, tails and voices of dogs, as well as their heads, are attributed to them. They understood, however, the language of the Indians. The reason for their name and their fictitious properties is evident from the circumstance that they kept big dogs for hunting wild oxen and other wild animals. If the use of dog-milk is attributed to them, this may have also been merely an invention, because it is said elsewhere that they used also the milk of goats and of sheep. The other things related of them show that they were a real nation, a tribe of the black aborigines.

They were acquainted with but few of the technical arts, had no houses or beds, but dwelt in caves and slept on couches of straw, leaves, or grass. They knew how to tan hides, and the men as well as the women wore very fine garments manufactured from them. The richest only possessed linen. They kept a multitude of asses, goats and sheep, and the greatest number of the latter constituted their wealth. Besides milk they used also as food the fruit of the Siptakhora tree, which they dried and packed up in plaited baskets and exported to the other Indians. They were very fast runners, good hunters, archers and hurlers of the javelin. They lived especially on the produce of the chase. The flesh of the animals which they killed, they roasted in the sun. Protected by their inaccessible mountains,

they were not attacked in war by their neighbours; they are represented as just men and
harmless.    They are said to have reached the age
of one hundred and seventy years, and some even
of two hundred.    They carried on trade with the
civilized Indians in their neighbourhood, and stood
in a free relationship with the Indian king.    To
him they brought annually two hundred and sixty
talents of dried fruits of the Siptakhora tree on
rafts, and as many talents of a red dye-stuff and
one thousand of elektron or the gum exuding from
the Siptakhora tree.    To the Indians they sold
these wares, and obtained from them in exchange
bread, oatmeal, cotton-clothes, bows, and lances,
which they required in hunting and killing wild
animals.    Every fifth year the king presented
them with three hundred bows, three thousand
lances, one hundred and twenty thousand small
shields, and fifty thousand swords.

This description throws a clear light upon the
position held by the Indian aborigines towards
the kings of the Aryan Indians, on their mutual
relations, on the intercourse of the civilized
Indians with their barbarous countrymen, and the
civilizing influence which they exercised upon them.
Secured from subjugation in their inaccessible
mountains, the latter must nevertheless have been
glad to live in peace with the neighbouring kings,
and to propitiate them by presents, and the former
to make them feel the superiority of their power.
On account of the need for the means of subsistence, and for the means for pursuing their occu-
pations, which they procured from their civilized
neighbours, the aborigines were obliged to accustom

themselves to have intercourse with them, and to
afford them also an opportunity, and to open a
door for the admission of their doctrines and laws
among them.

The Indian name of this people S u n a m u k h a,
*dog-faced*, has been discovered in a MS. which has
not yet been published.[53] This tribe, according to
it,[54] dwelt on the Indus. The Καλύστριοι considered
by Ktêsias to be synonymous with it cannot be
satisfactorily explained from the Sanskrit; but
it may have reached us in a corrupted form. To
deny that the Aryan Indians may have given to a
nation which they despised a name taken from the
dog would be unreasonable, because the dog was
a despised animal, and the name Svapâka or
Svapaka, *i. e.*, feeder of dogs, designates one
of the lowest castes. Nor is there anything to
object to the view that one of the aboriginal tribes
was specially addicted to the rearing of dogs, which
were needed for hunting, seeing that the wild
dog is widely propagated throughout India and
occurs in the Deccan, and probably also in Nepaul
as well as in the south and in the north, where the
K y n a m o l g o i dwelt. This tribe also has been
transferred to Ethiopia and Libya.[55]

The third of these tribes are the P y g m i e s,
whose name is Greek, and means ' a fist long.'
They are mentioned by Homer, and as fighting

---

[53] Wilford, *As. Res.* vol. VIII, p. 331, from the *Prabhâ-sakhaṇḍa.*
[54] Vans Kennedy explained this by *Kâlavastra*, clothed in
black, but the meaning does not suit.
[55] Herodot. IV, 191, and Agatharkhides, p. 44, ed. Hud-
son, who has drawn his account from Ktêsias.

with the cranes.[56]   It hence appears that the name
has been transferred to an Indian people. The
Indian Pygmies are described as very small, the
tallest of them being two ells in height, but most of
them only one and a half.   They dwelt in the interior of India, were black and deformed, had snub
noses, long hair and extraordinarily large beards.
They were excellent archers, and three thousand of
them were in the retinue of the king.   Their
sheep, oxen, asses and mules were unusually small.
They hunted hares and foxes, not with dogs, but
with eagles, ravens, crows and vultures, like the
Indians, followed the Indian laws, and were just.
They agreed further with the Indians in using
both sesame oil and nut oil, as already mentioned.
This is all that is stated regarding them in the
fragments of Ktêsias.   To determine what Indian
people is meant by this name, it must further be
mentioned that Megasthenês ascribes the battle
with the cranes to the T r i s p i t h a m o i, *i. e.* men
three spans long,[57] a name by which he could only
designate the Pygmies, and which he had probably
selected because it was an old word.   Ktêsias may
therefore be considered as one of those writers who
mentioned the battle of the Indian Pygmies with
the cranes. Now the Indians ascribe to the G a r u-
d a, the bird of Vishnu, enmity towards the people
of the K i r â t a, which for this reason is called
K i r â t â ś i n, *i. e.* the devourers of the K i r â t a,
and the name of this people has also the meaning
of *a dwarf.* It hence appears that the Kirâtas
were small men in comparison with the Arian

---

[56] *Iliad*, III, 3ff.
[57] *Ind. Ant.* vol. VI, p. 133, note †, and p. 135.

Indians, and may consequently have been easily
confounded with the Pygmies. The form of the bird
of Vishnu, as described by the poets, does not
exactly correspond with a real bird; in the pictures the form of a bird almost entirely yields to
that of a man. There is nevertheless some similarity to an eagle and to a vulture as well as to a
crane. If in mythology a simple bird of this
kind usually only occurs, it is to be remarked that
it passes at the same time for the father and king of
the divine birds, and there is nothing to hinder us
from believing that, according to the ideas of the
people a battle of this bird with the K i r â t a was
thought to have occurred. If the remark that
they lived in the interior of India does not agree
with their actual position, which is assigned to the
east of Bengal, in the Himâlaya, and further to
the north, it must be understood that foreigners
had attributed a wider extension to the name so
that it designated even a people in Orissa.[58] From
this further application of the names several characteristics attributed to the Pygmies explain
themselves, which partly suit the true K i r â t a s,
who like the Bhuta people are beardless, but on the
other hand wear long hair. Among them occur
also the flat noses,[59] but not the black complexion
by which the G o n d a and other Vindhya tribes
are on the contrary distinguished, so that here
also a commingling of characteristics must be
assumed. Both these people, however, are distinguished by their shortness of stature. If the

---

[58] *Peripl. Mar.* c. 62; *Ind. Ant.* vol. VIII, p. 150.
[59] Wilford. *u. s.,* mentions the *chipitanasika,* 'snubnosed.'

smallness of the Pygmies has been ascribed to their cattle also, it must simply be considered as an enlargement to the account made by foreigners. As we have seen above that the Arian kings kept female Kirâta slaves and hunters, while the Pygmies are described as very brave and hunters of wild animals, and even in later times, the people of that race appear in the royal retinue, the Greek report is confirmed in this point also, while it must further be correct in stating that, though not all, yet at least one tribe of this people had adopted the laws of the Arian Indians.

The Pygmies with their battle against the cranes have also been transferred to Ethiopia[60] from their original home in India. Whether the legend concerning them had already reached the Greeks at the time when the poems of Homer were composed, may be left undecided.

The preceding examination of the narrative of Ktêsias (which has reached posterity in so abridged and incomplete a form, and the author whereof had been accused by his own countrymen of mendacity) abundantly shows that Ktêsias has in most cases only repeated statements as he heard them from the mouths of the Persians, who themselves had received them from Indians who sojourned in their country, and so we have the reports, not directly from the Indians themselves, but from the Persians. From this circumstance, it is evident why the names, as far as they have been explained, are, with a single exception, Persian, and why some names attributed to the Indians are foreign. If we consider the cir-

---

[60] Hekat. *Frag.* 266, Müller's ed. p. 18.

cuits these accounts have made in reaching Greece from India, we cannot but be surprised that in general they still bear the stamp of their Indian origin. As has been shown, Ktêsias cannot be absolved from the charge of having in some instances adorned the statements he received and of having even allowed himself to tell untruths. He has also transferred Greek notions to Indian subjects, at least in the matter of the Pygmies. If we however consider his book in its original and complete form, then we see that he must have given a tolerably complete representation of the products of Western India, and of the customs and usages of the inhabitants, as well as several notices of the interior of the country. A few details serve even to elucidate Indian affairs, and there were no doubt many such, which have been lost, because after the Greeks had become more closely acquainted with India in the time of Alexander the Great, his work had been neglected by his countrymen. But the special significance of his narrative does not consist in these isolated elucidations of Indian antiquity, but in the fact that he had communicated to his countrymen the mass of the knowledge on Indian matters and the form which they had assumed among the Persians, and had marked thereby the extent of the knowledge gained regarding India before the time of Alexander. His work may have contributed to increase the desire of the Greeks to investigate foreign countries, but it exerted no influence on the development of geographical science, and just as little on the expedition of Alexander, as has already been remarked.

# APPENDIX.

## ON CERTAIN INDIAN ANIMALS.

### From Kosmas Indikopleustes[61] *De Mundo*, XI.

#### 1. *The Rhinoceros.*

This animal is called the rhinoceros from having horns growing upon its nose. When it walks about the horns shake, but when it looks enraged it tightens them, and they become firm and unshaken so that they are able to tear up even trees by the roots, such especially as stand right in their way. The eyes are placed as low down as the jaws. It is altogether a most terrible animal, and is especially hostile to the elephant. Its feet and its skin closely resemble those of the elephant. Its skin, which is dry and hard, is four fingers thick—and from this instead of from iron some make ploughshares wherewith they plough their lands. The Ethiopians in their language call the rhinoceros *arou* or *harisi*, prefixing the rough breathing to the *alpha* of the latter word, and adding *risi* to it, so that the word *arou* is the name of the animal, while *harisi* is an epithet which indicates its connexion with *ploughing* arising from the configuration of its nose and the use made of its hide. I have seen a living rhinoceros, but I was standing some distance off at

---

[61] A monkish traveller of the 7th century.

the time. I have also seen the skin of one, which was stuffed with straw and stood in the king's palace, and I have thus been enabled to delineate the animal accurately.[62]

### 2. *The Taurelaphos or Ox-deer.*

This is an animal found in India and in Ethiopia. But those in India are tame and gentle, and are there used for carrying pepper and other stuffs packed in bags; these being slung over the back one on each side. Their milk is made into butter. We eat also their flesh, the Christians killing them by cutting their throat, and the Greeks by beating them with cudgels. The Ethiopian ox-deer, unlike the Indian, are wild and untameable.

### 3. *The Camĕlopardalis or Giraffe.*

This animal is found only in Ethiopia, and is, like the hog-deer of that country, wild and untameable. In the royal palace, however, they bring up one or two from the time when they are quite young, and make them tame that the sight of them may amuse the king. In his presence they place before them milk or water to drink contained in a pan, but, then, owing to the great length of their feet, breast, and neck they cannot possibly stoop to the earth and drink unless by making their two forelegs straddle. When they make them straddle they can of course drink. I have written this from my own personal knowledge.

### 4. *The Agriobous or Wild Ox.*

This is an animal of great size and belongs to

---

[62] Referring to the picture of the animal in his book.

India, and from it is got what is called the *toupha*, wherewith the captains of armies decorate their horses and their standards when taking the field. They say of it that if its tail be caught by a tree it no longer stoops, but remains standing through its unwillingness to lose even a single hair. On seeing this the people of the neighbourhood approach and cut off the tail, and then the creature flies off when docked entirely of its tail.

### 5. *The Moskhos or Musk-deer*.

This is a small animal, and is called in the native dialect the *Kastouri*.[63] Those who hunt it pierce it with arrows, and having confined the blood which collects at the navel, they cut the navel off, that being the part which has the pleasant fragrance known to us under the name of musk.

### 6. *The Monokerôs or Unicorn*.

This animal is called the unicorn, but I have never set eyes upon it. I have however seen *four* brazen statues of it in Ethiopia, where they were set up in the royal palace—an edifice adorned with four towers. From these statues I have thus delineated the animal. They say of it that it is a terrible beast and invincible, having its power all lodged in its horn. When it perceives that its pursuers are many and that they are on the point of catching it, it springs down from the top of some precipice, and during the descent through the air turns itself in such a way that the whole shock of the fall is sustained by the horn which

---

[63] This is still its Indian name.

receives no damage thereby.[64] The scripture refers to this peculiarity, which says : *save me from the mouth of lions and my humility from the horns of unicorns* ; and again, *the one beloved as the son of unicorns ;* and again in the blessings of Balaam wherewith he blessed Israel, he says twice over : *God led him out of Egypt even as the glory of the unicorn,* thus bearing witness to the strength and boldness and glory of the animal.

### 7.   *The Khoirelaphos or Hog-deer,*
### *and the Hippopotamus.*

The hog-deer I have both seen and eaten.   The hippopotamus however I have not seen, but I have had in my possession teeth of it so large that they weighed about thirteen pounds.   These teeth I sold here.   I saw many both in Ethiopia and in Egypt.

### 8.   *Piperi—Pepper.*

This is a picture of the pepper tree.   Each separate plant clings for support to some tall tree which does not yield fruit, being very weak and slender like the delicate tendrils of the vine.   Each cluster is enveloped within a couple of leaves. It is perfectly green like the colour of rue.

### 9.   *Argellia*[65] *or the cocoanut-tree.*

There is another tree of this sort called *argellia,* that is—the tall nut-trees of India.   It differs in no respect from the date-palm except in being taller and thicker and having larger leaves.   It pro-

---

[64] The ibex is said to fall in such a way that its horns sustain the force of the impact.

[65] The initial *n* must have dropped out as the word *no* doubt transliterates the native term for the cocoa, *narikel.*

duces no other fruit than two or three and as many nuts. The taste is extremely sweet and pleasant, being like that of the kernels of green nuts. The nut is at first full of a deliciously sweet water which the Indians therefore drink instead of wine. This very sweet beverage is called *rhongkhosoupha*. If the fruit is gathered at maturity, then so long as it keeps its quality, the water in the course of time hardens upon the shell, while the water in the centre retains its fluidity till it finally disappears. If however it be kept too long *without being opened*, the concretion on the shell becomes rancid and unfit for human food.

10. *Phôkê, Delphis, Khelônê—The Seal, the Dolphin and the Tortoise.*

When at sea we use the seal, dolphin and tortoise for food should they chance to be caught.[66] The dolphin and tortoise we kill by cutting their throat, but we cut not the throat of the seal, but despatch him with blows as we do large fish. The flesh of the tortoise, like that of the sheep, is dark-coloured; that of the dolphin like the pig's is dark-coloured and rank; that of the seal like the pig's is white, but not rank.

---

[65] According to the recipe for making hare-soup—" First catch your hare."

---

BOMBAY : PRINTED AT THE EDUCATION SOCIETY'S PRESS.

## ADDITIONAL NOTE.

In frag. XIII p. 43 it is stated that eagles were trained by the Indians to hunt hares and foxes, and Lassen (p. 81) expresses doubt as to whether eagles could be so far tamed. Here however Ktêsias must be judged to have written according to fact, for in Upper India eagles are trained to this very day for the purpose mentioned. Sir Joseph Fayrer informs us that when the Prince of Wales visited Lahore, there were among the people collected about Government House some Afghans with large eagles trained to pull down deer and hares. They were perched, he adds, on their wrists like hawks.

# INDEX.

\* n means *note*.

* See additional note on p. 97.

# JOHN W. McCRINDLE

# ANCIENT INDIA

## AS DESCRIBED IN

# CLASSICAL LITERATURE

**BEING A COLLECTION OF**
**GREEK AND LATIN TEXTS RELATING TO INDIA, EXTRACTED FROM**
**HERODOTOS, STRABO, PLINIUS, AELIANUS, KOSMAS,**
**BARDESANES, PORPHYRIOS, STROBAIOS, DION CHRYSOSTOM,**
**DIONYSIOS, PHILOSTRATOS, NONNOS,**
**DIODORUS SICULUS, THE ITINERARY AND ROMANCE HISTORY OF**
**ALEXANDER AND OTHER WORKS**
**TRANSLATED INTO ENGLISH, WITH COPIOUS NOTES, A CRITICAL INTRODUCTION**
**AND AN INDEX**

\* \* \*
\* \*
\*

Westminster 1901. Reprint 1971. XXI, 226 pages.
Cloth, 8vo. (*ISBN 90 6022 110 9)

PHILO PRESS / POSTBOX 806 / AMSTERDAM 1000 / HOLLAND

# BRIAN HOUGHTON HODGSON

# ESSAYS ON THE LANGUAGES, LITERATURE AND RELIGION OF NEPAL AND TIBET

TOGETHER WITH FURTHER
PAPERS ON THE GEOGRAPHY, ETHNOLOGY AND COMMERCE
OF THOSE COUNTRIES

CORRECTED AND AUGMENTED EDITION OF TWO EARLIER COLLECTIONS
OF ESSAYS

ENTITLED 'ILLUSTRATIONS... 1841' AND 'SELECTIONS... XXVII, 1857',

WITH A SUPPLEMENT OF

ADDITIONS AND CORRECTIONS FROM THE AUTHOR'S COPY,

EDITED BY MAHADEVA PRASAD SAHA

AND WITH OTHER ADDITIONS, OMITTED IN THE FORMER EDITION

PHILO PRESS / POSTBOX 806 / AMSTERDAM 1000 / HOLLAND

# EDWARD B. COWELL & ROBERT A. NEIL

# THE DIVYÂVADÂNA

## A COLLECTION
## OF
## EARLY BUDDHIST LEGENDS

SANSKRIT TEXT IN TRANSCRIPTION,

EDITED FROM THE NEPALESE MANUSCRIPTS IN CAMBRIDGE

AND PARIS,

WITH COMPARISON OF OTHER MANUSCRIPTS, WITH VARIANT READINGS,
APPENDICES,

NOTES TO THE TEXT AND AN INDEX OF WORDS AND PROPER NAMES

\* \* \*
\* \*
\*

Cambridge 1886. Reprint 1970. XII, 712 pages.
Cloth, 8vo. (ISBN 90 6022 079 X)

PHILO PRESS / POSTBOX 806 / AMSTERDAM 1000 / HOLLAND